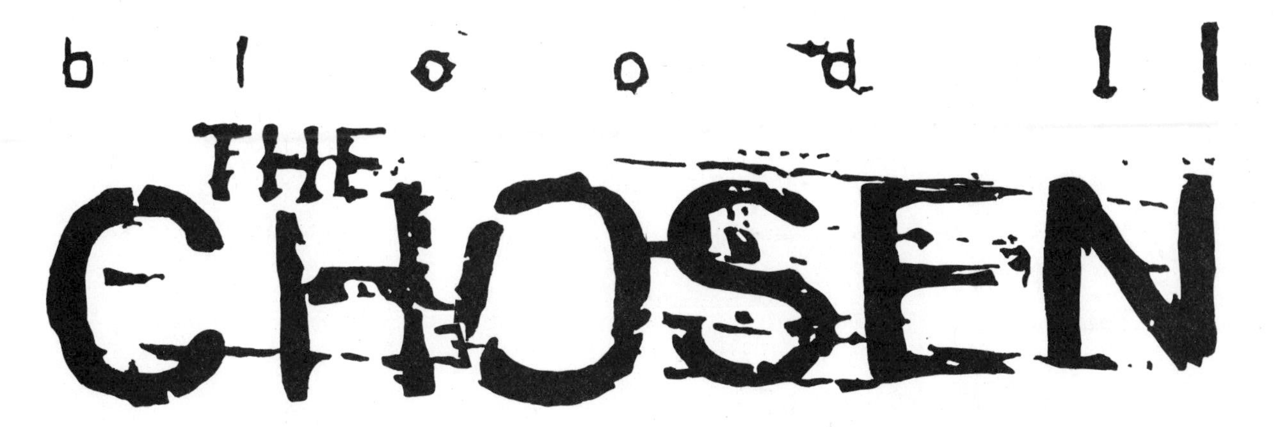

Official Strategy Guide

OTHER TITLES FROM GW PRESS

Civilization II—The Complete Guide to Scenario Design

Dominion: Storm Over Gift 3—Exclusive Strategy Guide

Duke Nukem 64—Official Strategy Guide

Duke Nukem: Time to Kill—Exclusive Strategy Guide

Duke Nukem Total Meltdown—Exclusive Strategy Guide

Oddworld: Abe's Exoddus—Exclusive Strategy Guide

Oddworld: Abe's Oddysee—Official Strategy Guide

Quake II—Authorized Strategy Guide

Rogue Trip Vacation 2012—Exclusive Strategy Guide

Star Trek: Starfleet Academy—Exclusive Strategy Guide

Total Annihilation—Exclusive Strategy Guide

Trans-Am Racing—Official Strategy Guide

Unreal—Official Strategy Guide

WarGames—Exclusive Strategy Guide

War of the Worlds—Official Strategy Guide

INTERACTIVE STRATEGY GUIDES
(on CD-ROM) from GameWizards

Blood

Duke Nukem 3D

Duke Nukem Atomic Edition

Lords of the Realm

Phantasmagoria II

Redneck Rampage

Shadow Warrior

Star Fleet Academy

Tomb Raider

Order information: Contact The WizardWorks Group, Inc., 2300 Berkshire Lane North, Plymouth, MN 55441 USA. You can also call toll free 1-800-229-2714.

Visit our web site at www.gwpress.com

Official Strategy Guide

Jamie Madigan

GW Press
A Division of GameWizards, Inc.
7085 Shady Oak Road
Minneapolis, MN 55344

www.gwpress.com

BLOOD II:™ THE CHOSEN—
Official Strategy Guide

Publisher
Shel Mann

Associate Publisher
Scott Grieve

Acquisitions/Development
Michael Koch

Design/Layout
Akeson Design

Published by
GW Press

A Division of GameWizards, Inc.
7085 Shady Oak Road
Minneapolis, MN 55344

ISBN: 1-56893-930-2

Library of Congress Catalog Card Number: 98-84116

Printed in the United States of America

99 00 01 10 9 8 7 6 5 4 3 2 1

CONTENTS

PART I: BLOODY BASICS

PART II: BLOODY WALKTHROUGHS

PART III: MULTIPLAYER BLOODBATH

PART IV: BEHIND THE BLOODY SCENES

APPENDIX:

ACKNOWLEDGMENTS

This is the time when I get to stop being selfish and recognize all the people who you should *really* thank for making this book possible. I guess it's best to do this first, since I can also blame them for all my stupid jokes, too (but just the ones that aren't funny). First on the list would definitely have to be my editor, Michael Koch, who was gracious enough to give me a shot at doing this sort of thing. He took a risk, and I hope I met all his expectations. A close second would be fellow strategy guide author Craig Wessel, to whom I ultimately owe this opportunity, and who was always open and willing to share his advice.

And of course, there's those folks at Monolith, who took care of that minor detail of creating the game. Very special thanks go to Karen Burger, who patiently returned my (probably annoying) phone calls and emails, and answered my long lists of questions. Thanks also to Jay "Shade" Wilson, who volunteered some of his precious time for an exclusive interview. And while I'm at it, I'd like to thank Jay and everyone who hung out on the Official Blood 2 Messageboard at http://www.the chosen.com. You all were a great wealth of information, whether you knew it or not.

I had originally wanted to dedicate this book to the one person who helped me the most through the process: Mr. Coffee. However, something tells me that I would be better off in the long term dedicating it to my wonderful and beautiful wife, Geralyn. It was her, after all, who offered me constant encouragement and tolerated my getting up at 5:00 a.m. many mornings to work on this thing. She was also quite convincing when she pretended to be interested in conversations about Singularity Generators, Shikari, Focus, the Tchernobog, and Bloodbaths. Thanks, hon.

About the Author

Jamie "Thrrrpptt!" Madigan has been playing computer games since the days of *Wizardry: Proving Grounds of the Mad Overlord* in the early 1980's. He grew up with computer gaming and plans to die with it, as well. He has written online strategy guides for *Hexen II* and *Quake II,* and for some reason just loves doing this sort of thing. He will complete his Ph.D. in psychology in early 1999—a prospect that many people, Jamie included, find frightening. He plans to continue working his day job as an Industrial-Organizational psychologist, providing companies with expensive organizational development consulting. Jamie lives in St. Louis, Missouri, with his wife, Geralyn, and his cat, Wolfgang.

FOREWORD

Three years ago I came onto the *Blood* team as a level designer. The team was small—Nick Newhard, Peter Freese, Kevin Kilstrom, Dan Leeks, Craig Hubbard, and myself. We spent most of the development working out of Nick's family room. It was a hard two years, but at the end of that time we created a game that we all enjoyed playing over any other game on the market. We were gamers making a game for other gamers, and I'm proud of what we achieved, and honored to be among the incredibly talented group that was the Blood team.

Any time you have a success like *Blood*, the immediate reaction is to follow it up with a sequel, and so we have *Blood 2*. But I view *Blood 2* as much more than a sequel to *Blood*. My hope was to create a game that lived up to *Blood*, while at the same time taking it to a new level. At its core, though, I wanted *Blood 2* to have its feet firmly planted in the spirit of the first game. In many ways, I view *Blood 2* as a tribute to *Blood*, not a departure. Many of the ideas and concepts were taken from the original *Blood* spec, things that for one reason or another didn't make it into the original game. The most important thing I wanted *Blood 2* to be, though, was fun, and I think it accomplishes that goal in spades.

As proud as I am of being a part of *Blood*, I'm even more proud of being a part of *Blood 2*, and the team that created it. Thanks to everyone on the *Blood 2* team. And thanks to you for buying *Blood 2* and this guide. You'll find plenty of helpful tactics within this book that have been gleaned directly from the *Blood 2* team. As mentioned before, *Blood 2* is the culmination of nearly four years of work in the *Blood* universe by the *Blood* and *Blood 2* teams, so I hope it gives you a hard time. The writer and editor of this guide are kind enough to offer you some advice, but I'm here to tell you that you shouldn't expect the same kindness from the *Blood 2* team. We're the enemy. Every time a maniacal group of Cabal fanatics guns you down, we're there. Every time a Soul Drudge thumps you on the head with a pipe, we'll be smiling. Every time some nasty thing sneaks up behind you in a nasty place, make sure and think of us. Good luck, and I hope you enjoy kicking our butts. I know we'll enjoy kicking yours...

Watch your back, or something else might watch it for you.

JAY "SHADE" WILSON

Blood 2 Lead Designer
Kirkland, Washington

INTRODUCTION

When *Blood* hit the shelves a couple of years ago, it made a big bloody splash with great game play, logical and inventive level design, and ridiculous amounts of gore. Even though it was built on the somewhat outdated build engine, gamers loved it.

Well, the folks at Monolith were determined to do it again. Enter *Blood II: The Chosen*. This game has a flavor all its own and can stand up to even the most popular, mega-hyped first-person shooters out there. Instead of licensing one of the existing gaming engines; the folks at Monolith spent the sweat and blood (pardon the pun) required to come up with their own 3D LithTech engine. While other first-person shooters offer uninspired mission objectives like "Find exit; kill all enemies," *Blood II* presents engaging mission-based episodes in an interesting story line of classical gothic horror with a futuristic twist and a dash of macabre humor. And perhaps best of all, you won't have to play as a single, faceless, cookie-cutter antagonist. Instead, you get four anti-heroes with their own unique drives and personalities. In addition, the game comes with shiny bells and sharp whistles, including dynamic lighting, 3D accelerator support, 3D sound, and realistic environments.

How to Use this Book

This manual will aid you on your quest to overthrow the Cabal and complete *Blood II: The Chosen*. It is divided into four parts and an appendix. **Part I, Bloody Basics,** gives you all the basic information on the Chosen, game play tips, weapons, items, and enemies. **Part II, Bloody Walkthroughs,** takes you step-by-step through the labyrinthine levels of the game. Think of it as a guided tour, and if you're stuck, you'll find the answers to your queries here. **Part III, Multiplayer Bloodbath,** gives you the basic information you'll need to get started in Bloodbath, *Blood II's* multiplayer mode. **Part IV, Behind the Bloody Scenes,** includes an interview with Jay Wilson, the lead project manager behind the game, as well as insider tips and strategies from the development team. Finally, the **Appendix** conveniently lists all the cheat codes and other commands you could want.

BLOODY BASICS

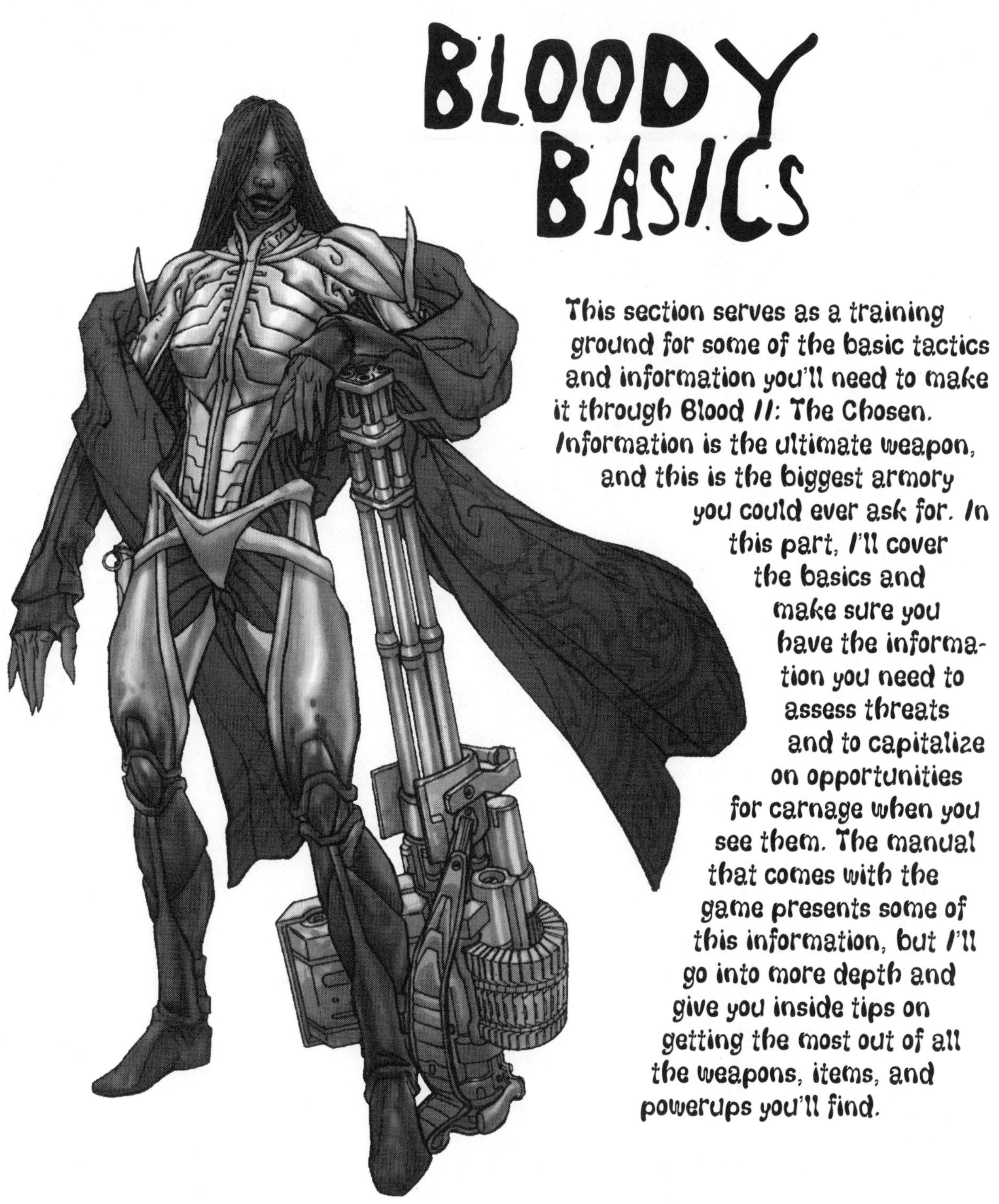

This section serves as a training ground for some of the basic tactics and information you'll need to make it through Blood II: The Chosen. Information is the ultimate weapon, and this is the biggest armory you could ever ask for. In this part, I'll cover the basics and make sure you have the information you need to assess threats and to capitalize on opportunities for carnage when you see them. The manual that comes with the game presents some of this information, but I'll go into more depth and give you inside tips on getting the most out of all the weapons, items, and powerups you'll find.

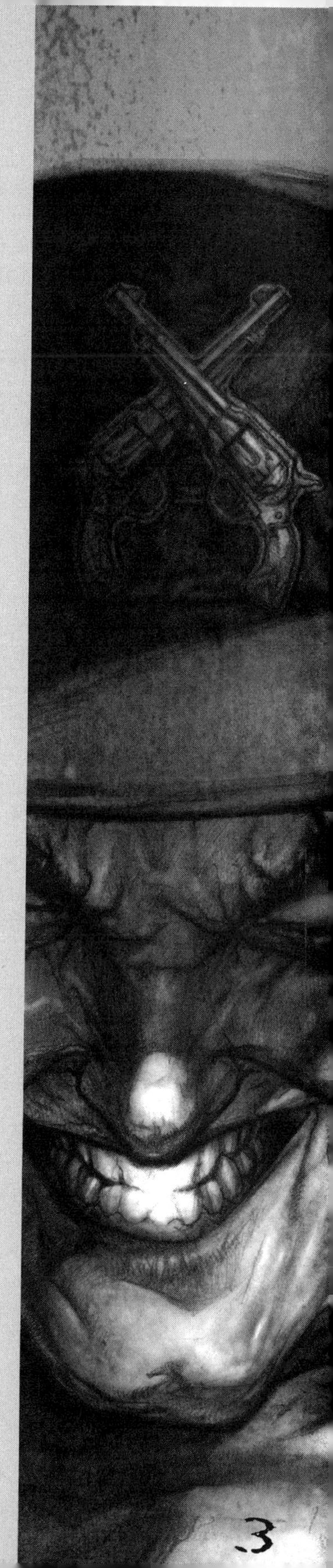

JOINING THE CHOSEN

It's a tough road ahead of you. You've got this Gideon guy and his army of gun-toting geeks busting your chops, and there's no end in sight. Think you can just say "time out" and go home? Think again. You're going to have to fight your way out. Ancient philosophers of war advised you to "know thy enemy," but an even better piece of advice is "know how best to mow thy enemy down in a flurry of bullets." Even before you make one bloody footstep on your path to victory, you've got to know the facts and think ahead.

BLOOD II: THE CHOSEN STORYLINE

Blood II is painted against the backdrop of a gothic future inspired by *The Crow* and *Blade Runner*. The year is 2028, and the world has not aged well. Its inhabitants trudge below spires of soot-stained concrete linked by cobwebs of black electrical wires. This is a world ruled by the few who have managed to wrench power and wealth from the hands of the weak. The heads of giant corporations trample the planet and its people with impunity, leeching the lives away from those that are forced to serve them.

Atop the most powerful of these corporations, we find a familiar old enemy: the Cabal. As fans of *Blood* remember, the Cabal is an organization whose roots creep past the beginnings of recorded history. On the surface, the Cabal has always been about power in all its facets—social, magical, financial, technological, and political. The few that have seen below this surface know that the Cabal is actually driven solely to furthering the wishes of Tchernobog, often called "The One That Binds," or "The Sleeping God." Depending on Tchernobog's current incarnation, the Cabal serve it in different ways. In this day and age, the Cabal are serving it as a juggernaut megacorporation named (appropriately enough) Cabalco.

Occasionally the Tchernbog's incarnations are benign. For example, the 5th incarnation, a Buddhist high priest, had the Cabal striving for spiritual purity. Other times, however, the Tchernobog's nature leans toward the much more malign. Perhaps the most frightening example of this was the 16th incarnation, which swelled the ranks of the Caleb to the size of an army and pushed them toward world domination.

This was the Tchernobog that threatened the early 20th century world in the original *Blood*. To spearhead its conquest, "The One That Binds" gathered its four most vicious, cunning, and powerful warriors—the Chosen. The leader of the Chosen was a killer named Caleb, whose ambition, paired with his derision for almost everyone around him, finally compelled him to rebel against the Cabal. Enraged, Tchernobog cast down the Chosen, killing them all except for Caleb, who was simply too stubborn and too driven to die. Even hanging an inch from death, Caleb still had enough in him to take on the entire Cabal army.

In retaliation for the Tchernobog's attack, Caleb donned his gunbelts and fought his way through the Cabal, mauling whoever crossed his path. He eventually vanquished this incarnation of Tchernobog, draining and absorbing all of its vast energy to use as his own. However, instead of the admiration, subservience, and boatloads of cash that he expected from the Cabal, Caleb only received the burning hatred of every remaining member.

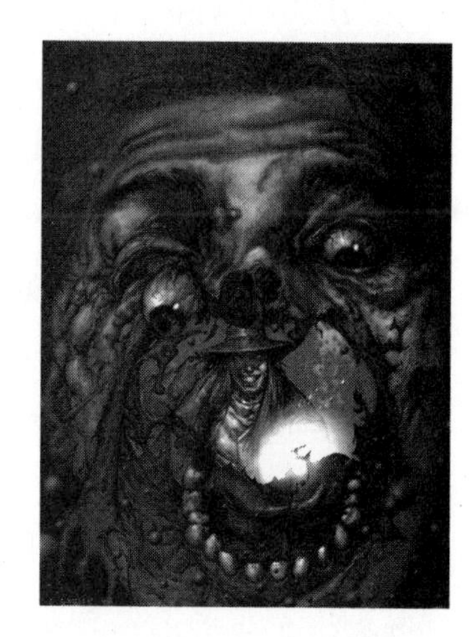

Caleb was unable to establish domination over the Cabal, which to this day he views as his birthright. Instead he was branded as "The Great Betrayer." As a result, Caleb spent nearly a hundred years wandering the Earth, shunned and despised by the secret society that he burned to rule. Even through the mystic power of the vanquished Tchernobog filled the undead gunslinger to the brim, he found little use for it. Occasionally, he would use it to get chicks in some seedy bar, or to get out of the parking tickets—nothing really fitting of that sort of power.

While this was probably good for the world at large, certain powermongers don't like to see that sort of potential go untapped. One such individual is Gideon, the current leader of the Cabal and C.E.O. of Cabalco. Under Gideon's command, Cabalco has achieved immense power and near world domination with minimal bloodshed through worldwide economic and political influence. Still, Gideon views the unused power Caleb leeched from the Tchernobog with great envy. And unlike Cabal, Gideon has plans for that power. Nasty plans. *Really* nasty plans.

To make things worse, Gideon views Caleb's continued existence as a sort of personal insult. If Caleb is allowed to live much longer, Gideon will view it as a failure on his part. And this kind of man does not allow failure. Still, Gideon is a villain of the old school tradition, and as such, he must taunt and toy with Caleb before doing him in. Fortunately for you, this means you'll have a chance of turning the tables.

Think you can do it?

Start the game and find out.

GAME STRUCTURE

Blood II: The Chosen offers a lot of variety when it comes to game structure. Some levels are stand alone, which means you start at the beginning, move through to find the exit, and move on to the next level. Other levels (or maps), however, serve as "hubs" for a set of levels. In this case, you may find yourself returning to the same map to find things slightly changed, with paths that were previously barred now open and leading to new areas. Still other areas, such as the Airship levels, are too big to be contained in one map, and you will find yourself moving between sets of maps as you complete various objectives. Don't be afraid to go through an exit if you find one. If you weren't meant to exit the level yet, the game wouldn't have let you. If you need to come back, it'll let you know.

All told, you'll blast through 30 levels before your final confrontation with the Ancient One. You'll see all kinds of level themes on your way, including crumbling urban deathtraps, a flying fortress, high-tech research labs, subterranean mazes, forgotten ancient cities of magic, and much more. Just make sure you don't stand gawking at the landscape so much you get a bullet between the ears.

SETTING UP YOUR GAME

The manual that comes with your game should give you the bare bones on how to get started, but we'll add some flesh to those bones here. Certain game features are discussed in more depth so you can make all the informed decisions you'll need to make in order to start a game.

Once you launch *Blood II*, the main screen will present you with three choices: start a SINGLE-PLAYER game, start a MULTIPLAYER BLOODBATH game, or change your options. Let's skip the first two right now. Starting a BLOODBATH game is covered in Part III of this book, and we'll come back to starting a SINGLE-PLAYER game. Go to the OPTIONS menu. Many of the options you will find here are self-explanatory, but let's take a second to go over a few of the ones that are more important to game play:

- **GENERAL OPTIONS**—This menu contains several miscellaneous options that are important to game play. It's a good idea to turn on ALWAYS RUN, and MOUSE LOOK if you're using a mouse to aim. You can also turn on the CROSSHAIRS here if you like.
- **KEYBOARD OPTIONS/MOUSE OPTIONS/JOYSTICK OPTIONS**—This is where you assign keys to movements, actions, weapons, and items. Spend some time here to experiment with various setups until you find one you like. It's a good idea to assign hotkeys for commonly used items that are close to the hand or hands that you have on the keyboard. You don't want to be searching for the right key in a time of crisis.
- **SAVE CONFIG**—If the mood strikes, you can save different configurations. Maybe you have one you like for Bloodbath and another you like for single player. If so, save them under different names.
- **LOAD CONFIG**: Use this option to load previously saved configurations.
- **ACCEPT CONFIG**: Make sure you select this option after making any changes. If you don't, your changes will not be applied and you'll have to do it all over again.

After you have set your configuration options, select the SINGLE PLAYER menu. Here you can either load a previously saved game, start a new game, or play a custom level. When you start a new game, you can select from different difficulty levels. The hardest setting is indeed difficult, so don't take it unless you feel like taking a lot of punishment.

NOTE

Depending on what difficulty level you choose, you will encounter more or fewer enemies, health, ammo, and other items. The higher the difficulty, the more you'll have to do with less resources. The strategies and walkthroughs in this book are written for the Normal difficulty level.

CHOOSING YOUR CHOSEN

When you start a new game, you are asked to select with which of the four Chosen you wish to play the game. Each of the Chosen has unique advantages and limitations, and your choice and how you customize him/her will determine what special ability you have, how much ammunition you can carry, and how the game's story unfolds. Choose carefully, because once you start a game, you won't be able to change your character without starting all over. This section discusses the four single-player options: Caleb, Ophelia, Gabriella, and Ishmael. You have more choices (and more customization) in multiplayer games, which are discussed in depth in Part III, Multiplayer Bloodbath.

TIP

Blood II gives you the choice of playing in Story Mode in which you play Caleb, or Action Mode in which you can play any of the Chosen. You should play in Story Mode the first time you play through single-player Blood II. This is because the intricate storyline and interactions with the other Chosen center around him. If you play in Action Mode as one of the other three Chosen, you will miss out on all the dialogue and cut-scenes.

Caleb

The protagonist ("hero" would probably be a misnomer) from the original *Blood* is back and ready for more action. Caleb is fairly well rounded, but has more strength than magic ability. Because of his reliance on strength over magic, he will be able to carry more ammunition for conventional weapons and control less Focus for magic weapons. Because Caleb has over a hundred years of practice in brawling, he fights with unusual bloodlust. This special ability enables him to increase his bloodlust meter with every kill he makes. The meter will slowly run down if the kills don't come quickly enough. Once the meter is full, the undead gunslinger gets ten seconds of bloodlust in which he is resistant to 95 percent of damage (the same effect as the Willpower powerup). Caleb can also extend the duration of his bloodlust by slaying more foes—every additional kill adds two seconds, up to a maximum of ten additional seconds. Use Caleb if you prefer the straightforward approach, and leave secrecy and stealth to others.

Strength:........................ 5
Speed:........................... 3
Resistance:...................... 3
Magic:........................... 1
Special Ability:................. Bloodlust
Maximum Health:.................. 300
Maximum Armor:................... 100

Ophelia

Where Caleb draws on tremendous strength and moderate resistance, the love of his (after)life does quite well relying on great speed, moderate strength, and moderate magical power. Ophelia won't be able to carry exceedingly large amounts of ammo or control tons of Focus, but she will be able to call on superior speed to help her do her dirty work. If you're going to play Ophelia, play her right—sneak by enemies when you can, and don't be afraid to run in order to save your hide. You will be aided in this by her special ability to hide. If Ophelia stands perfectly still for two seconds, she blends into her surroundings and becomes completely invisible. Once she moves or attacks, she will become visible again, but by then it's probably too late. If you must fight head-to-head, then use your superior speed to fullest advantage. Don't ever stay still, and always keep a weapon trained on your target.

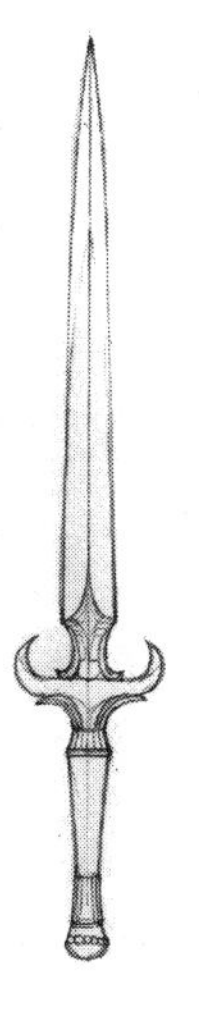

Strength:............. 2
Speed:................ 5
Resistance:........... 1
Magic:................ 4
Special Ability:....... Stealth
Maximum Health:........ 100
Maximum Armor:......... 250

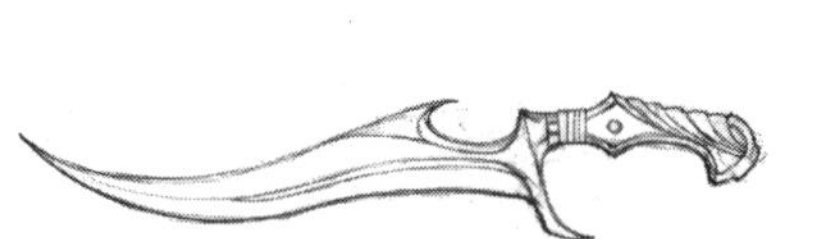

Ishmael

Ishmael has forgone physical training and combat in favor of his studies on dark magic. With little muscle to lug much ammunition for conventional weapons, he relies on his supreme magical prowess to slay his foes. He is aided in these efforts by moderate speed and resistance ratings. Besides being able to stockpile great amounts of Focus to be used as ammunition for magic weapons, Ishmael benefits from defensive magic in the form of a mystic shield. This shield will protect Ishmael from up to 100 points of damage, but it is easily disrupted by the slightest attack. Thus, the shield will protect from an attack doing one point of damage or a hundred, but either attack will shatter it. Once down, the shield slowly regenerates itself, leaving the Indian warlock defenseless until it is fully restored.

Strength:.................... 1
Speed:....................... 3
Resistance:.................. 3
Magic:....................... 5
Special Ability:............. Shield
Maximum Health:.............. 100
Maximum Armor:............... 300

Gabriella

Slow and steady wins the race. In this case, it wins the race by killing off all the other runners. Gabriella towers over even Caleb, and likewise relies on her brute strength to make things happen her way. While she possesses outstanding strength and resistance to damage, these attributes leave her with practically no speed or magical ability. Gabriella won't be able to control much Focus for magical weapons, but she will be able to tote truckloads of ammunition for all the conventional weapons. On top of all this, Gabriella has a chance to critically injure any foe she attacks. Each attack she makes has a five percent chance of inflicting double damage. Think strafing and dodging are for wimps? Well, then, you might want to consider giving this hulking Haitian warrior a try.

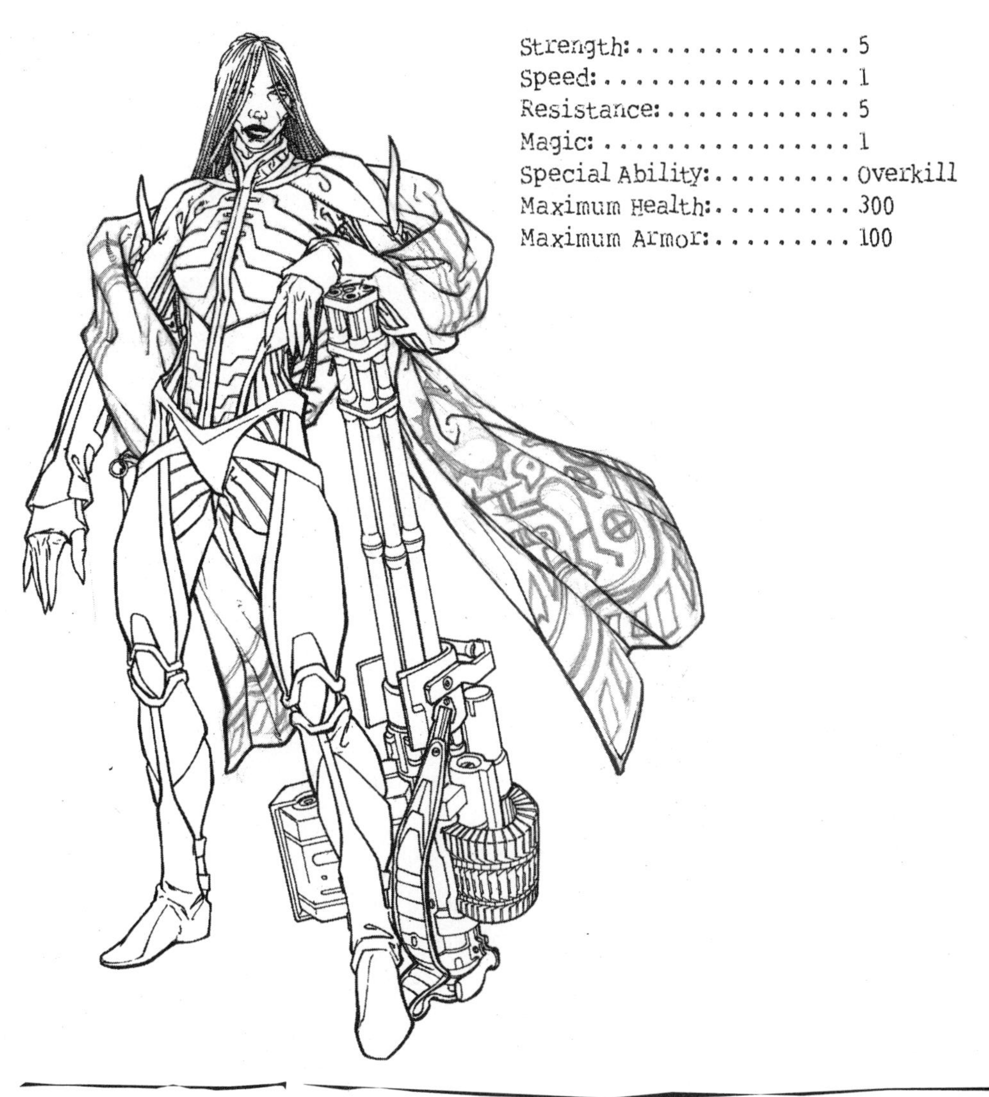

Strength: 5
Speed: 1
Resistance: 5
Magic: 1
Special Ability: . . . . Overkill
Maximum Health: 300
Maximum Armor: 100

WINNING TIPS AND STRATEGIES

Here is a quick list of some of the winning strategies that will help you along your way to dominion over the Cabal. Some of these tips are generic to most first-person shooters, others are specifically tailored to *Blood II*. However, they all represent good points to keep in mind. Here goes:

- **Use the Mouse!** Probably the biggest factor that separates great players from human targets in first-person shooters is the use of a mouse/keyboard combination for controlling the game. It takes a little practice to get used to mouse aiming, but it's *well* worth the trouble. Crank up the mouse sensitivity so that you can make a quick 180-degree turnaround with a simple flick of the wrist, and you'll be amazed at the number of bodies that pile up around your feet.

- **Pick the right weapon for the situation!** When it comes to wreaking havoc and blasting your foes in *Blood II*, you have a lot of choices. When wandering through cramped hallways where you're likely to see action at closer range, keep your Shotgun or Tesla Cannon ready, and think twice before popping off a grenade. Conversely, keep the Assault Rifle, Sniper Rifle, or other good long-range weapons out when you're in big open spaces.

TIP

Weapons generally fall into two categories: projectiles and instant damage. Some enemies will dodge projectile fire (like the Tesla Cannon or the Napalm Launcher), especially in open spaces. Instant damage weapons like the Baretta or the Vulcan Cannon, however, can't be dodged. Still other weapons like the Singularity Generator offer unique effects. Pick the right type of weapon given the circumstances.

- **Aim Carefully.** *Blood II* offers localized hit damage for certain body parts. This means that the more eagle-eyed shooters can do extra damage by shooting an enemy in the head. For added gib-filled excitement, you can even blow arms and legs off.

- **Use Bombs.** Don't underestimate the three different types of bombs you can accumulate in *Blood II*. There's nothing quite like the satisfaction you get from luring a pack of Cultists into a carefully lain trap with a remote or time bomb. You shouldn't have any of these toys left when you finish the game.

- **Keep moving!** Don't just *stand* there! If you keep on the move, enemies will have a harder time tracking you and lining up a shot. If you're following my advice and using the mouse to aim, you should be able to strafe from side to side while keeping your crosshair on the target. It just takes a little practice.

- **Trash the place!** Cabalco isn't exactly the most environmentally conscious megacorporation out there, so you shouldn't feel too bad about littering their establishments and busting up everything in sight. Crates and barrels often hide health, ammo, and powerups, so take the time to crack them open and see what goodies you can find. If you're low on ammo, make sure you use your knife.

- **Don't get overwhelmed!** Some enemies, like the Soul Drudge and Shikari, like to attack in packs and surround you. In the heat of battle, it's easy to get caught in a corner when you run backwards while firing at the enemy. Don't let this happen to you. If you need to, try luring the enemy away one at a time to make things more manageable.

- **Don't break up fights!** Remember as a kid how it was always a bad idea to break up two dogs in a fight. No? Well, trust me, it was. You'd most likely be the one to get bitten. Likewise, if two or more enemies in *Blood II* start going after each other, back off and let them duke it out. Then you can reward the victor with a shiny new bullet between the eyes. Saves health, saves ammo. An even better tactic is to trick them into fighting each other by putting one between you and the other. If the foe in the back shoots at you, it might hit the other, who will try to return the favor.

- **Listen up!** And down. And around. Sounds are sometimes as important as sights. If you hear a pack of Fanatics a corner, bounce a grenade their way. Likewise, if you're strolling along and suddenly hear gunfire, *move*! It likely means somebody is looking at you down the sight of his rifle and you need to take quick cover. Also, most enemies sound a unique alarm when they first spot you. Hearing it gives you an extra second or two to take cover or locate the threat.

- **Look around!** Take the time to thoroughly explore every nook and cranny of the level, especially the ones off the beaten path. Secrets and powerups are rarely hidden in plain sight, so do your best to find all the out-of-the-way places where they could be stashed. It'll be well worth it.

- **Proceed with caution!** Some places look dangerous because they really are. When entering a new area, take a second to check all directions, including overhead, for threats. Don't stroll into an ambush. Even better, if you have Binoculars or the Sniper Rifle, use them to scope out an area from a distance.

That's all the advice I can give you at this point. Mark my words and proceed to the Armory, where I will fill you in on your weapons and other goodies.

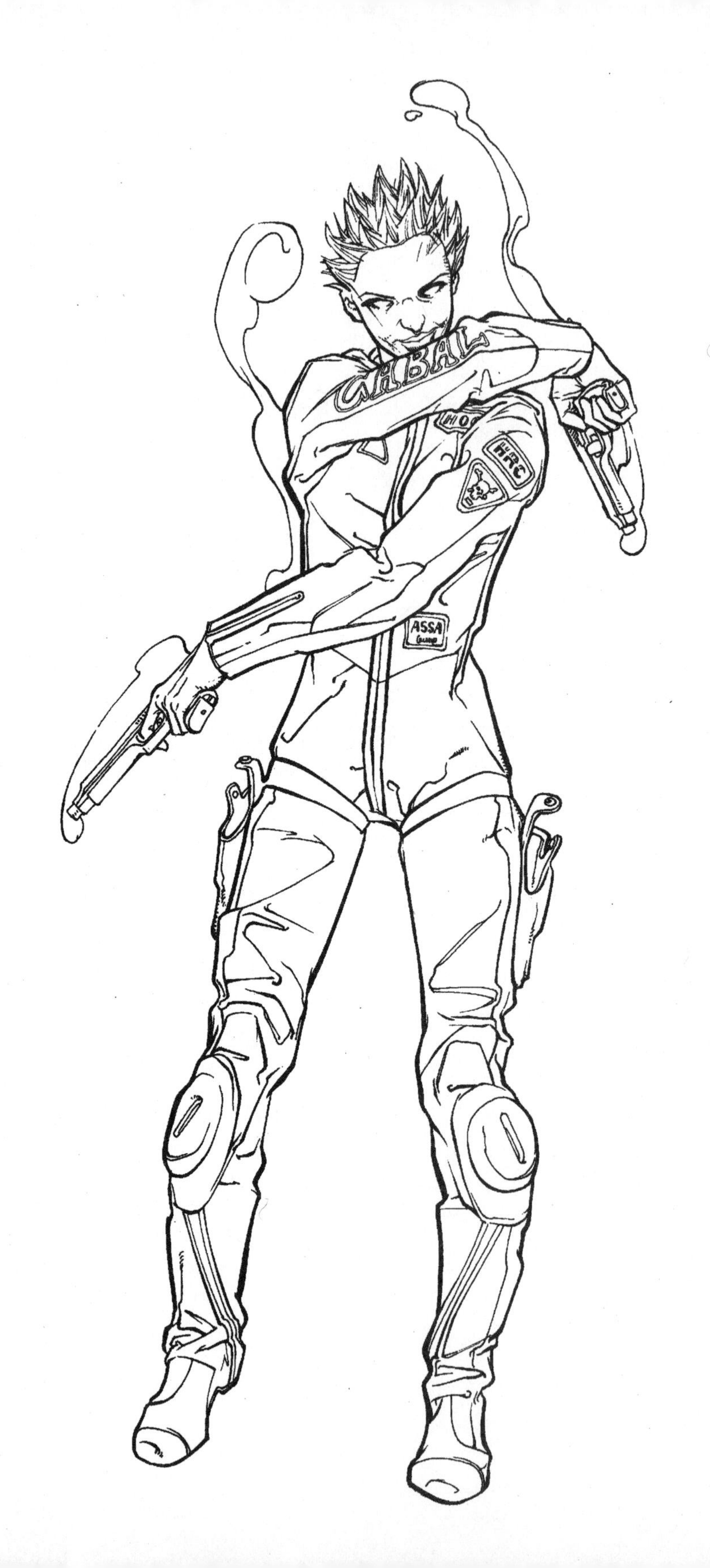
CABAL
HRC
ASSA

THE ARMORY

Rumor has it that early in the *Blood II* development cycle, the team at Monolith had some revolutionary plans for dealing with the other creatures you encounter in the game. Enough senseless violence and unbridled hostility. This was to be an enlightened game for the 1990's. For example, hitting one key would ready "Open-Minded Conversation," while hitting other keys would arm you with "Empathy for Others" or "Group Hug." Fortunately, this concept did not sit well with early customer focus groups, and the *Blood II* team decided to equip the players with a much more exciting array of weapons, items, and powerups. They did a heck of a job, too. Read on to find out more.

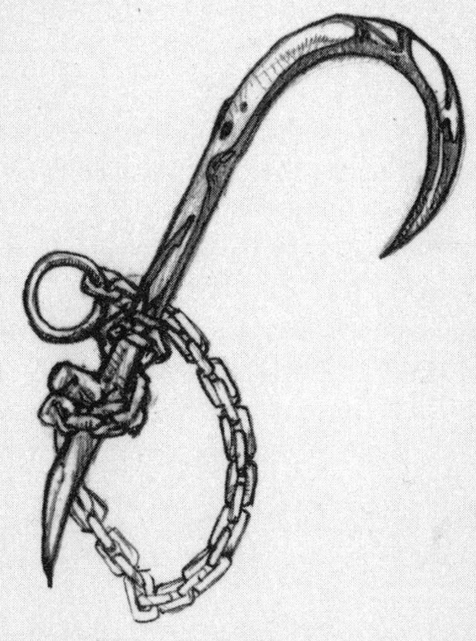

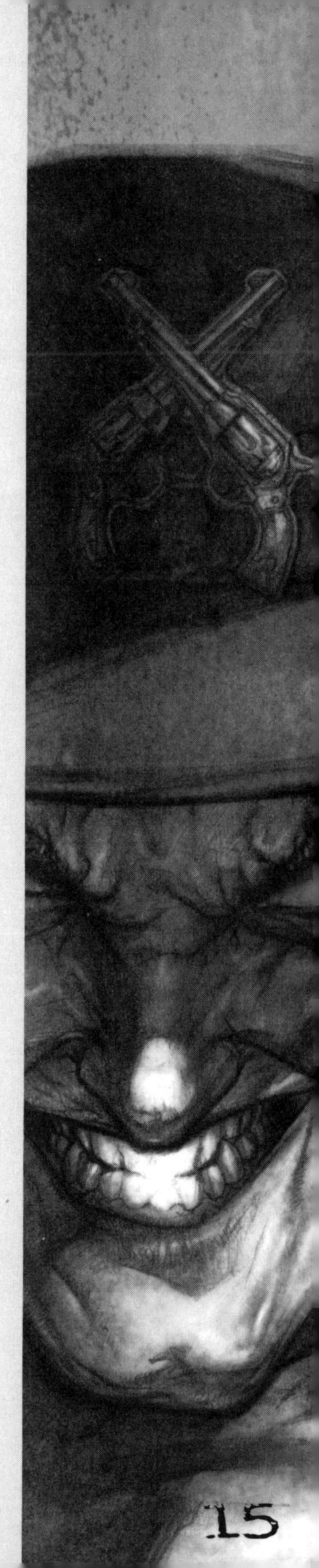

WEAPONS

Weapons in this game fall into four groups: conventional weapons that typically use bullets or shells; demolitions that usually result in gratuitous explosions and flame; futuristic energy weapons that use different forms of energy as their power base; and magical weapons that rely on a player's magic ability. The type of ammunition that each weapon uses is listed with its other statistics. Also, two tables at the end of this chapter present players' capacities for each type of ammunition at each level of strength and magic ability.

NOTE

So many choices! Even the superpowered Chosen have their limits, so you'll only be able to carry a maximum of ten weapons at a time in single-player mode (actually, the Knife plus nine others). You may have to drop an old weapon and leave it behind in favor of a new one. Just make sure that you have the whole spectrum covered—bullet weapons, demolitions, energy, and magic—when you have to choose your final array of arms. Also, don't carry too many weapons that use bullets or you'll run out of ammo too often. Plus, all dual-handed weapons take a higher strength value to wield. While this won't be a problem in a single player game, you'll have to make some choices in a bloodbath to get the most balanced assortment of weapons.

Conventional Weapons

Ah, gunpowder. For many purists, there's nothing like it for decimating your foes. Most of the weapons in this category use bullets or shells as ammunition, so be sure to keep an eye on your ammo reserves.

KNIFE

It's a knife. Use it to cut things—with the sharp end. If this is all you've got, then you should really be looking hard and fast for a better weapon and ammo. The knife doesn't use any ammo, so it does come in handy for smashing stuff when you want to save your limited ammunition for things that will actually shoot back at you. For a little variety, you can use the alternative fire to do a fancy slicing motion for a little more damage.

BARETTA 92F AUTOMATIC PISTOL

Not an extremely powerful weapon all things considered, but quite serviceable and easy on the ammo (bullets). Things get a little more exciting and stylish after you've acquired two of these little toys—you can hold one in each hand for twice the fun! This pistol takes bullets, so pick them up whenever you can. For added flair and a faster firing rate, the alternative fire will shoot the gun in "gangsta" fashion.

INGRAM MAC-10 SUB-MACHINE GUN

Getting better. Also often referred to as "the Uzi," this is a great tool for thinning out unwelcome crowds of Cabal agents. Just hold down on the trigger and the air will soon be thick with bullets and pointless pleas for mercy. The alternative fire mode will unlatch the shoulder-stock and fire a little slower, but with much more accuracy. Like the Baretta, you can hold two of these weapons to double your pleasure.

NOTE

This weapon is extremely inaccurate. Hence it is relatively ineffective at long ranges, but great in tight areas, as its spread makes it hard to miss.

SAWED-OFF SHOTGUN

Nothing really says, "Hi, I'm one of the Chosen and I'm here to blast you to Kingdom Come" like a sawed-off shotgun. Caleb's weapon of choice, this monster sprays a deadly cloud of buckshot that will take a bite out of just about anything. While very ineffective at a distance, this weapon is downright devastating at close range. It's a good weapon to keep readied when you're wandering through dark, confined hallways where you could come face-to-face with an adversary without notice. If you can find two of these beauties, you can double-fist them. The alternative fire will let loose with both barrels at once for two shells and twice the ventilating power.

BARRET .50 BMG SNIPER RIFLE

Originally designed for taking out enemy artillery and vehicles, using this monster rifle against personnel is a bit over the top—just as it should be. The ultimate long-range weapon, the Sniper Rifle's alternative fire button actually enables you to zoom in on your unsuspecting victim and aim a shot right up its left nostril. This weapon uses BMG shells as its ammunition.

M16 ASSAULT RIFLE

Every good undead interior designer knows that sometimes you need to spread a *little* Cabal blood on those walls, and sometimes you need to smear *a lot*. In the latter case, the Assault Rifle is an obvious choice. This rapid-fire bullet-eating beauty will make short work of just about any crowd. Even better, this rifle is actually two weapons in one! The alternative fire will pop a can of explosive and toxic bug spray into the midst of your foes, complete with economy-sized explosions and fiery death. Just make sure you're well out of the way when it goes off. If you're lucky enough to find a pair of these weapons, you can wield them both at once, but doing so makes the "grenade" launcher inaccessible.

NOTE Unlike the Mac-10, the Assault Rifle is EXTREMELY accurate. It does more damage, but has a slightly lower firing rate.

VULCAN CANNON (MINIGUN)

Subtle? No. Devastating? You bet. This definitely isn't you're typical pea-shooter. Just hold down the fire button to let rip with a steady stream of high-speed bullets that will shred anything unlucky enough to cross your path. The tradeoff is that it takes a couple of seconds to cycle up, and accuracy is very low, but it's well worth it.

HOWITZER

Major league devastation. The Howitzer is usually found mounted on top of some vehicle since no ordinary mortal could wield it, but the Chosen don't exactly fall into that category, do they? Use this weapon with care, because the blast radius from its rockets can take you out, too. The alternative fire mode takes a second to load up four rockets, and then lets fly with all at once, resulting in a larger area of effect.

Demolitions

For those times when you need a big bang to clear out a room full of enemies, there's demolitions. Most of these weapons result in fire or explosions of some sort, so be sure to take care when using them. You'll do more than singe your eyebrows if you fire them off in cramped quarters. Demolitions use a variety of ammunition types, so you have a lot more options to keep track of. You should make sure to save the rarer ammo for when you really need it.

FLARE GUN

Blood Etiquette Rule #1: It's generally considered impolite to ignite people. Blood Etiquette Rule #2: Be impolite at every opportunity. The Flare Gun's projectiles do little damage in and of themselves, but they do stick to targets and set them on fire. Said targets will burn for a while, taking damage every second. What more could you ask for? Well, how about the alternative fire mode in which the flare shatters shortly after leaving the barrel, sending eight happy little bursts of flames that spread to whatever they contact? Players with a flair (pun intended) for pyromania can even hold two Flare Guns at once.

NAPALM LAUNCHER

Warning: Point away from face when discharging. That's good advice to keep in mind while using this weapon of mass destruction. The Napalm Launcher fires flaming balls of jellied gasoline that explode quite violently on impact. This is definitely not the type of weapon you want to be using in close quarters, as you'll end up roasting yourself as well.

Energy Weapons

Science has given us many wonderful things: the ability to communicate freely, healthy living conditions, drugs to fight disease, and devastating energy weapons to reduce our opponents to twitching piles of gibs. Like demolitions, though, some of these weapons have dangerous area effects. Many energy weapons use chemical batteries as their ammunition, so be careful not to run out.

Insect-A-Cutioner

Apparently giant insects are still a nuisance in the future. Seeing a chance to make a quick buck, Cabalco created "Mr. Happy's Yummy Bug-B-Gone Juice" to kill even the biggest pest. After a rash of unfortunate poisonings, a class action lawsuit forced them to change the name to "Die Bug Die!" brand bug spray. However, since the directions on the can still read "Extremely toxic! Flammable! Do not expose to skin!", this makes for a handy weapon for taking out pests of the otherworld type at close ranges. And, being the clever Chosen that you are, you've even taped your lighter to the end so that the alternative fire turns the Insect-A-Cutioner into a makeshift flamethrower.

Death Ray

Perfect for slicing bread, trimming toenails, and cutting up pesky opponents bent on your destruction. The Death Ray emits a short burst of energy that's both accurate and deadly. These bolts even reflect off surfaces, so you can bounce them around corners and off floors. The alternative fire mode eats more energy but fires a short continuous stream of Death Ray goodness. Watch your ammo gauge, though, because this one sucks up the chemical batteries fast.

TW-X59 Tesla Cannon

Hot apple pie, freshly cut grass, honeysuckle, and the sickening smell of charred Cabal flesh carried on the soft summer breeze. These are all the smells that are reminiscent of a typical child's youth. Now you can relive these olfactory delights with the help of the Tesla Cannon. In normal firing mode, this state-of-the-art piece of artillery draws on your chemical batteries to fire a near continuous stream of energy balls that do a great amount of damage. Even more impressive is the alternative fire mode, which creates a giant ballooning ball of electricity that lashes out at everything in its vicinity with deadly bolts. Quite impressive. This monster weapon can even be wielded two at a time.

SINGULARITY GENERATOR

This is the ultimate weapon for heavy crowd control. Got a boring bunch of party guests that you want to get rid of? Just point the Singularity Generator at them and tell them to grab their coats, because they're heading out. If you have enough juice in your chemical batteries, this weapon creates a localized singularity at its point of impact that lasts for several seconds. We're not sure what a localized singularity is, but the results are impressive: Whoever gets caught standing in its area of effect is sucked in and takes constant damage until the singularity collapses on itself. The alternative fire mode creates a localized singularity around you that follows you around and drags items and enemies toward you, doing damage to them (but not you) the entire time.

TIP

Use the Singularity Generator wisely. The black holes it creates in normal fire mode are just as dangerous to you, so don't fire it right at your feet or the wall right in front you. Since it drags enemies and holds them in place for a few seconds, this weapon can help you elude stronger enemies. Even better, place the singularity such that enemies that are sucked into its grip will drop off ledges or into harmful environments when they're released. If the singularity doesn't kill them, the fall will.

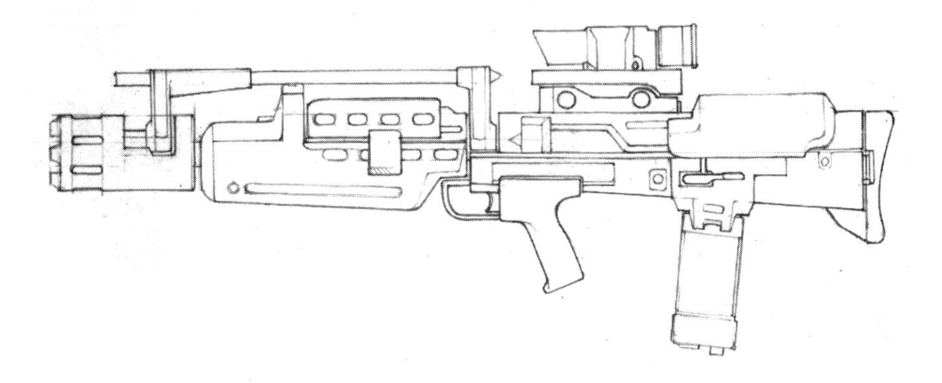

Magic Weapons

We're not talking about pulling rabbits out of top hats here. Magic has a lot of destructive potential. All magic weapons use the player's focus as their ammunition, which regenerates over time. The maximum amount of focus the player can control and how quickly it regenerates is determined by his/her magic rating.

Voodoo Doll

This is no child's dolly (unless, of course, your child is a masochistic voodoo priestess). When this weapon is "fired," the player sticks the doll with a pin, resulting in damage to the target plus a variety of effects depending on where on the doll the pin goes. Sticking the eyes temporarily blinds the opponent; sticking the arms causes the target to holster its weapon; sticking in the leg slows the target down for a couple of seconds; sticking in the chest or groin (!) causes normal and double damage respectively. The alternative fire uses much more Focus, but does double damage to every enemy in view and gives them Wonky Vision ™ if they survive. Just make sure the doll has something to focus on when you stick it, or it will backfire and do a lesser amount of damage to you.

Life Leech

Nothing kills like a shrunken head on a stick. Especially if that shrunken head fires deadly balls of life-stealing magic. While it takes you a second to ready the Life Leech and point it at what you want to die, holding down the fire button causes it to keep firing at a fast rate. The alternative firing mode slams the butt of the staff on the ground, causing a large global shock wave around you. It does less damage, but it's a good way to clear out a room full of weaker enemies or shove bigger enemies into areas they'd rather not be.

THE DECAPITATOR

This weapon looks like a small metal ball with nasty blades jutting out of it. Don't get the Decapitator mixed up with Fido's ball or you're in for a tragic game of fetch. When you let the Decapitator loose in normal firing mode, it flies in a straight path until within range of a moving target. Then it automatically seeks out that enemy, and starts drilling into them. It's much worse than that little drill your dentist uses. Once the Decapitator attaches to a victim, it will do constant damage until it is destroyed or the player runs out of Focus. In alternative mode, you can go "into" the Decapitator so that you see its view and control its movements. However, if the orb is destroyed while you're controlling it, you suffer damage and become temporarily blinded.

WARNING

Using the Decapitator in alternative fire mode not only uses up a heck of a lot of Focus, it makes your body extremely vulnerable. When you use this weapon in such a way, make sure you're well hidden or otherwise safe from harm.

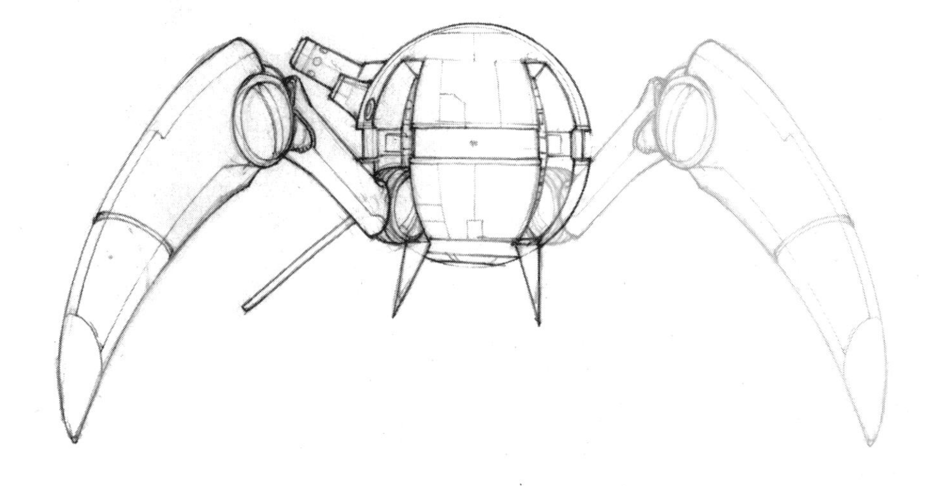

Ammunition Table

The amount of ammunition you can carry for firearms, demolitions, and energy weapons depends on your strength score. Similarly, the amount of Focus you can control for magic weapons and how quickly it regenerates varies with your magic score. Table I-1 lists the maximum ammo capacity for each level of strength. Table I-2 lists the maximum Focus capacity for each level of magic.

TABLE I-1. Ammo Capacities for Firearms, Demolitions, and Energy Weapons

STRENGTH	1	2	3	4	5
Bullets	100	200	300	400	500
Shells	50	75	100	125	150
Howitzer Rockets	20	40	60	80	100
Bug Spray Cans	10	20	30	40	50
Flares	20	40	60	80	100
Napalm Fuel	10	25	50	75	100
BMG (Sniper Ammo)	20	40	60	80	100
Batteries	100	200	300	400	500

TABLE I-2. Focus Capacity and Regeneration Rates for Magic Weapons

MAGIC	1	2	3	4	5
Max Focus	100	200	300	400	500
Regeneration Rate	1/sec.	2/sec.	3/sec.	4/sec.	5/sec.

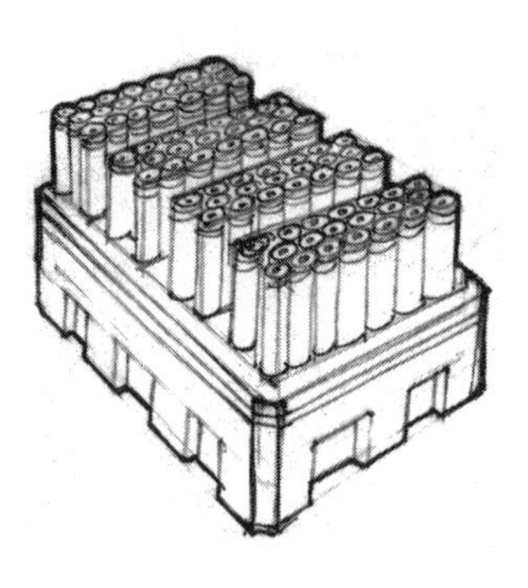

ARMOR

As much as you try to blast your foes into oblivion, some of them get off a few lucky shots. To lessen the damage taken from enemy attacks, pick up some magical wards to act as armor. The maximum amount of magical protection you can control at once depends on your magic rating. See Table I-3 for maximum armor values for each level of magic. Wards are automatically used when you pick them up, and slowly disintegrate as they absorb damage. Such protection comes in two types:

WARDS

Wards offer you the least amount of protection (25 armor points), but are cumulative in effect. That means that you can pick up multiple wards to boost your protection up to its maximum.

NECROWARDS

The "big brother" to the regular Ward, Necrowards can boost your armor protection 100 points at a time. Get lucky enough to find multiple Necrowards and boost your armor through the roof. Grab them whenever you can.

TABLE I-3. Maximum Armor Protection

MAGIC	1	2	3	4	5
Max Armor	100	150	200	250	300

INVENTORY ITEMS

Inventory items can be picked up and tucked away for later use when you really need them. You can carry as many inventory items as you like at any given time.

FLASHLIGHT

They haven't done away with crime, poverty, or oppression in the 100 years Caleb has spent wandering the Earth, but they have managed to create a darn powerful flashlight. While the Flashlight can be used to illuminate your way and uncover anything hiding in dark corners, it has the disadvantage of revealing your location and making you a giant, well-lit target. Considering this, it may not be a good idea to keep it on all the time. Besides, eventually the Flashlight will run out of juice. It will start at 100 percent and burn its charge at 1 point a second.

NIGHT VISION GOGGLES

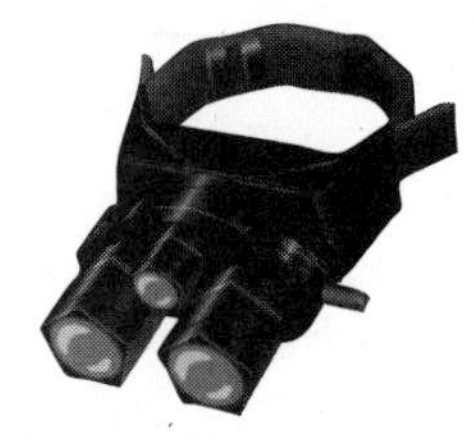

A fashion accessory every undead Chosen should have, the Night Vision Goggles allow you to see in the dark without actually lighting up your surroundings. As such, they're safer to use than the Flashlight since they won't give your presence away. Your Night Vision Goggles will start at 100 percent and burn their charge at 1 point a second.

MEDKIT

Not much to explain here. The Medkit starts off with 100 points worth of healing supplies, and can be used to regain health up to that amount.

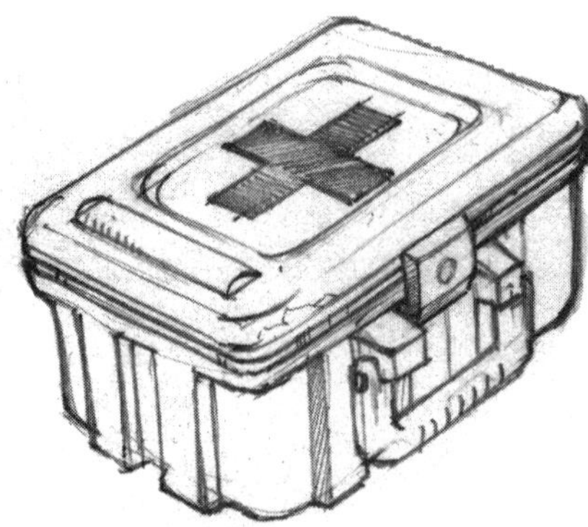

THE ALL-SEEING EYE

Nobody said that stealth, subterfuge, and spying couldn't be gross. Players possessing this item can drop it on the ground by pressing its assigned hotkey, move away, and look through the Eye by pressing its hotkey again. It's ideal for collecting information about an area or keeping an eye out (literally) for when the coast is clear. If the Eye is destroyed while the player is looking through it, it's not pleasant and the player will be temporarily blinded, but the Eye automatically returns to the player's inventory. This item can also be returned to the inventory by simply picking it up again. You may also be able to throw the eye and have it stick to walls.

BINOCULARS

This item is ideal for investigating areas from a safe distance. Often times a little advance reconnaissance will mean the difference between life and death—preferably your life and their death. Once you have acquired a Sniper Rifle, however, one can use it to the same effect, leaving the Binoculars to just take up space in your inventory.

PROXIMITY BOMB

One of three types of bombs you get to play with, the Proximity Bomb can be thrown (normal fire button after selecting the bomb's hotkey) or laid on the ground (with the alternate fire button). It will lie in waiting until some unlucky soul ventures too close, at which point they will get a face full of explosive plastic. The player can have up to 10 of these items in his/her possession.

Remote Bomb

For those times when you want to detonate a bomb at your leisure, there's the Remote Bomb. This bomb is dispatched in the same manner as the Proximity Bomb (select it with the hotkey, then regular fire to throw). After placing multiple bombs, the player can detonate them by pressing the alt fire key. These bombs are extremely useful when you're being chased—drop one as you run and detonate it when you think your pursuer is running over it.

Time Bomb

The third type of bomb at your disposal, the Time Bomb does more damage and goes off after a specified time period. To arm the Time Bomb, select it with its hotkey, then press and hold down the alt fire key to set the time from 5 to 60 seconds. The longer you hold the alt fire key, the longer the timer is set for. Once the timer is set to your satisfaction, press the normal fire button to throw, or the alt fire button again to drop.

POWERUPS

Powerups are automatically used when you pick them up, and represent some of your greatest opportunities to increase your offensive and defensive capabilities. The effects can be permanent or temporary, depending on the item.

Life Essence

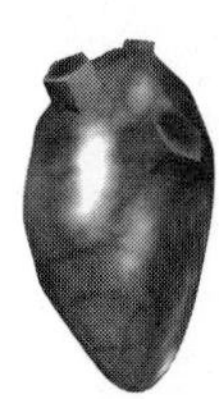

Represented by little floating hearts (not the Valentines ones—these are anatomically correct), these talismans restore 25 health points to the player, up to their maximum. See Table I-4 for a list of the maximum health by strength level.

TABLE I-4. Maximum Health by Strength Level

STRENGTH	1	2	3	4	5
Max Health	100	150	200	250	300

LIFE SEED

Grab these whenever you see them. The Life Seed talisman jacks your health up by 100 points, and can extend it beyond the normal limits.

WILLPOWER

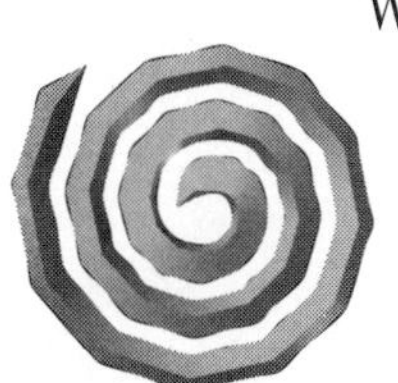

Whenever you come across one of these talismans, get ready to go on a righteous killing spree with almost complete impunity. The Willpower talisman absorbs almost all (95 percent) of damage from your foes, making you the closest you'll get to unstoppable. But hurry up and do your damage, because the effect only lasts for 30 seconds.

STEALTH

What else is there to say? This talisman makes you almost completely invisible for 30 seconds. Don't get too carried away, though, because you can still be heard and your enemies can still roughly identify your location from your actions.

THE ANGER (TRIPLE DAMAGE)

Increases the damage done by all weapons for a duration of 30 seconds. A must-have for wreaking true mayhem and making it through the toughest firefights.

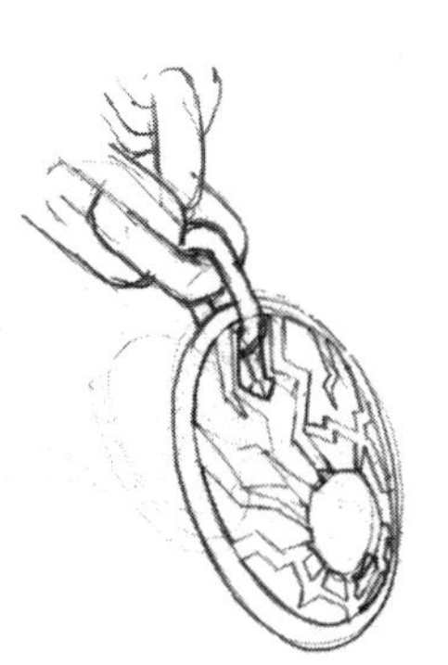

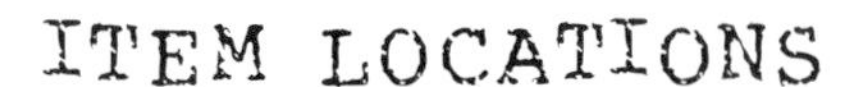

ITEM LOCATIONS

For your gaming convenience, Table I-5 lists the locations of every secret or difficult to find item in the game (Note: levels that don't have secrets are not listed). Weapons, ammo, and health from slain enemies or pedestrians are not listed, nor are items found lying in plain site. If you think you've found everything, give this list a glance and you may find out differently.

TABLE I-5. Item Locations

LEVEL	ITEMS	LOCATION
2	Health	Trash can at start of level
	Ward	Trash bags at start of level
	Bullets	Trash can on ledge above escalators
	Health	Trash can on ledge above escalators
	Flashlight	Trash bin outside Crazy Eric's
	SMG & Ammo	Crazy Eric's shooting range
	Health	Trash can outside Laundrohut
	2 Remote Bombs	Trash bin outside Laundrohut
	Life Seed	Bloody Laundry Machine in Laundrohut
	Flares	Tipped dumpster outside Motel Hello
	Health	Trash can outside Motel Hello
	Ward	Trash bag in playground
	Health	Trash bag in playground
	2 Proximity Bombs	Ledge above playground
3	Health	Trashcan outside museum
	Ward	Trashcan outside museum
	Health	Trashcan under fire escape
	Willpower	Rooftop
	Ward	Crate in loading bay
	Ward	Crate beyond loading bay
	Health	Crate beyond loading bay
	3 Proximity Bombs	Up on beam in area beyond loading bay
	The All Seeing Eye	Outside Bathrooms
	Various ammo	Crates where Gabriella is raised
4	Various ammo	Crates in condemned building
	Ward, Flashlight, Medkit, Life Seed	Hidden room in condemned building (shoot out window in 1st room, climb ladder from ledge, shoot out skylight & drop down)
5	Health	Under the stairs at the start of the level
	Various ammo	Crates by 1st lever
	Wards	Crates after metal bridge
	Various ammo	Crates by Drudge Lord
	Necroward, Remote Bombs	Lair of the Predator (behind pipes in Maintenance area)

LEVEL	ITEMS	LOCATION
6	2 Health	Inside computers in first computer room
	Ammo	Cabinet near Soul Drudge pin
	Medkit	Cabinet in Examination Lab
	Necroward	Elevators near security station
	Flashlight	Cabinet in CRU
	Tesla Cannon	Cabinet in janitor's closet
	Necroward, Life Seed	Vending Machines near Prophet
7	2 Wards	Crates above first red force field
	Various ammo	Crates near first red force field
	Life Seed	Crate under ship (climb down ladder from first catwalk)
	Various ammo	Crates after first catwalk
	Various ammo	Crates after second catwalk
	Various ammo	Trunks in barracks
	4 Healths	Cabinets and shelves in Galley kitchen
	Various ammo	Cabinets in Armory
8	Insect-a-Cutioner	Shack in second construction area
	Ward	Trash can in alley after playground
	Ammo	Trash can in alley after playground
	Health	Trash can in alley after playground
9	Ward, health, ammo	Urns past first set of stone doors
	Ammo	Urns in main cathedral room
	Assault Rifle, ammo	Urns in antechamber near first key
	Health	Stone cross near first key
	Night Vision Goggles	Under stairs near first key
	Health, ammo	Urns near spiral staircase
	Various ammo, 2 health	Urns after shattered rooftop
10	Medkit	First aid box in third car
11	Ammo	Apartment on first floor labeled "Wilson"
	Flashlight, Remote Bomb, ammo	Construction site on first floor
	Night Vision Goggles	Apartment on first floor labeled "Mattingly"
	Ammo, Life Seed	Apartment on first floor labeled "Hendrickson"
	Ammo	Apartment on first floor labeled "Kettel"
	Medkit	Apartment on first floor labeled "Bouwman"
	Shotgun	Under table between vending machines in second floor balcony
	Ammo	Apartment on second floor labeled "Kelvin"
	Life Seed	Hidden underwater tunnel in trench near exit
13	Various ammo	Crates where you start the level
	Life Seed, Necroward	On ledge beneath blood pipe
	Various ammo	Crates outside meat plant entrance
	Various ammo, Binoculars	Cabinets in office area

LEVEL	ITEMS	LOCATION
13	Willpower	Box of meat near room with large vats
	The All Seeing Eye	Counter near gristle separating machine
	4 Health	Bodies hanging in meat room beyond Processing area
14	Medkit	Behind counter in motel
	Ammo	Crate in motellobby
	Binoculars, Sniper Rifle	First room in motel
	The Anger	Right-hand stall in train station bathroom
15	Ammo	Ledge next to subway overpass
16	Medkit	First aid box in last car of first train
17	4 Time Bombs	In alcove just before train station lobby
18	Stealth	Up on ledge at Shikari ambush
19	Various ammo	Crates behind garage door in tower
	Ward, Anger, ammo	Crates near playground
	Various ammo	Crates in room with catwalk and red ladder
20	Various ammo	Crates in parking garage
	Life Seed	Next to desk in recruiting office
	Various ammo	Inside desk in recruiting office
	Medkit	In chest in barracks room labeled "J.Spaid"
	Various ammo	In chests in other barracks rooms
	Various ammo	In crates near pools of toxic waste
21	Life Seed, Necroward	Bottom of watery sarcophagus in the first room
	Life Leech	Antechamber on second floor.
	Various ammo	Crates in rooms after falling from bridge
	Medkit, ammo	Crates in room after riding elevator back up
	Life Seed	Other side of broken bridge
22	Necroward	Vending Machines in hardwood hallway
	Medkit	Inside filing cabinets in office near vending machines
	Stealth	Upstairs in office near vending machines
	Life Seed	Under stairs in room with giant Cabalco floor mural
23	Ward	Under stairs in the Sector 2 pit
	Medkit	Behind grate on wall (shoot it out) of Sector 3
	Various ammo	In narrow hallway behind Sector 4
25	Life Seed	Second biosphere
	Ward	Lab with two Shikari in cages
	Ward	First padded cell
27	Ward	Vending machines near first key
	Medkit, Necroward, Life Seed	Rooftop below the crosswalk in the second office area
	Necroward	Vending machines near top of stairway to second office area
	Various ammo	Janitor's closet, second office area
	Life Seed	Inside safe (shoot painting on the wall) in large office near exit
28	Life Seed	Window washer platform hanging over the side of the building
29	Medkit, Ammo	Across tightrope up on the ledge near the bridge
	Various ammo	Crates in second "Cabalco Expedition Team" base
	Willpower	Narrow alley just before you get to the bridge

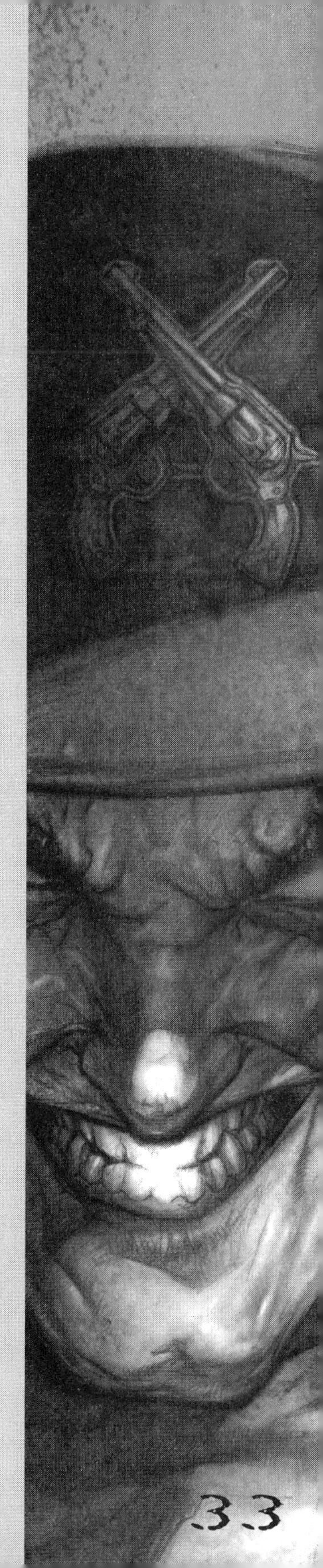

AGENTS, CREATURES, AND BOSSES

It's not going to be easy hacking and blasting your way to the end of this game. There are a lot of people (and things) that want to stop you, and you can bet your last bullet they're going to do their best. But you can better your odds of coming out on top by taking the time now to learn about your enemies (or, as I like to call them, "targets"). There are three general categories of enemies: Cabal Agents, Otherworld Creatures, and Bosses.

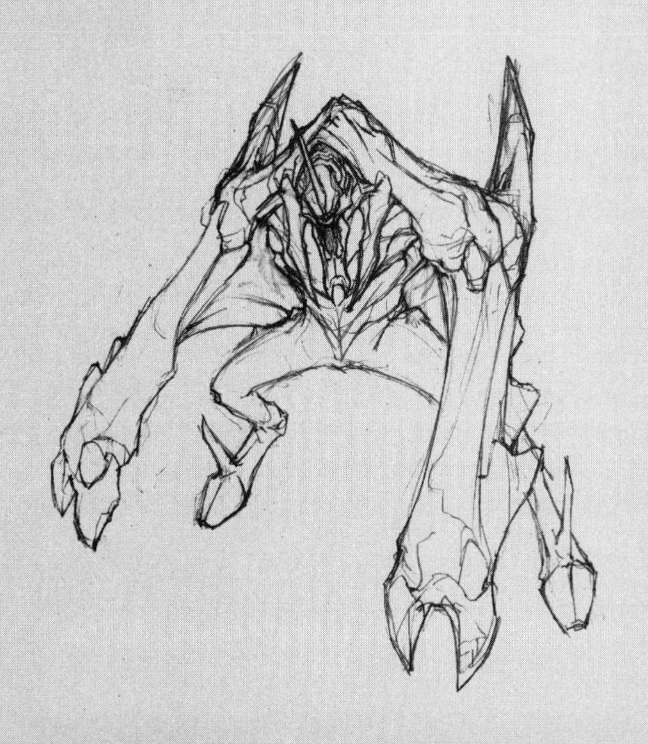

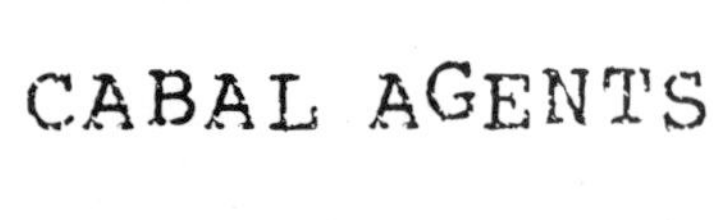

CABAL AGENTS

The Cabal represents a vast rogues' gallery of foes, all of which would prefer to see you bullet-ridden and six feet under. The Cabal has transformed from a hoard of robed mystics to a megacorporation full of militaristic soldiers. Still, they all bleed easily enough.

NOTE Most Cabal Agents will take area specific damage. That is, they'll take 50 percent less damage from shots to their appendages, but die instantly from head shots. The exception is the Prophet.

CABAL CULTIST

These are the "rent-a-cops" of the Cabal army. While they don't look like your typical cultist dressed in their snazzy business suits, don't let it fool you. They've sworn to serve the Cabal, so feel free to fill them with your ammunition of choice. Don't waste the heavy artillery on these guys, though, since they're typically only armed with Baretta pistols (though they can sometimes carry better weapons) and can't take much punishment. Moreover, they're not that bright, panic easily, and have only average tracking ability.

CABAL FANATIC

Fanaticism has its rewards in the ranks of the Cabal. Not only do you get to wear cool urban camouflage and a gas mask, but you get your very own Assault Rifle and 10 percent off day-old sandwiches at the Cabalco cafeteria. Before you can acquire some heavy firepower of your own, these guys can be a real nuisance. To make matters worse, Fanatics can occasionally activate a special canister that injects chemical stimulants directly into their brain. This drives them into berzerker mode, spiking their health to 60 and their armor to 50. Take them out fast and try to separate them if you find them in groups. To make matters worse, Fanatics have been known to trade in their Assault Rifles for even more dangerous weapons. Note: Fleeing Fanatics will drop proximities to discourage the player from following them.

ZEALOTS

Like the Fanatics, the Zealots represent some of the Cabal's most elite shock troops. However, while Fanatics rely on military weapons, Zealots rely on dark magic to try to separate your head from your shoulders. They have three means of attack: First, they can shoot deadly blue balls of mystic energy that travel quickly. Second, they can attack with magical fire, also at a good distance. Third, if you get too close for their comfort, they can erect a magical shield that pushes you back to a safer distance. Zealots often travel in groups with other Zealots and Fanatics. Take them down as fast as you can with a medium-range weapon. Zealots self-destruct shortly after death. They also can heal themselves if left alone, and they may be able to heal others.

PROPHETS

They don't get much nastier than this. Prophets are kept in reserve by the Cabal for the times when real power is needed. Heavily armored and armed to the teeth, these guys can put you in a world of hurt, especially when in groups. Prophets are not affected by body-specific damage (like head shots), and they can use any weapon. Get out some of your heavier artillery to punch through their armor and take them out.

MAD SCIENTIST

Remember that nerdy little guy you used to stuff into trash cans in high school? Well, he grew up, joined the Cabal, underwent extreme genetic mutation, and spends his time trying to spring traps on you from his safe little control room. Paybacks are hell. The Mad Scientist never attacks you directly, but rather activates traps and other environmental effects to try to do you in. If you can make your way to his control room, he'll just try to run away and beg for his life.

OTHERWORLD CREATURES

As you progress in the game, you'll encounter more and more creepy creatures from beyond the great abyss. No, not from New Jersey—from the Otherworld. These foes are more frightening for good reasons. A lot of them can really put some serious hurt on you without even blinking. Play it smart and try to save your ammo/focus for the right occasions.

BONE LEECH

Ewwww...that pretty much sums up the Bone Leech. These little parasitic worms are vulnerable outside of their hosts, which is part of the reason they'd like to scurry up your chest and attach to your throat. And this symbiotic relationship isn't like that bird that sits on top of the hippopotamus in those nature television shows. Bone Leeches are nasty! They don't have many health points, though, so squash them before they can annoy you too much.

SOUL DRUDGE

A tracheotomy gone bad, the Soul Drudge is the first step in the parasitic Bone Leech's evolution after attaching itself onto a victim. The Bone Leech controls the former human by grafting onto its throat and spinal cord, and will attack anything that looks threatening (hint: *you* look threatening). The good news is these guys don't have the coordination to handle firearms, so all they can do is try to close in on you and hack you with their crowbars, knifes, axes, or whatever else is handy. Keep your distance, pick them off, and don't let yourself get hooked with the chain or backed into a corner. Soul Drudges can only be defeated by doing damage to the head or chest, so target those areas. As with the Cabal Agents, soul drudges are affected by body-specific damage, just like humans are.

TIP

Here's a great strategy for easily taking out enemies with a melee attack, especially Soul Drudges or the Drudge Lords: run like a maniac and get right in their faces. This will cause them to switch from ranged attack mode to melee. When they rear back to take a swipe at you, backpedal and fill them full of lead while they finish their swing. Repeat until they're dead. Just be careful trying to use this tactic in a crowd—you can get surrounded easily.

DRUDGE LORD

Given time to grow, a Soul Drudge will evolve into the more powerful and more dangerous Drudge Lord. These unpleasant fellows will try to skewer you with giant bone hooks protruding from their forearms, and they won't stop until one of you is dead—again. Metal plates over their chest and neck make Drudge Lords harder to kill, and when damaged they occasionally drop a Bone Leech parasite. These monstrosities are capable of a magical ranged attack in the form of a fireball, but it's fairly easy to dodge. When battling Drudge Lords be on the lookout for other threats; they like to keep Soul Drudges around as lackeys. Drudge Lords take 50 percent more damage from head shots, and only 25 percent normal damage from appendage shots.

DRUDGE PRIEST

The top rung in the evolutionary ladder of the Bone Leech, the Drudge Priests possess magical powers that make them quite dangerous. They float above the ground, the former human body host hanging like a gestation sack for more Bone Leeches. Put them down however you like, but be careful—they often drop more Bone Leeches when they die.

SHIKARI

These spindly creatures are full of predatory rage and ferocity. Shikari are always out looking for a good meal, and you look as tasty as anything else. Once they set their sights on you, they'll relentlessly pursue you, swimming, climbing, jumping, and even scaling walls or ceilings so they can rip you apart with their claws. They can dodge, shimmy, and jive their way out of danger, and can leap forward to close gaps between themselves and their prey. And as if that weren't enough, they can spit streams of powerful acid at you from across great distances. Once a Shikari takes its prey down, it will ignore everything else while it gorges itself. Shikari take body-specific damage like the Drudge Lord.

CHOKING HANDS

Waste not want not. Fresh, whole corpses to be made into Soul Drudges or zombies to serve the whims of the Cabal aren't always available. As a result, the mad scientists have to make due with what they have. Often that's just a spare hand or two. What these things lack in menacing appearance they make up for in determination and zeal. Don't let them get too close, or they'll grab onto your face and start squeezing it harder than an old lady testing melons at the supermarket. If they do manage to get the drop on you and start giving you the old cranial massage, you'll have to shake them off by pressing the "use" key repeatedly.

THIEF

This creature has elevated taking advantage of others to a whole new level. The Thief is a small, stealthy, spider-like creature that attacks from behind attaching to the base of the skull, injecting a poison that slowly destroys the victim's nervous system until death occurs. If the poison does not immediately cause death it will cause extreme disorientation. Kill it quickly.

DEATH SHROUD

The death shroud is a creature composed almost entirely of fell magic. It is in a state of constant fluctuation between our world and the Otherworld, causing it to fade in and out of sight, especially when endangered. You're often nose-to-nose with these nasties before you even realize you're in their presence. Not only can they take a fair amount of damage, they can turn almost completely invisible. In intense firefights where you can't keep your eye on them, this can be problematic. Death Shrouds attack by launching jets of flame that attach to whatever they contact, including you. Take them out quickly and don't turn your back on them.

BOSSES

What global megacorporation would be complete without big bad bosses? You'll have to fight or maneuver your way through a few really tough fights to round off each chapter of the game, but don't fret—you've got information on your side (though a Napalm launcher couldn't hurt, either).

BEHEMOTH

This giant predator serves as the boss at the end of the Chapter 2, and even makes more appearances later in the game. Fresh off the buss from the Elder God dimension, the Behemoth spells trouble if you're not ready for him. It will attack whatever it comes across, but has little ability to track you over distances or around many corners. This creature is very difficult to kill, due in no small part to its tough armor. Then you've got to kill it again. Going toe-to-toe with a Behemoth isn't really advisable; a much better strategy is to find a place up high, if possible, where you can snipe at it until it goes down. Just be careful, because it is capable of ranged attacks. You'll be facing two of these creatures as you go along.

NAGA

Big, ugly, and lots of trouble for those without heavy artillery, the Naga serves as the boss of Chapter 1. Keep moving, and try to find some cover you can duck in and out of. The Naga is big, which makes it a bit intimidating, but it also means it can't follow you a lot of places. Find those places and use them strategically.

GIDEON

The current leader of the Cabal and C.E.O. of Cabalco, Gideon is the reason behind many of your troubles, but you'll have to wait until the end of Chapter 3 to thank him for it. He's fast, tough, wily, and loaded up with enough magic to tear you apart with ease if you're not careful. If you've got any heavy weaponry or powerups lying around, now would be a good time to use them.

UNDEAD GIDEON

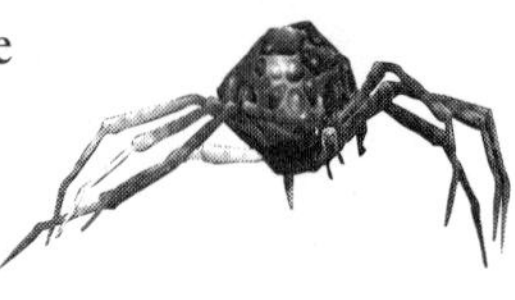

The head cheese at Cabalco makes an encore appearance at the end of Chapter 4. He looks, acts, and smells exactly like the Gideon you fought at the end of Chapter 3, but once you crack his outer shell his undead form reveals itself and his attacks are renewed.

THE ANCIENT ONE

He's the final Boss. I don't want to give away too much information, since your fight with this guy is one of the high points of *Blood II*, and you may not want to spoil the surprise. It's really nothing like what you may be expecting. If you need information on him/her/it and tips for coming out of the final confrontation alive, they're provided in the walkthrough for the last level.

Part II

BLOODY WALKTHROUGHS

For a guy like Caleb, taking a hundred years off to gather your thoughts is really an extraordinary thing to do. Oh, sure, there's been the occasional act of senseless violence (always to somebody that had it coming, rest assured), but a hundred years without any direct assault on one's sworn enemy is a hard thing to wait through. Well, the wait is over. Time to strap on the old gunbelts and show the Cabal who's the boss. And it sure as heck isn't that skirt-wearing geek Gideon! Blood II: The Chosen is roughly divided up into four chapters, each of which culminates in an intense encounter with a "boss" enemy. Load up and read on.

Level 1

CABALCO TRANSIT SYSTEM

Things start out easy, but don't expect a leisurely ride on the city's mass transit. Gideon, the head of the Cabal, has finally tracked you down and has sent some of his goons to get in your way. The game starts with Gideon's rudely interrupting your leisurely subway ride with his plans to wear your internal organs as fashion accessories. You really shouldn't stand for that sort of insult. He's got nowhere to hide, so slap a fresh clip in your Pistol and make a bee-line for the conductor's booth.

OBJECTIVES: .... Catch up with Gideon at the front of the subway train.

ENEMIES: .... Cultists

ITEMS: .... Health

WEAPONS: .... Pistol

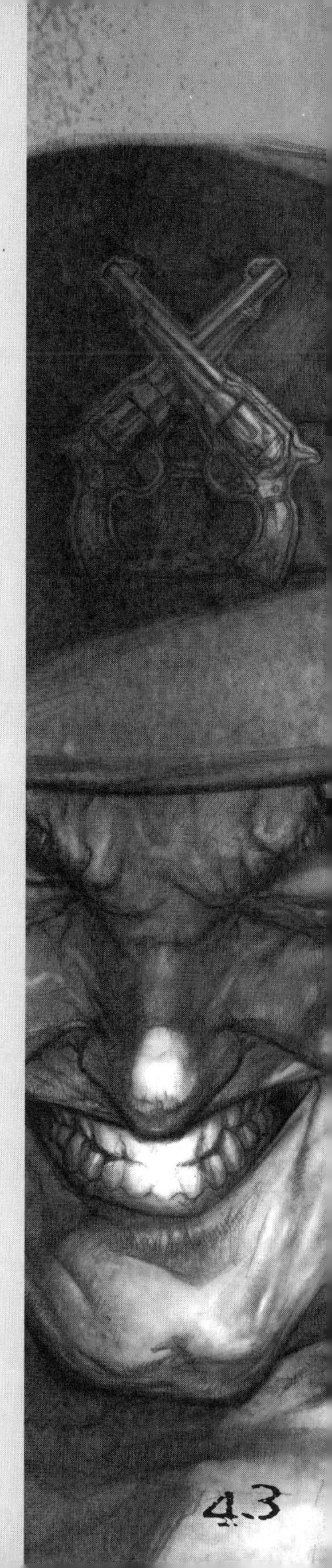

This level is pretty straight forward. As a matter of fact, if you go any way *but* up the middle of the train you'll fall to your death on the tracks. You don't have much to work with besides your starting weapons, but that's not too bad. All you'll encounter here are a few Cultists with pistols. If you prefer, take care not to mow down the terrified passengers, but be warned that the Cultists won't share your humanity and will gleefully spray the car with bullets to take you out.

Gideon is always just out of range in this level, but keep on after him. Once you reach the **front of the train (1)**, the level will end with Gideon's escape and attempt to kill you (and everyone else on board) by crashing the train.

Level 2

PICKMAN ST. STATION

Gideon almost did you in with that crashing subway bit, but he just doesn't understand that you're too stubborn to die that easily. Either that or he's just toying with you, like evil geniuses do sometimes. Still, he made a mistake either way, because you're going to track his skinny butt down and nail it to the wall. You wake lying on the cold pavement where you were thrown clear of the subway when it crashed. Pick yourself up, dust yourself off, and get ready to tear through downtown with guns blazing. Gideon can't make it far.

OBJECTIVES:........ Make your way through the city so you can continue your pursuit of Gideon through the Museum.

ENEMIES:........... Cultists

ITEMS:............ Ammo, Health, Wards, Life Seed, Flashlight, Remote Bombs, Proximity Bombs

WEAPONS:........... Pistols, SMG, Flare Gun

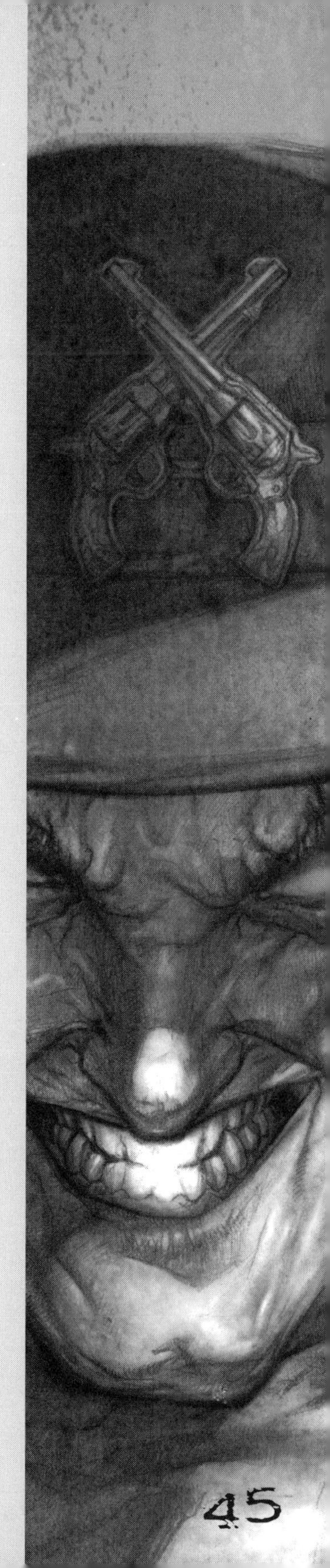

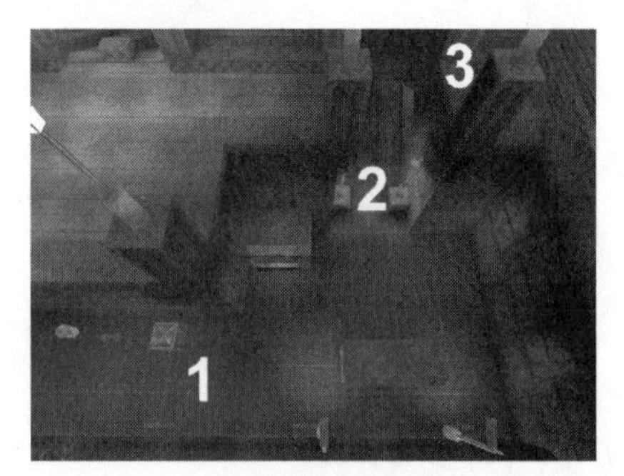

After you regain your senses, bust open the nearby trash sack and trash cans to get a **Ward** and some **health.** Then carefully walk around the fence (1). Don't jump or fall down onto the subway tracks or you'll be electrocuted. Walk past the magazine stand and take the escalators (2) to the upper platform. Mow down the Cabal Cultists waiting at the top, then jump across to the ledge (3) above the escalators to **score some ammo** and **health** inside the trash cans. Jump back across and go through the archway to the right of the escalators, gunning down Cultists as you go.

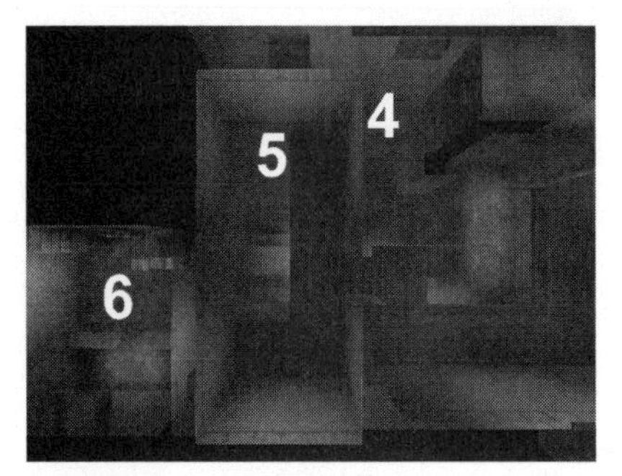

Follow the hallway around to the entrance of "Crazy Eric's Guns and Ammo"—your kind of store! Before letting yourself in, gun down the Cultists, then climb on top of the pipe opposite the store so you can dive across to the dumpster to find a **flashlight**. Jump back out and let yourself into Eric's, watching for the Cultists that will attack from the catwalk overhead. Notice Eric behind the bar. He's crazy. He's armed. He's annoying. It's a good bet Gideon has been through this way. From the front door (4), go through the only other doorway leading out of the room opposite you. Follow the hallway around until you come to some stairs (5). Don't go up yet, but rather stop in at the nearby shooting range (6) to stock up on **ammo** and grab a **sub-machine gun**. Eric won't mind. After you've grabbed all you can, fight your way up the stairs (5).

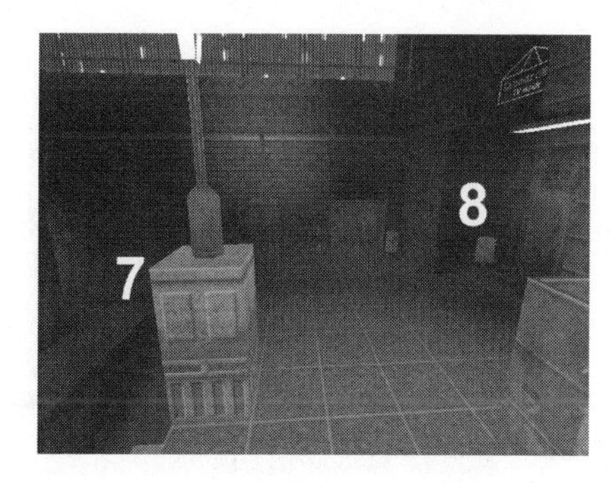

Cross the catwalk above the main shop floor and go through the hole in the wall to the alley with a Cultist outside. Follow the alley until you come to an outside area with one set of steps leading down into a drainage sewer (7) and another leading up to the entrance to the LaundroHut. Go up to the entrance to the LaundroHut and **push the barrel (8)** up against the nearby trash dumpster to the right of the door. Hop up onto the barrel and then into the dumpster to find **two remote bombs**. There is also a **health** in the trash bag to the left of the door. As much fun as watching clothes spin in a drier sounds, forgo the LaundroHut for now and head down the steps into the sewage drain. Swim through the open tube straight ahead since the one to the right is blocked.

NOTE

The Laundromat will eventually lead you into the Steam Tunnels, but that path is blocked right now. Still, you may want to stop in and shoot the washing machine that has acquired a taste for human blood. This will grant you a Life Seed. Go back outside after doing so.

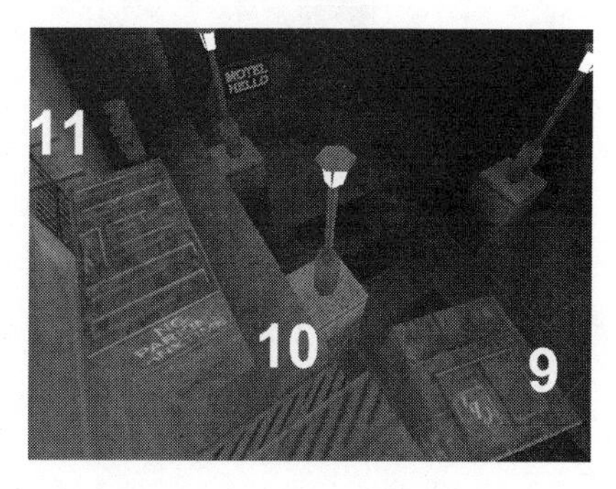

Surface on the other side of the tunnel with guns blazing, because there will be a few Cultists waiting for you. After you've cleared the area, climb the stairs in front of the Motel Hell. Look inside the capsized dumpster (9) to find some **ammo**. Hop onto the dumpster, jump across to the ledge opposite it (10), then onto the second dumpster to your right. From there, hurdle the fence (11) and drop into the alley beyond.

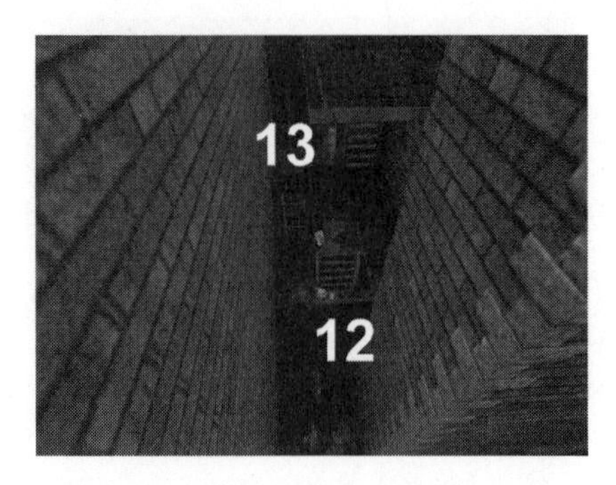

Follow the alley around until you come to a fire escape and another dumpster. Take out the Cultists lurking nearby, then climb the fire escape ladder (12) to the second level. From there, jump across the fence (13) to the courtyard beyond. Clear the court of Cultists and then tear open the **trash bags** and cans to find a **Ward** and a **health**. When you're done, jump onto the dumpster and proceed down the alley opposite the court to enter the Museum.

TIP

If you're really slick, you can jump from the trash dumpster to the top of the narrow "No Dumping" sign, then to the ledge over on your right. If you can pull this tricky jump off, you'll SCORE A COUPLE OF BOMBS.

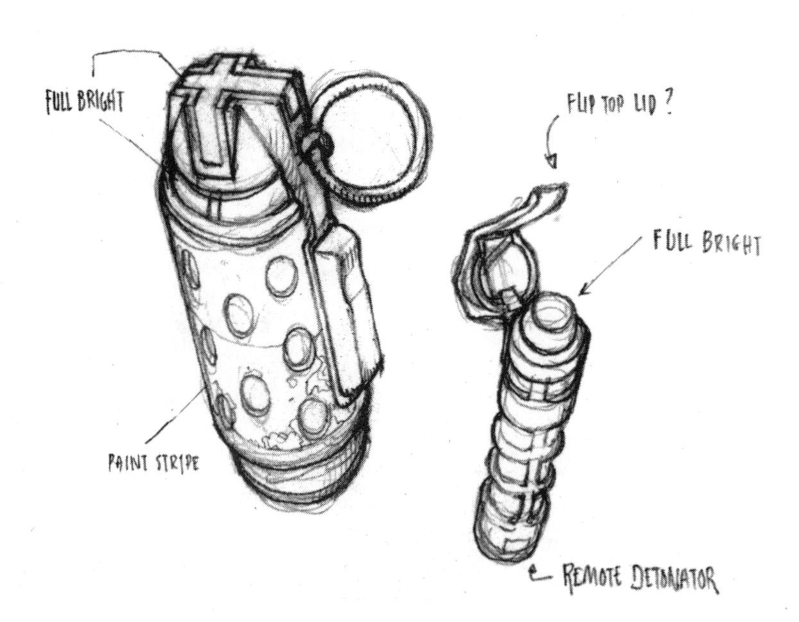

Level 3

LAFAYETTE MUSEUM OF ANTIQUITIES

You've got Gideon trapped inside the Lafayette Museum. Time to go tear him a new one, and break some priceless art while you're at it! It's after hours, so at least you don't have to worry about any civilians getting in your way. Still, something doesn't quite feel right about this. The more cautious part of you thinks you might want to reconsider charging headlong into the museum. Too bad the part of you screaming for bloody murder is much more persuasive.

OBJECTIVES: . . . . Find your way through the Museum and Catch up with Gideon

ENEMIES: . . . . Cultists, Fanatics

ITEMS: . . . . Ward, Necroward, Willpower. The All-Seeing Eye

WEAPONS: . . . . Pistols, SMG's

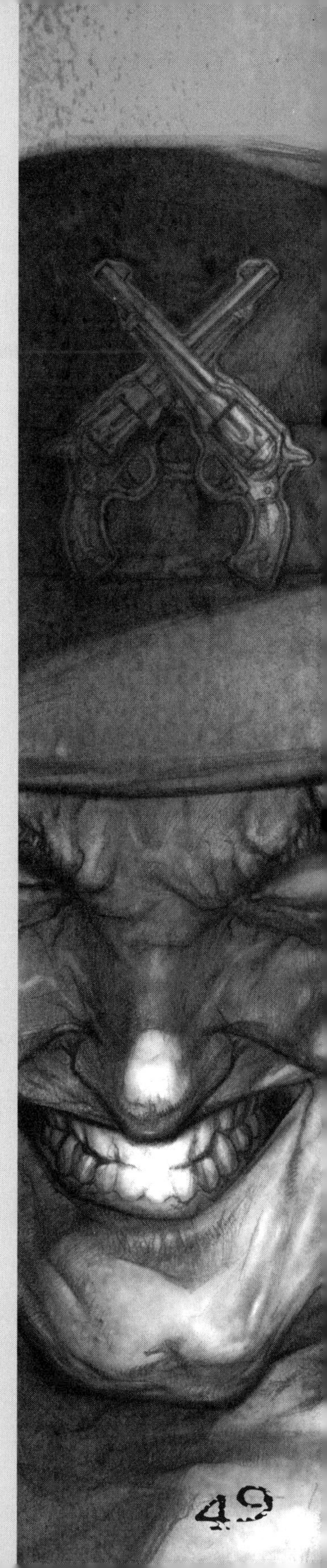

When you start this level, you have two choices right off the bat as to how to proceed. If you decide to go the direct route, you can blast the lock off the front doors (1) and go through shooting. Or, to take a saner approach, you can walk around the alley to the right of the front door, climb the fire escape, and, from a safe distance, **blast the flammable fuel line** on the side of the building (2). While this isn't exactly quiet and stealthy, it does create a ridge on the side of the building that you can climb to access a Willpower powerup on the roof. Either route you take, spend a moment searching through the trash cans outside the museum to get a **Ward** and some **health.**

TIP

If you prefer, you can go through the front doors, but you'll meet with some pretty tough resistance in the form of Fanatics. Since you probably don't have really heavy artillery at this point, it's easier on the health and ammo if you follow the alternative route described here.

The ridge leads you to a shaft that empties out onto the roof. Go all the way at the other end of the roof and grab the **Willpower** powerup behind the skylight. Quickly **shoot out the skylight** and jump down in the middle of a gang of Fanatics below. Send them to oblivion before your powerup wears off. Climb the steps to confront Gideon...or so you think. What a wuss. Mr. Big Stuff can't even face you directly; he has to taunt you through holograms. Notice, however, that the doorway behind you is now blocked by security lasers and you have a hoard of Fanatics and Cultists breathing down your neck. One of the Fanatics is even wielding a **Shotgun.**

WARNING

Those security lasers hurt. Don't get too close, and for heaven's sake, don't try walking through them. They're just Gideon's way of herding you through the level on the path he'd like you to take. Not too much you can do about it at this point, though. Watch the Fanatics. One will be wielding a Shotgun.

Shoot out the glass on the display in front of you (3) and slip through the lasers to get the Necroward. Then turn around and go through the left-hand hallway (4), since it's the only one unblocked by lasers. Go through the doorway labeled "West Wing" and follow the hallway (notice that the security lasers activate behind you).

Follow the hallway until you come to a short flight of stairs guarded by a Cultist. Climb them to have your second confrontation with a Gideon Hologram. Fight your way up the stairs to your left (5) and go through the doorway at the top (6). Follow the hallway through another set of security lasers and a set of double doors guarded by Cultists.

After going through the double doors, blast past Fanatics on your way down the green-tiled stairway (7) then go through the security lasers on your right (8) to the North Wing. Follow the hallway around to another holographic Gideon in the lair of the Mecha-Tchernobog!

Hit the button on the left wall (9) to activate the robotic Tchernobog (10). Uh oh...Looks like someone wasn't maintaining Mr. Tchernobog very well. He sort of blew up. That's going to be hard to explain to the Museum curator in the morning. On the plus side, it did leave an interesting looking hole in the floor. **Drop down** and see what you can find.

After dropping down you'll find yourself in the museum storage area. Take a right at the truck and follow the hallway full of crates and Fanatics until you come to a door labeled "Exit" on your left. Go through and walk through the blue-lit room with a vase on display. Take the short stairway on the left (11) leading down from this room. Follow the hallway through another set of lasers to a room with more crates.

NOTE

In the last room, you'll be confronted by Gideon. It turns out the museum was supposed to be a trap for you, but the joke's on him as he accidentally raises Gabriella from a rift. Always the chicken, Gideon and his lackeys then make their escape.

After fighting off the Fanatics, go through the archway on the right (12) and **shoot out the fire extinguisher** down the hall on the left to rip open a passageway to the next level.

Level 4

CONDEMNED TENEMENT

You made it out of the Museum alive (or whatever it is you are), but your pursuit of Gideon isn't over yet. You're going to have to track him through the downtown hub level again. Things have changed a little since you were here last, so keep a sharp eye out. You'll have your first encounters with two Otherworld creatures: the Soul Drudge and the Bone Leech.

OBJECTIVES: .... Trudge back through the City Hub to access the Steam Tunnels.

ENEMIES: .... Cultists, Soul Drudges, Bone Leeches

ITEMS: .... None

WEAPONS: .... Flare Gun

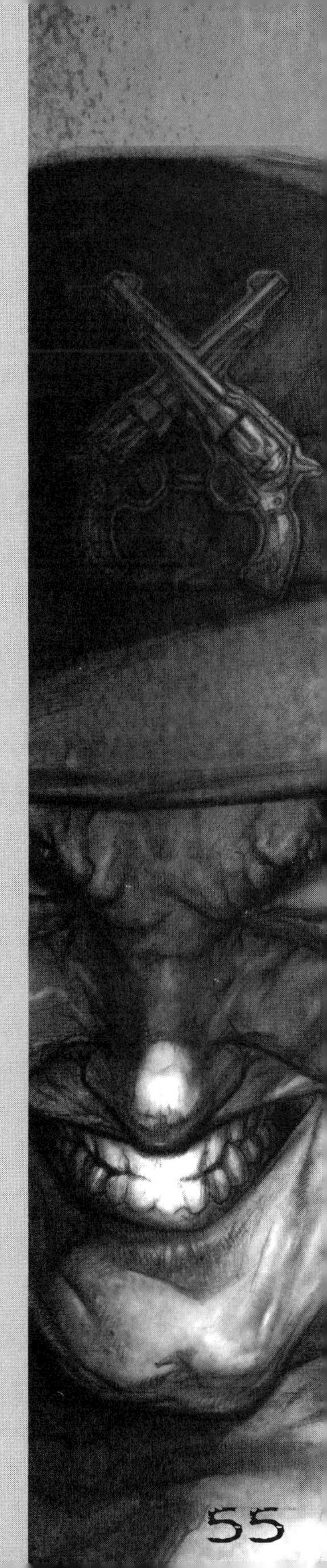

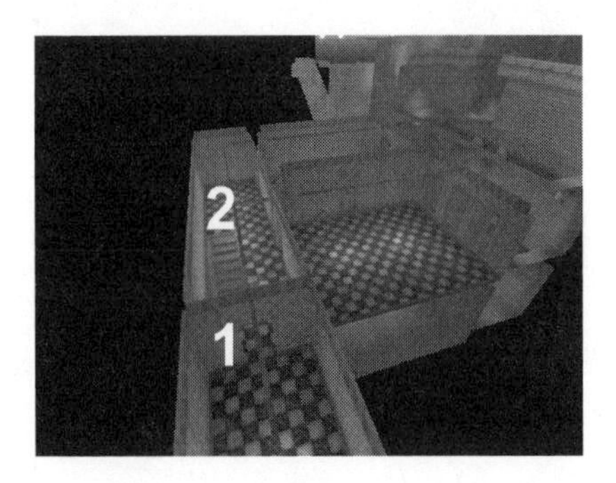

You start this level inside a condemned apartment building. Things don't look too safe here, and it's not just because of the crumbling support beams and sub-standard ventilation. If you listen carefully, you can hear something unpleasant on the other side of the doorway before you (1). Carefully investigate the rooms beyond. Once you've dispatched the Soul Drudge, go down the stairs (2), finish off a couple more and a Cultist, then exit the building. Once outside, turn to your left and drop down through the broken tiles into the sewer below.

While crawling through the sewer, you'll need to take special care to watch out for Bone Leeches. They're hard to see under the water, so keep an eye out. Your knife makes an excellent weapon to use against these little pests.

TIP

If a Bone Leech does manage to grab on to your face and get a little too intimate, you can shake it off by repeatedly hitting the "use" key.

Swim down the tunnel and go right when it forks. You'll come out in front of the entrance to the LaundroHut. Kill off any more Bone Leeches, Soul Drudges, and Cultists. Go through the doors (3) and from there walk around to the back and enter the Steam Tunnels (4).

Level 5

STEAM TUNNELS

To get through this level you're going to have to navigate some pretty treacherous environments. To make things worse, it looks like most of the city's sanitation workers have been infested with Bone Leeches, turning them into Soul Drudges ...or worse. Don't zip around corners too quickly on this level, since danger awaits you everywhere. The Shikari are often particularly troublesome, since you may stilllack really heavy artillery. You might consider running at certain points, or tricking the beasts into falling into the water.

OBJECTIVES:........ Shut off all steam vents so you can continue through the tunnels to the CDM.

ENEMIES:........... Soul Drudges, Drudge Lord, Shikari, Fanatics

ITEMS:............ Medkit, Night Vision Goggles, Remote Bombs, Life Seed

WEAPONS:.......... None

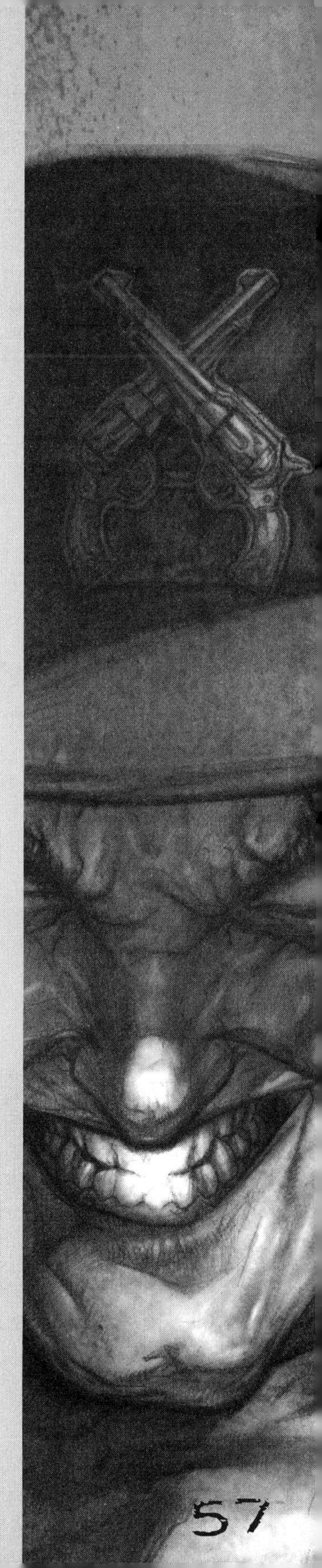

If you took a beating on the last couple of levels, there's a wealth of **health** underneath the stairs (1) you start out on. Grab it, then go through the door to the right of the elevator. Once in the room beyond, climb the stairs, shoot the Drudge Lord at the top, and **throw the lever** (2) to shut off the steam vents before you. This lever also shuts off some vents that would have blocked your path later in the level. Make sure you take the time to bust open the nearby crates to find some **ammunition.**

WARNING

The steam vents you encounter throughout this level are extremely dangerous. Contacting any of them will result in your death (although your clothes will all be crisp and neatly pressed). To get past the vents and progress, you'll have to shut them off with various controls throughout the level.

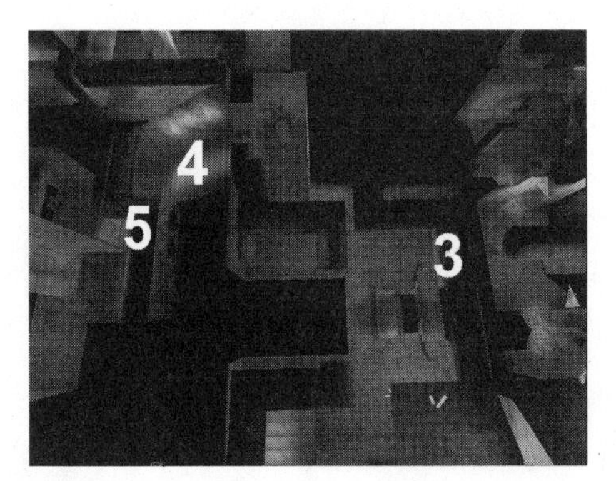

Backtrack to the icky pool underneath the elevator and move forward past the burning barrel. Gun down the Soul Drudge that comes out to greet you, then follow the hallway, go down some stairs, and come to an area with a door labeled "Valve Control" (3). Follow the hallway to the left, go down some more stairs (4), and carefully skirt past two active steam vents (5). You'll encounter several Drudge Lords along the way, so make sure you're ready for them.

On this level and every other level in the game, make sure ou break open any breakable crates you find lying around. They're like big presents wrapped in wood just like your crazy uncle Elmo used to give you on your birthday. And just like uncle Elmo's gifts, most of these crates contain live ammuniton. Use your knife when opening them to save ammo.

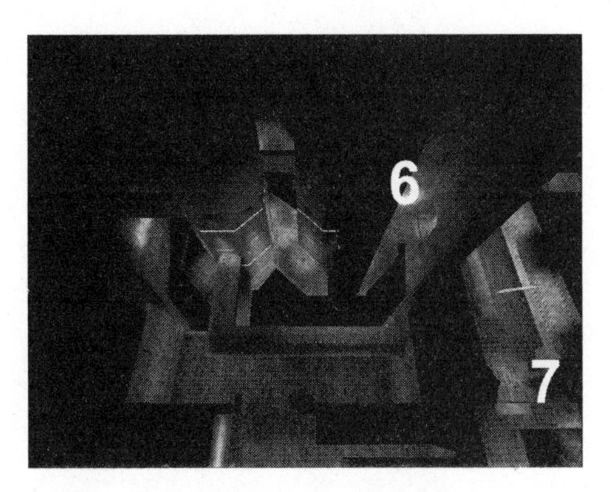

You'll come to a more open area with two great columns rising out of a sewage pool. It's here that you'll have your first run-in with one of the deadly Shikari. It'll be coming from the right, so don't let it catch you unawares. Once you're done with it, run up the twisting ramp over the pool and go through the door labeled "Sewer Access" (6). Follow the hallway and **shoot out the boards** blocking the door at the end (7) to gain access to the Shikari-infested Storage area.

Once in the Storage area, feel free to bust things up while fighting off the Shikari. Also be sure to grab the **Medkit** and **Night Vision Goggles** in this room. When you're done, shoot out the pipes blocking the hole in the wall opposite the door you entered through. Jump up, climb through, and waste the Soul Drudge waiting on the other side. Follow the short hallway, go through a door, and come into the Maintenance area. Be ready for the Shikari on the other side.

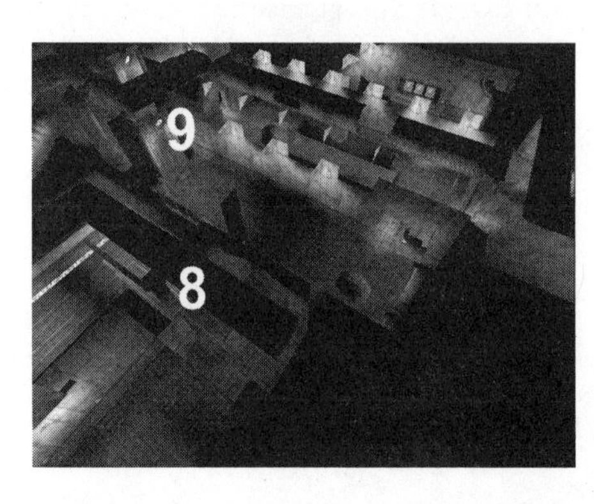

Follow the hallway around the corner until you come to a passage with a grated floor leading off to your left (8). Turn left into this passage and follow it to the Valve Access room. Blast past the Soul Drudge you meet on the way.

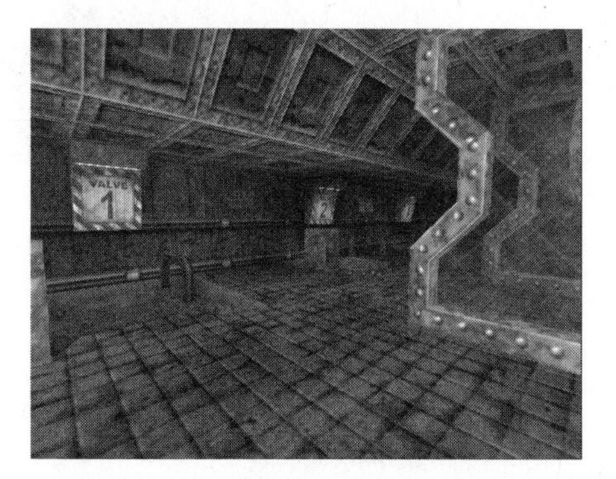

In this room you will find three elevators labeled 1 through 3 (and a Soul Drudge hiding in the corner). Ride down each one to the main steam tubes and **turn the wheel hidden behind each of the tubes** to deactivate them, carefully walking around the catwalk. Watch out for the Shikari lying in ambush above, though. After you've done one tube, ride the lift back up and do the next. After you've deactivated all 3 tubes, you'll have access to a new area of the level.

WARNING

If you fall in the water, watch out! There's a suctionfan near the ladder where you climb out of the water.The fan will suck you down and chew you up if you get too close.

Retrace your steps through the passage with the grated floor and turn left at its end. You'll come to a wide hallway with an active steam vent blocking a doorway on your right and a lever down the hall on your left (9) guarded by a Shikari and Soul Drudge. **Throw the lever** to deactivate the vent so you can go through the doorway.

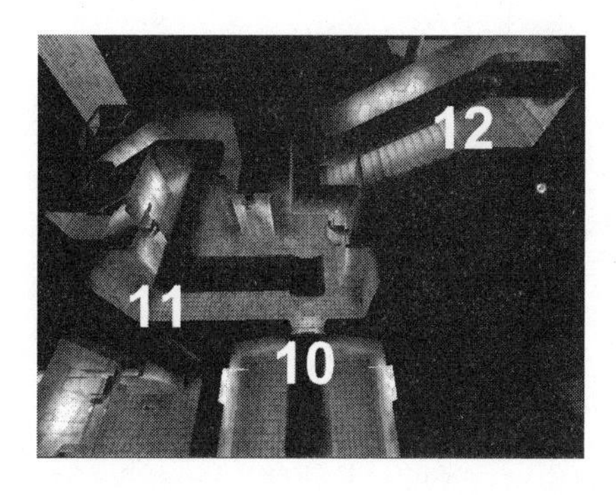

You will now be in an area with a bridge to your left running over more sewage, flanked by two deactivated steam vents. A couple of Soul Drudges will try to detain you—blast them and cross the bridge. Once on the other side, go through the door (10). After you've taken down the gang of Drudge Lord and the Shikari on the other side, take the hallway to your left (11) instead of climbing the stairway opposite you (12).

NOTE

You can view one of Blood II's many hidden tributes to the horror genre near the bridge flanked by steam vents. Before crossing the bridge, go through the door labeled "Maintenance". Kill the Soul Drudge, then walk between the two giant pipes in the back of the room. Follow the tunnel to the lair of the Predator, where you can score some Remote Bombs and a Necroward.

Follow the hall down some stairs until you come to a room with two great columns rising out of a moat of sewage. The room is guarded by Shikari and a Soul Drudge. There are **three levers** to your right (13). **Throw them in the following order** to deactivate the steam vents on the other side of the moat: **left, right, middle.**

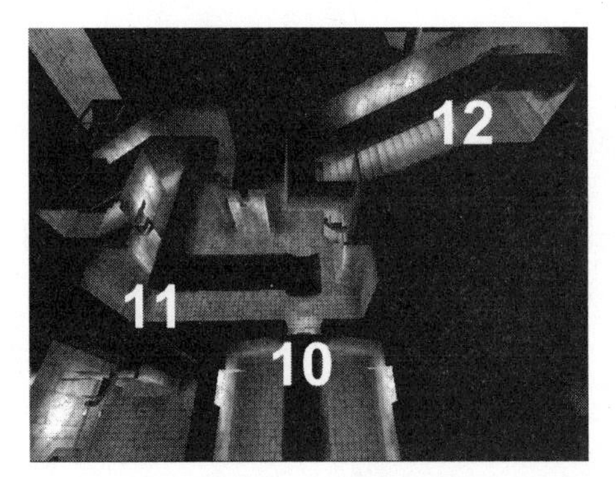

Don't bother trying to swim the moat; you can't climb out the other side. Instead, turn around and retrace your steps to the stairs (12) opposite the door you came through when you crossed the metal bridge (10). Climb the stairs and meet up with a Drudge Lord and his Soul Drudge buddies. After you're done playing with them, pick up the Life Seed the Drudge Lord drops. Then follow the hallway at the top until you come to a fourth elevator similar to the three you rode down earlier to deactivate the main steam tubes. Kill the Soul Drudges guarding it, and then **take the elevator down**. Walk past the deactivated vents on your right follow the hallway through a number of Shikari and Soul Drudges. Once you come to a doorway on the left-hand wall, take it and clean out the Shikari and Fanatics guarding the entrnace to the Center for Disease Management.

Level 6

CENTER FOR DISEASE MANAGEMENT

The many arms of Cabalco never fail to amaze. What other company could produce children's toys *and* biological warfare agents? Try not to breathe too deeply on this level, because you're heading straight into the heart of the Cabal's disease management (and creation) center. You're not a very welcome guest, though, so you'll have to be clever and find alternative routes in. You're also in for some of the most intense firefights in the game, so get your heavy weaponry ready at the beginning of this level. You'll need it.

OBJECTIVES: .... Infiltrate the CDM and track down Gideon

ENEMIES: .... Fanatics, Cultists, Prophet, Shikari, Soul Drudges

ITEMS: .... Flashlight, Stealth

WEAPONS: .... M16 Assault Rifle, Pistols, SMG, Sawed-Off Shotgun, Sniper Rifle, Tesla Cannon, Voodoo Doll, Death Ray, Sniper Rifle

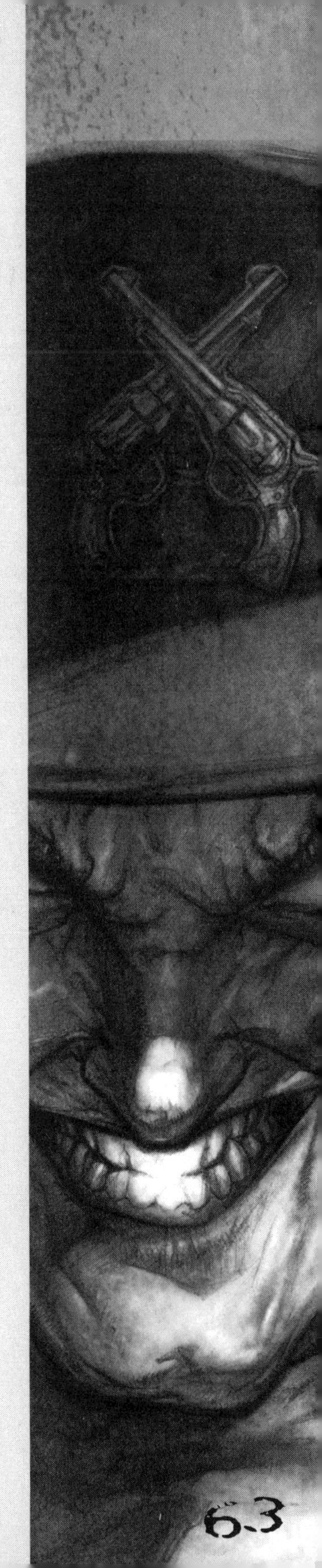

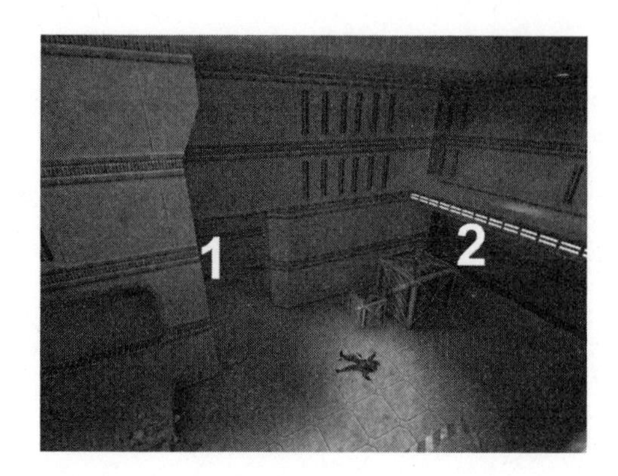

Step off the elevator, go straight forward, and turn left into the computer room (1) gunning down the Fanatics that try to get in your way. You can safely pick any remaining Fanatics off one by one by dodging in and out of this room. After you've cleared the area, scope it out. Notice the conveyor belt (2) running from out of the wall into a nasty looking red pool. You're going to need to return to this belt soon.

WARNING

Don't climb up that conveyor belt yet. There's a grinding machine that cuts up whatever is supposed to come down the belt. It will also cut up whatever is *not* supposed to come down the belt (that is, you).

TIP

You can activate the controls in the small computer room to open the metal doors out in the main area. You can then grab the AMMO and PISTOL on top of the crate in the room on the other side of the glass.

Follow the hallway opposite the computer room you ducked into (1). Go through the door and gun down the Fanatics that run out to greet you. Go through the door they came through and kill off a few more. Don't feel bad. They were probably getting hazard pay for working here. Turn right and go through the door labeled "Examination Lab" (3).

TIP

Mowing down the Scientists can be fun and therapeutic, especially if any of them happen to look like your high school biology teacher. However, it's generally a waste of ammo and is likely to distract you from things that will actually shoot back.

Mow down the Fanatics and grab the guns and **Ward** that they drop. Follow the hallway to the right until you come to a room labeled "Mainframe Access" (4). Also notice the pool of partially dissolved bodies on the other side of the glass opposite the door. Believe it or not, you're heading there soon. Go through the door and find the computer panel in the back of the room. Shove the scientist out of the way and **activate the computer** to disarm the grinding mechanism on the conveyor belt back in the beginning of this level.

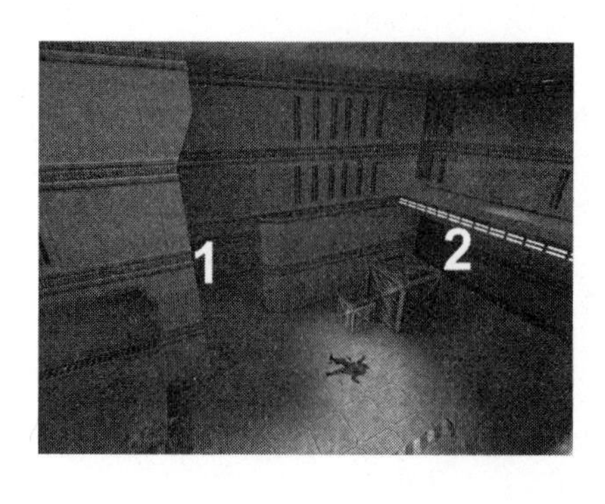

Retrace your steps back to the door leading into the Examination Lab (3), then turn left and backtrack to the PC1 room you started the level in. **Jump up on the conveyor** (2), crouch down, and follow it up into the narrow, red-lit tunnel.

Follow the conveyor belt until you come to that pool of half-dissolved bodies you saw earlier. Gingerly step off the belt onto the ledge over on your right (5), gun down the Fanatic guard and grab his **ammo,** then follow the large pipe (6) down a tight hallway.

WARNING

The pool of green acid is painful, but it's worth a quick dip to grab the LIFE SEED. Jump in, swim across, and grab the powerup. Then jump back as far as you can and quickly scamper up the ladder next to the conveyor belt.

Follow the hallway past several pipes, until you come to a ladder. Watch out for the Shikari ambush on the way. Climb up the ladder through the hole (7) and wave hello to the Fanatic on the other side of the green glass. Blast him when he walks around to ask you for your identification. Go through the door on the right (8) then follow the hallway around to your right. Fight off any Shikari or Fanatics that you encounter on the way and find yourself up on the catwalk overlooking the area where you entered this level.

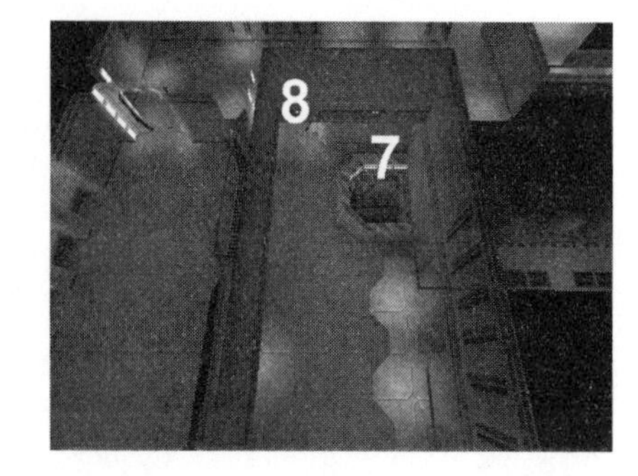

Follow the catwalk all the way around to the passageway on the other side. Gun down the **Tesla Cannon**-wielding Fanatic and take his weapon. Go through the passage and find yourself on another catwalk overlooking a medical lab. Take out any Fanatics and Shikari you find in the area.

NOTE

You'll notice an interesting blue-lit area on your left with security lasers over on your left. You'll be returning here shortly, but you have to find a security pass to disarm the lasers first.

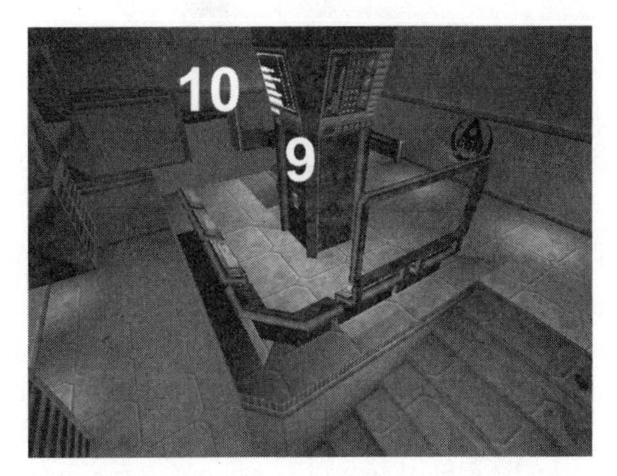

Continue following the catwalk around to the doorway on the other side. Go through and into the PC2 area. Follow the hallway to a security center. Gun down the Fanatics guarding it and go up the stairs to the controls. **Activate the handprint control** (9), which turns off the security lasers over to your left (10).

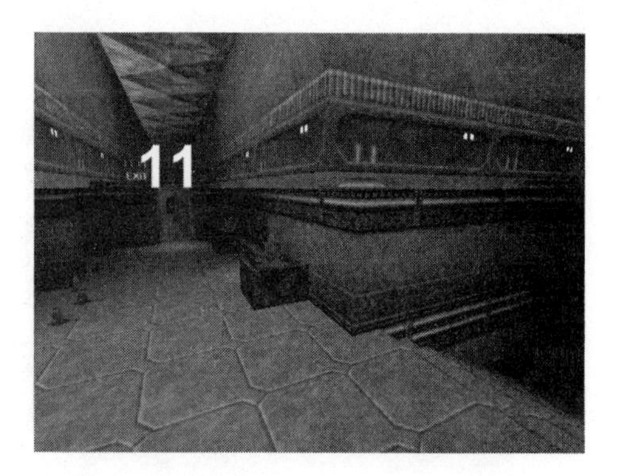

Go through the doorway past the deactivated lasers and climb the stairs on the other side (10), through a Shikari ambush. Walk past the broken elevators on your left and through the door ahead (11) into another computer room. Grab the **Cabalco Access Pass** at the other end of the room on your left.

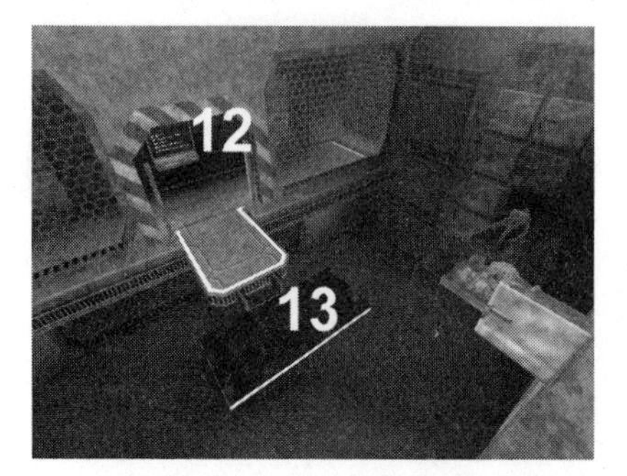

Retrace your steps all the way past the security controls, to the catwalk over the medical lab near the blue-lit area with security lasers. Now that you have the security pass, you can **activate the computer** (12) near the lasers, thus deactivating them. Turn around, enter the morgue and clear it of Shikari and Soul Drudges. After it's safe, jump down and grab the **Voodoo Doll.** Climb back up the ladder and **jump onto the floating platform** (13) when it comes by. (You may have to wait a minute.)

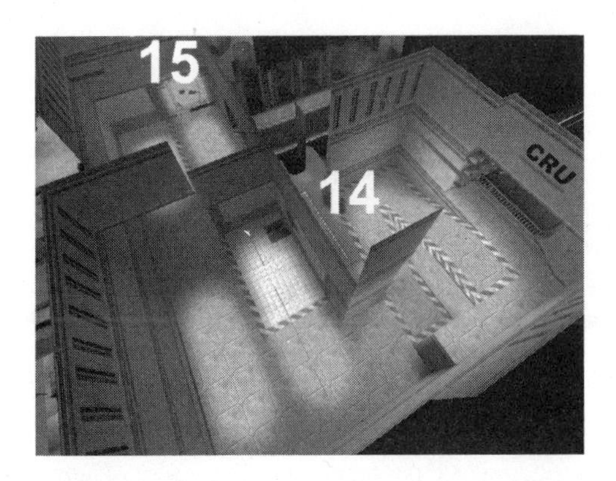

Ride the platform up to the Cryogenic Retrieval Unit. Hop off and blast any Cultists you can find. Walk down the ramp (14) and follow the room until you come to a doorway (15). Just make sure you shoot the cabinets to grab the **Flashlight** and retrieve the **Stealth powerup** from the CRU chamber. Go through the doorway and nail the two Fanatics and Soul Drudges flanking the other side of the door. Pick up any **ammo** and weapons they drop.

Walk around the hallway to your left, past some more broken elevators, and go through the door into the storage area. **Shoot the cabinets to find a Cabalco Death Ray.** Also pick up the lab key lying on the ground, then retrace your steps to the door leading into the Cryogenics area. Walk past it, following the hall in the other direction. Duke it out with the Fanatics guarding the elevator to the rooftops (16).

Open the door to the right of the elevator (you need the key from the storeroom to do so) and enter. **Grab the Security Pass** on the counter (17). Then go through the door on the left-hand side of the lab (18) **shoot the cabinets,** and score some **Proximity Bombs.** Go back out into the hallway, enter the elevator, and activate the controls.

NOTE

You must have the second Security Pass from the nearby storage room to activate the elevator and proceed to the end of the level. A new map willload once you activate the elevator.

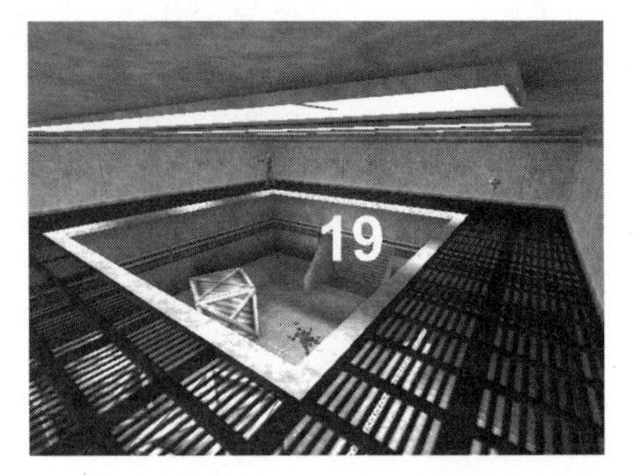

Man, that was one long elevator ride. You can see your house from up here. It's on fire. Darn riots. Turn around, exit the elevator, and walk past the vending machines to the cargo bay door. Open it and have your first meeting with a Prophet. Gun him and his flunky Fanatic friends down, then quickly lay a Proximity Bomb for the Fanatics that rush out the second cargo door (19). If the Prophet dropped his **Sniper Rifle** within reach, grab it. Then go through the second cargo bay door (18) and board the airship.

Level 7

CA'S REVENANT

Man, the Cabal sure know how to fly first class. They've got a veritable flying city at their disposal, and you just bet it would make one heck of a big crater if it were to crash. Only one way to know for sure, though. This level is so large that it's split up into two maps, and you'll have to move between them. You'll encounter mostly Cultists and Fanatics on this level, but the latter are so numerous that you'll be tripping over their bodies before you're done. The good thing, though, is that there are mainly tight corridors where it's easy to find cover and dodge around corners.

OBJECTIVES: .... Access the Bridge and stop this crazy ride.

ENEMIES: .... Cultists, Fanatics, Prophet

ITEMS: .... Wards, Life Seed, The Anger, Parachute

WEAPONS: .... Pistols, Assault Rifles, SMG's, Insect-A-Cutioner, Flare Gun, Sniper Rifle

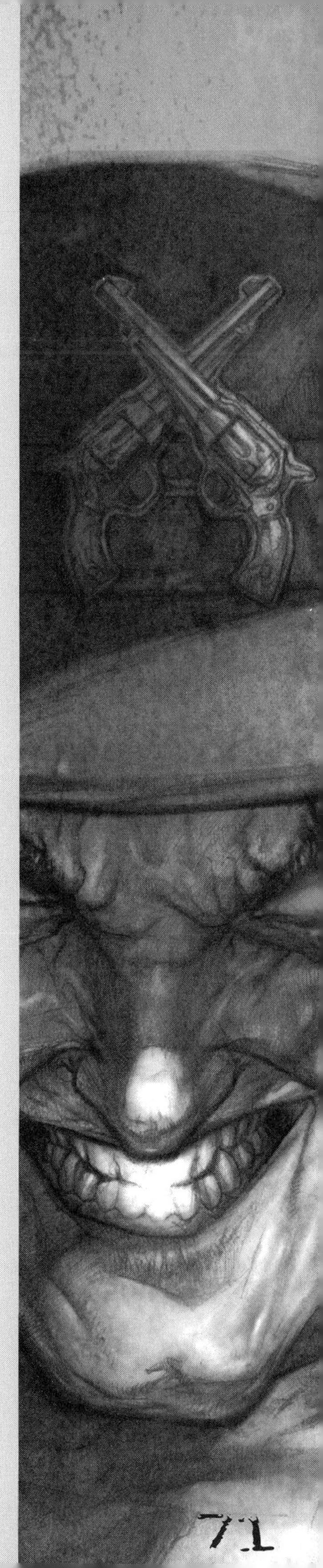

You start this level off by clinging for dear life to the side of the *CAS Revenant.* Step onto the airship's tail. Looks like most of the Fanatic guards haven't noticed you yet, so gently tap the ones nearby on the back of the skull with some bullets. Once the other Fanatics on the other side of the airship's tail notice you, though, you'll have to run for cover. Run down the catwalk and go through the door leading inside (1).

Gun down the Fanatic and Cultists on the other side of the door and **activate the two computer consoles** they were guarding. This deactivates some security measures elsewhere on this level. Go back outside and run across the catwalk to the other side of the airship's tail. Go through the door at the end of the other catwalk (2).

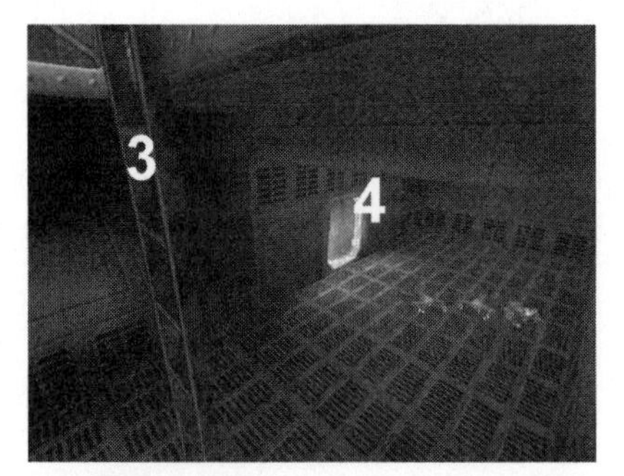

Kill the Cultists and Fanatics on the other side of the door, then **shoot the crates** to get a couple of **Wards**. Climb down the ladder (3) and dispatch the gang of Cabal agents below. After you've retrieved the **ammo from the crates**, proceed through the red-rimmed door (4), across the short catwalk, and through the other door.

You're in for a bit of a firefight here, as Cultists and Fanatics try to take you down from the ground and the catwalk above. After you're done with them, open all the crates to get some **ammo**, go through the doorway (5) and back across the short catwalk to the other side of the plane. Be sure to say "excuse me" when you pitch the Fanatics over the side of the catwalk railing.

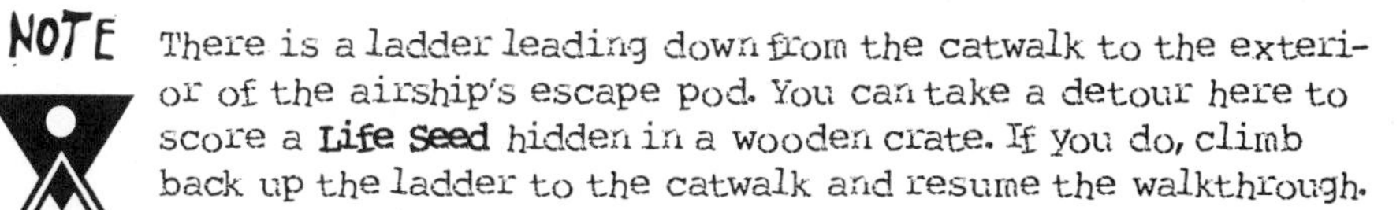

NOTE There is a ladder leading down from the catwalk to the exterior of the airship's escape pod. You can take a detour here to score a **Life Seed** hidden in a wooden crate. If you do, climb back up the ladder to the catwalk and resume the walkthrough.

After you make it through the intense shootout upon reentering the ship, don't bother with the computer panel next to the red force field. Instead, open up all the crates in the area (they contain **ammo**), then climb the ladder (6). At the top of the ladder, follow the hallway back outside to another catwalk (with a Fanatic). Cross the catwalk and follow the hallway to the interior of the *CAS Revenant.*

The map will change at this time.You can return to the exterior of the airship if you like, but it won't be necessary to complete the airship level.

Walk down the short hallway until it forks to the left and right. Gun down the Fanatics on your right, then go down the ladder on your left. Climb down into a small area with a Fanatic and a machine gun cubby hole. While facing the ladder, shoot out the grate on the right (7) and creep through the crawlspace.

Follow the crawlspace until you come to another grate. Shoot it out and come to a room with a giant propeller behind blue glass. Climb up the nearby ladder (8) to another area with a grated floor and Fanatics up on a ledge overhead. Climb another ladder up, then follow the ledge around to a airlock door. Go through.

Come out of the airlock door (10) into a room with two other doors. Walk past the short stairway (11) and go through the far airlock door (12). Follow the hallway and climb the ladder at the end. Climb up to a small room with a Fanatic and a computer terminal. **Activate the terminal** to unlock the first set of doors leading to the Bridge. Climb back down the ladder and return to the room with three airlock doors. This time go through the middle door at the bottom of the short stairway (11).

Follow the tunnel through a few Cultists and another airlock door. On the other side of the door, walk past the entrance to the Bomb Bay and take the ladder leading up on your right (13). This takes you to another small room with a Fanatic and a computer terminal. **Activate the terminal** to grant you access to the Bridge.

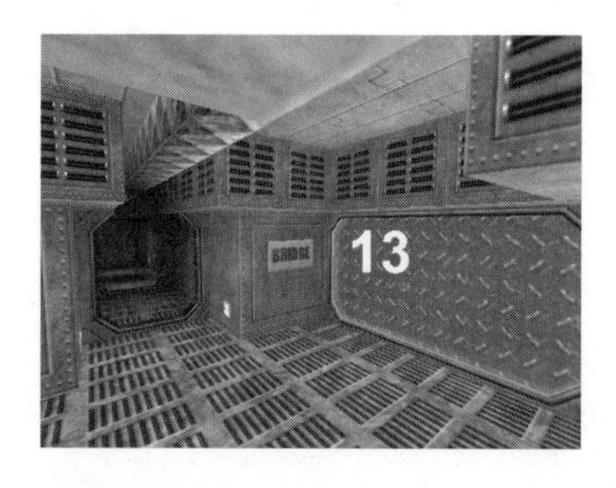

Turn around and go through the doorway opened by the computer terminal. Turn left and walk until you see a double set of open, red-rimmed doors on your right. This leads you to the entrance to the Bridge (13), which is unfortunately blocked by a red force field. Turn right, gun down a Fanatic, and go down the hall until you see a door on your right labeled "Galley."

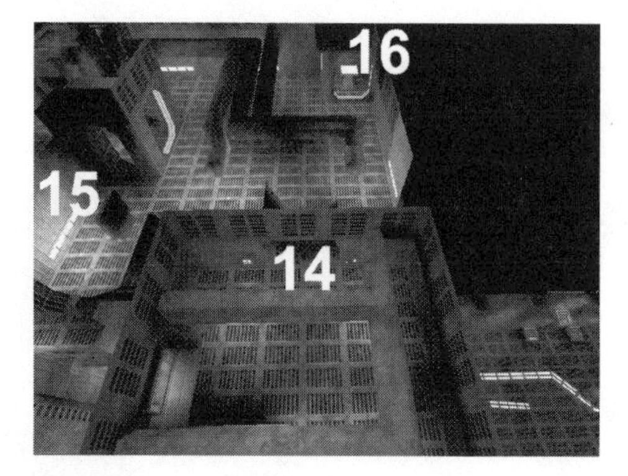

Go through and blast the Fanatic getting ready to sit down and have a nice bowl of soup. Enter the kitchen area on your left and shoot the fire extinguisher (14), which will rip an opening to the Armory beyond. **Break open all the cabinets** to get the ammo inside, then **activate the computer panel** on your left (15), which will shut off the room's force fields, as well as the one blocking your access to the Bridge. Grab the **Anger** from its pedestal (16) and clean up any remaining Cabal agents.

TIP The barracks down the halls to the left and right of the Bridge entrance are loaded with ammunition. Take a minute to go through and break open all the chests and cabinets you can find so you can replenish your supplies.

Make your way back to the Bridge and ride the elevator down. Take down the Cultists and the Prophet in the area, then go through the doorway (17) on the lower level to the escape pod. Open the bars and go through the small door on the other side. Finally, since you "really mean it," **shoot out the glass and hit the self-destruct button**.

Uh oh... You didn't think this through too well, did you. Forgot the fact that you were still on board the airship when you set the self-destruct, didn't you? Well, don't stand there smacking your palm against your head. Get the heck outta Dodge! Run back through the Bridge and go through the now deactivated force field opposite the self-destruct chamber. Follow the tunnel past a few Fanatics and Cultists until it forks. Go right and follow it until you see the entrance to the Bomb Bay on your left. Climb down the ladder and go through the airlock door. Mow down any Fanatics in the area, then activate the computer controls on the right (18) to deactivate the Bomb Bay force fields. Don't jump yet, though; you'll crater. Go through the red-rimmed doorway on the bottom level (19) and grab a parachute from behind its protective glass. Return to the Bomb Bay and dive through the hole in the floor.

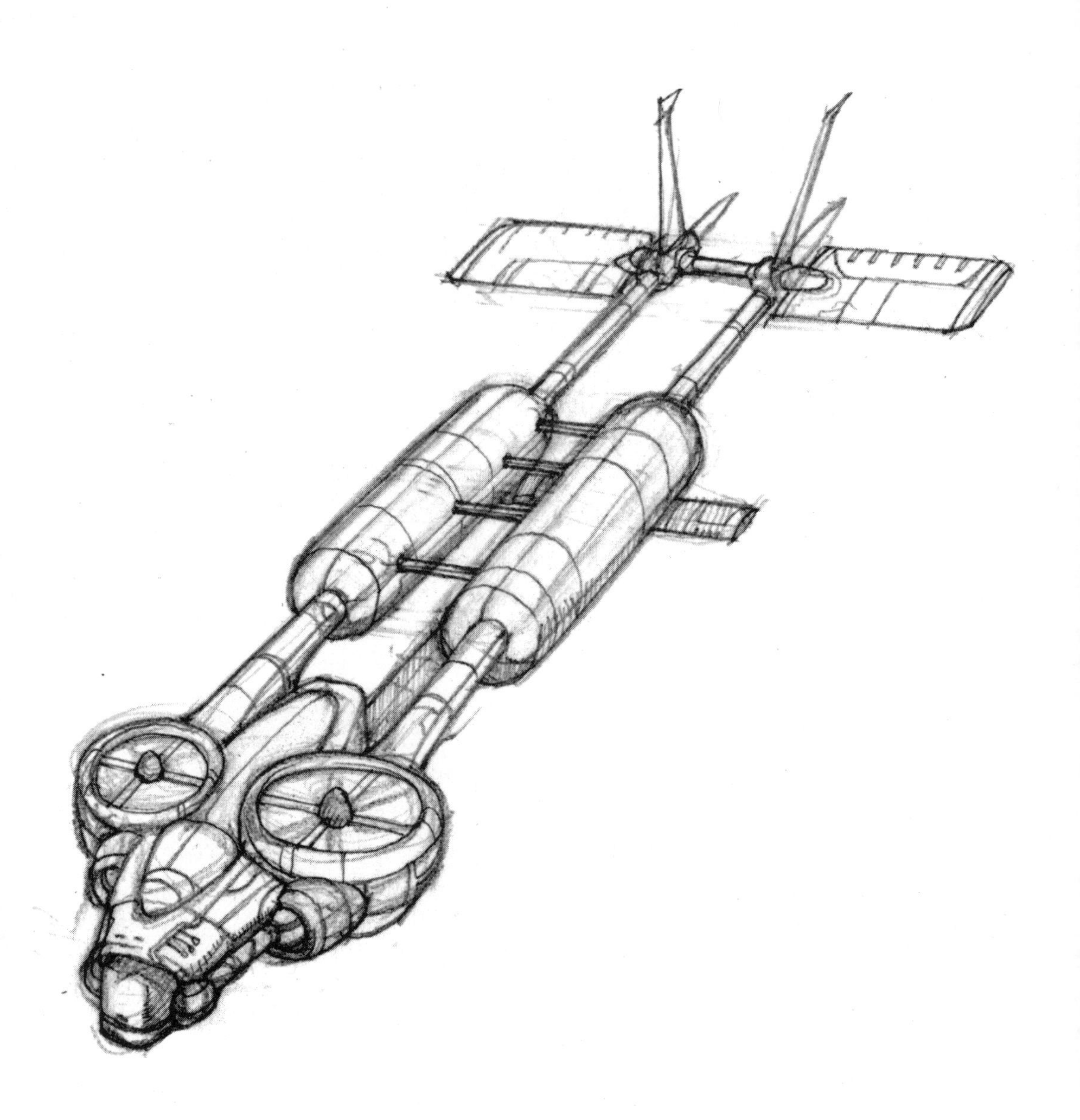

Level 8

HARD HAT AREA

Your narrow escape from the flaming remains of the CAS Revenant deposited you on top of a condemned building back in the city hub you frequented earlier in the game. You'll revisit a different area of this level this time as you track your way through the cityscape in search of Gideon. Be careful on this area, because it involves some tricky jumps at great heights. However, you do get to add an impressive weapon to your arsenal if you so choose: The Insect-a-Cutioner!

OBJECTIVES: .... Navigate the construction zones and find the entrance to the Cathedral.

ENEMIES: .... Bone Leeches, Soul Drudges, Shikari, Cultists

ITEMS: .... None (unless you left some behind earlier)

WEAPONS: .... Insect-a-Cutioner

After you've slain the Soul Drudges in the area, **push the metal crate** (1) up against the fence so you can hurdle it and land in the alley beyond.

Follow the alley around until you reach an area with narrow ledges running the parameter of a collapsed building. There is a sewage ditch with drainage tunnels (2) far below. After dealing with the Shikari down below, carefully jump down from the upper levels to the ledge on the second level. You may take a little damage from the fall, but not much. Creep along the ledge until you can go through a gap in the wall (3) above the sewage trench.

Go through the gap into another area with ledges overlooking a small shack (4). There are more Shikari here to deal with. Run down the collapsed beam (5) and shoot the barrels around the shack. If that doesn't blow it up, give it a few extra hits with your favorite weapon. Inside you will find an **Insect-a-Cutioner**.

The shack explodes once you've pounded on it enough, and explosions are generally painful. Don't be standing next to it when it goes, and for Pete's sake don't stand there and whack at it with your knife to get it to explode!

After you've collected the bug spray, climb back up the collapsed beam (5) fight off the new wave of Shikari, then go back into the area overlooking the sewage ditch (2). Jump down and crawl into the sewage tunnel. Again, watch out for Bone Leeches in the water as you make your way along.

Follow the tunnel until it empties out in front of the LaundroHut again (6). Don't get out of the water. Instead, turn right and swim through the short drainage tunnel there (7) to the pool outside the Motel Hello. Deal with any Shikari or Soul Drudges that appear.

NOTE

From here, you're basically going to be retracing your steps to the Museum level that you visited earlier in the game. However, you'll diverge from that path at the last moment when you reach the basketball court and playground.

Climb out of the water and up the stairs opposite the hotel entrance. Hop up the trash dumpsters (8) and over the fence as you did before. Follow the alley to the fire escape. Climb up the first level and hop across the fence to the playground full of Cultists.

Once in the playground, climb the rubble in the alley on your left (9) and follow the alley to the entrance Cathedral. You'll have to walk a ways, fight through some Soul Drudges and Shikari, then smash some crates to uncover it, but you can't miss it.

Level 9

CATHEDRAL

Time for a big change of pace.Your next destination is a charming cathedral located in the heart of downtown where Gideon is expected to appear. You've heard strange rumors about this cathedral, and you've always suspected that it serves as a gathering place for the Cabal. Well, it was polite of them to all get together in one place. It makes shooting them all that much easier. At the end of this level, though, you're in for a pretty tough fight as you show down with this episode's boss, the Naga.

OBJECTIVES:........ Fight your way through the old Cathedral to confront the Naga.

ENEMIES:........... Fanatics, Zealots, Soul Drudges, Drudge Lord, Shikari, Bone Leeches, Naga

ITEMS:............ Health, Life Seed, Night Vision Goggles, The Anger, Necrowards

WEAPONS:........... Shotgun, Assault Rifle, SMG, Life Leech, Voodoo Doll

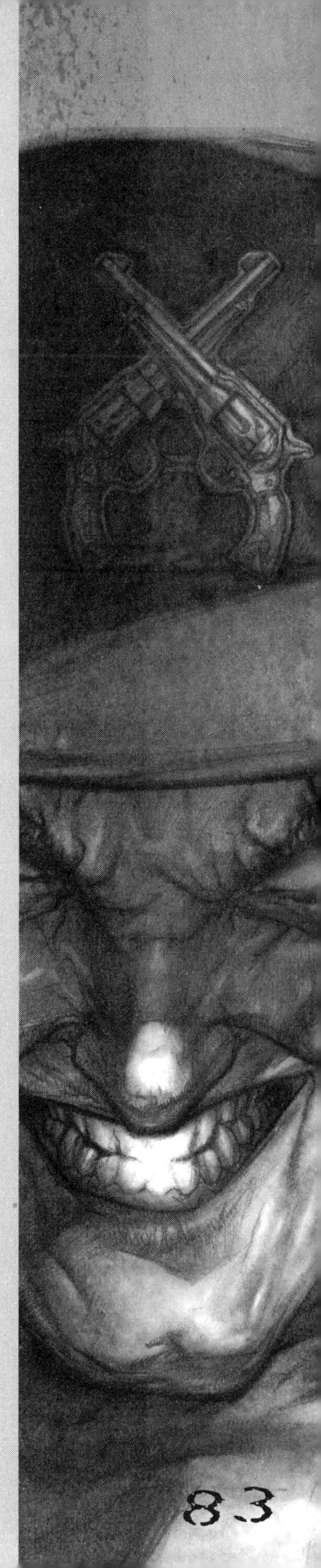

You start this level before the entrance to a huge gothic cathedral, but you have the feeling that it's been a while since anybody has gone to Sunday school here. You'll notice that there's a welcome wagon of Cabal agents waiting to greet you. Show your appreciation with massive amounts of gunfire. Ascend the steps and open the huge stone doors leading into the Cathedral's foyer. Fight off the Shikari and open the second set of mammoth stone doors and enter the main Cathedral area. Two Zealots will warp in to harass you.

There are doors on either side of you once you enter this area, but you'll be too busy to notice right away. Go through the door on the left to enter twp antechambers, one containing a pair of **Night Vision Goggles**, the other containing a **Skeleton Key**. fight some more Otherworld creatures. After you do so, go back into the main cathedral and use the Skeleton Key to go through the door on the right (1). This will lead you to an antechamber with two doors. Again, take the right door (2), which leads to a broken spiral staircase. (Hint: Break all vases and urns you find on this level. Like crates, they often hide ammo and health.)

Part of the staircase is collapsed, so you can only climb so far before you'll have to find another way to proceed. Fortunately, somebody was kind enough to rip you a nice big hole in the wall. Climb through and find yourself overlooking a blue pool of water and Bone Leeches some distance below (3). Jump down into the water, then quickly climb out. Go through the breach in the wall to fight a Drudge Lord for possession of a **Necroward** and a **Skeleton Key** you'll need shortly. To continue your ascent, you'll have to climb using the protruding bricks and fallen beams. This is a little tricky, and may take a couple of tries, especially when the Zealots warp in to bother you. Once you reach the top, climb through the window and climb the spiral staircase the rest of the way to the top, where a Soul Drudge is waiting for you.

At the top of the stairs, go through the door way and—WOAH! Back up! Looks like an errant lightning bolt has struck the rooftop, and the ancient Cathedral is literally crumbling under your feet. Too bad for the Soul Drudges who happened to be standing on it. Unfortunately, you still need to get to the door on the other side (4). To do so, you're going to have to hop and skip across the fragile skeleton of buttresses. Take it slow and easy and watch for the Shikari that warp in or you'll fall to a rather painful death below.

TIP

If you're feeling uncoordinated, or don't feellike playing the jumping game, it would be a good idea to save your game at this point. If you fall, you can simply reload it and try again.

Once you make it across the rafters, go through the door and the small room on the other side. Follow the hallway to a breach in the wall. Go through it. Wow, you're actually on the outside of the Cathedral now, overlooking the neighboring buildings. You might also notice the Fanatics and Shikari spraying gunfire and acid your way. After you've cleared the area of threats, you'll need to find a way to get back inside, but it's going to be tricky. Not only do you have to watch your step so that you don't fall, but there's Fanatics and Zealots scattered about that will try to knock you down. You're much too high to survive a fall, so make sure you save your game at this point.

Start by walking along the narrow ledge to your left and down the nearby buttress (5). Walk around the parameter of the connecting building and jump across to the building with the misbehaving "Hotel Corral Essex" sign (6). Watch out for Fanatics. From there, jump straight across to the opposite ledge (7). Turn left (away from the Cathedral) and creep along the narrow ledge—very carefully.

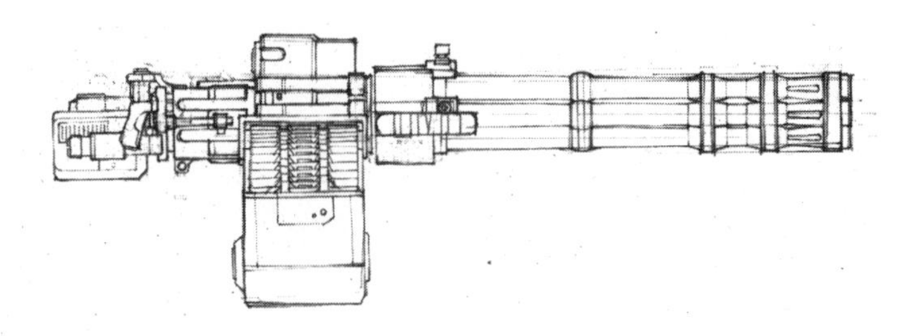

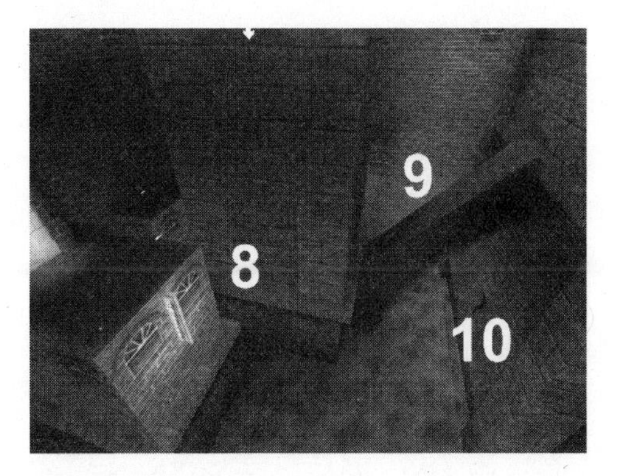

Follow it until you can jump across to another ledge near a blue "Hotel" sign (8). Walk under the sign and jump across again to a new ledge of a building with another buttress leading up to the Cathedral again. Walk past the buttress and jump diagonally to the nearby rooftop with some **ammo** and a **SMG** (9). Turn to your right and see another breach in the Cathedral wall (10). Jump across to the ledge and climb through the breach. Descend the spiral staircase into the lair of the deadliest foe you've gone up against yet—the Naga!Once you kill the two Shikari in the are, the Naga warps in. Let loose with everything you've got. Duck in and out of the pillars on either side of the room and the Naga will have a tough time hitting you. Grab all the powerups on the upper ledge by jumping up the rubble against the wall. Continue darting back and forth until Gabriella appears to lend a hand and finish the beast off.

Level 10

CABALCO TRANSIT SYSTEM 2

All you wanted to do was take a nice relaxing train ride after your encounter with the Naga. Well, the Cabal are still hot on your trail, and the soothing clickity-clack of the tracks has been replaced by the painful ratta-tat-tat of M16 Assault Rifles. You can bet that Gideon is in on this again, and you're starting to develop a serious disliking of subways.

OBJECTIVES: . . . . Fight your way to the front of the train.

ENEMIES: . . . . Fanatics

ITEMS: . . . . Health, Medkit

WEAPONS: . . . . M16 Assault Rifles

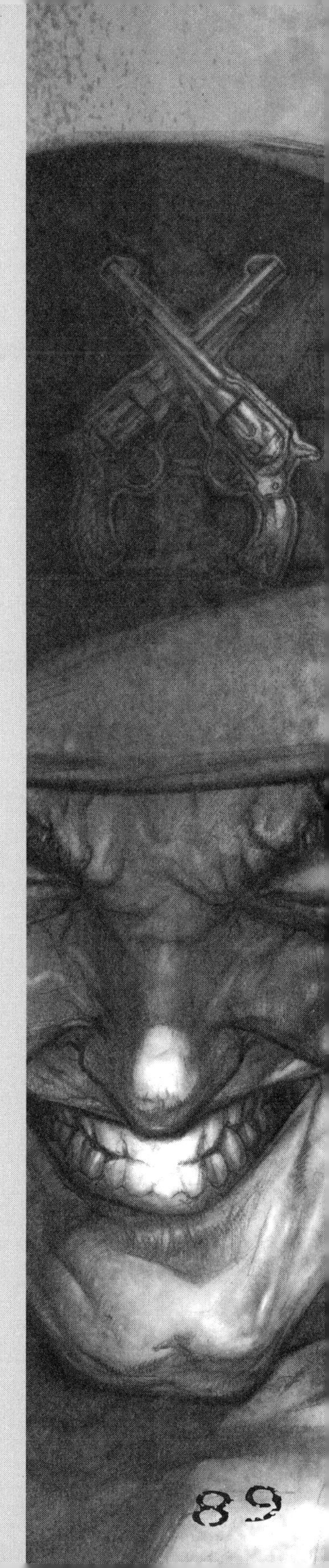

Same as the subway ride you took at the beginning of the game, you have to fight your way to the front again. Only this time, you have to deal with unruly Fanatics with assault rifles blocking your way, instead of wimpy Cultists. This can be a tough fight. Use the doors strategically, and don't be afraid to run for cover when you need to. You won't live long with six assault rifles trained on you at the same time. About halfway through the level, notice the first aid kit on the wall to your left (1) . Shoot it to get the **Medkit.** Make it to the front of the train alive to progress to the next level.

Level 11

CABAL SAFEHOUSE

Ouch. You just don't seem to have much luck with trains. Gideon managed to crash your subway car again, but you managed to stay alive and the chase goes on. Gideon has picked up his skirts and made a run for one of the Cabal's safehouses in the old downtown district. He'll be hard to track down here, and you'll have to fight your way through an army of Cabal agents and Otherworld fiends. But hey, you didn't have any plans for today anyway.

OBJECTIVES: .... Pursue Gideon to the roof; escape from the safehouse.

ENEMIES: .... Cultists, Fanatics, Zealots, Soul Drudges, Shikari, Thieves

ITEMS: .... Health, Medkit, Flashlights, Remote Bombs, Time Bombs, Night Vision Goggles

Weapons: .... Assault Rifles, SMG, Shotgun, Howitzer

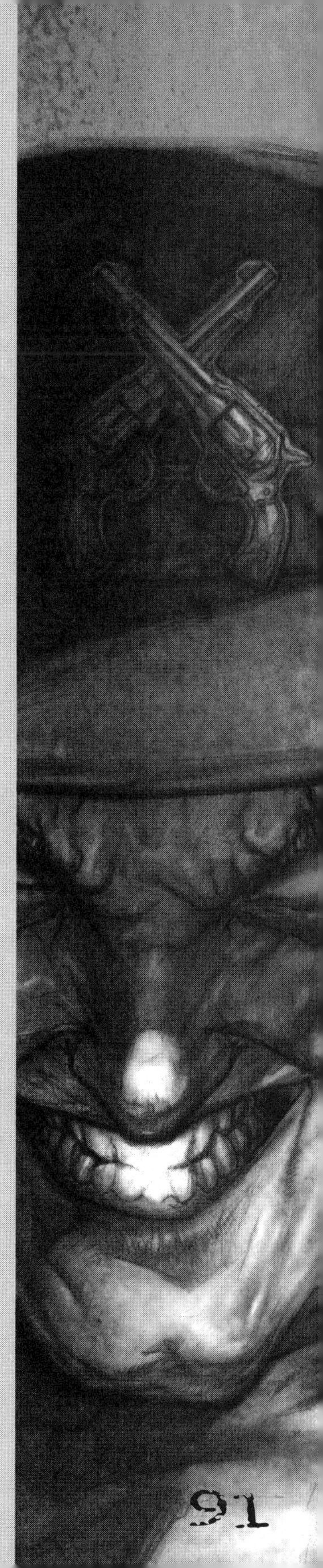

That was one wild ride…again. Pick yourself up and **shoot out the subway car window** above you. Then climb the fallen beam and pull yourself out. Wipe out the welcoming committee of Soul Drudges, Thieves, and Shikari, then run down the tracks, through the crack in the wall, and climb up onto the train station platform on your right. Zealots will warp in and try to surprise you, so be ready. Run forward through the train station exit (1) and up the stairs to the streets above. Just watch out for the massive Shikari and Fanatic ambush on the way.

Clear the area of Drudge Lords, then climb the stairs leading to the Cabal safehouse (2). Go through the doors, up the narrow staircase, and follow the hallway to your right at the top of the stairs, mowing down Fanatics as you go. Go until you see an open room on your left with a couple of nasty couches and doorways leading out to the left or right. Grab the **ammo** next to the vending machine, then go through the doorway on the left.

NOTE

There's a lot of this level that you don't have to go through in order to go on to the next, but it may be a good idea to go exploring. You can pickup a few items and ammo that may come in handy in the future. Just find your way back to this room on the ground floor to continue on. Also, Some of the names on the doors you see throughout this level are those of the Blood II development team.

Follow the hallway until you come to a construction area with concrete floors and a number of concrete bags stacked up. Clean out any enemies and grab the nearby **Remote Bombs** and **Howitzer**, as well as the **flashlight** through the door on the right-hand wall (3). Then go back the way you came and backtrack to the room with the couches and vending machines.

NOTE

Here is one of *Blood II*'s many "Easter eggs" and references to famous horror icons. There are two girls at the end of the hallway you follow from the room with couches and vending machines. They want you to come play with them...forever. The girls vanish as you approach. This is one of two tributes to the movie *The Shining*. The other is in the hallway one floor up near the hatchet and door labeled "Stephens".

Proceed past the vending machines and follow the hallway opposite you. Grab the **health** if you need it. Go all the way to the end of the hallway and take the stairs on your right (4). Take the stairs up and go through the broken door at the top. The door labeled "Roof Access" on your right is locked, so you'll have to find another way up onto the roof.

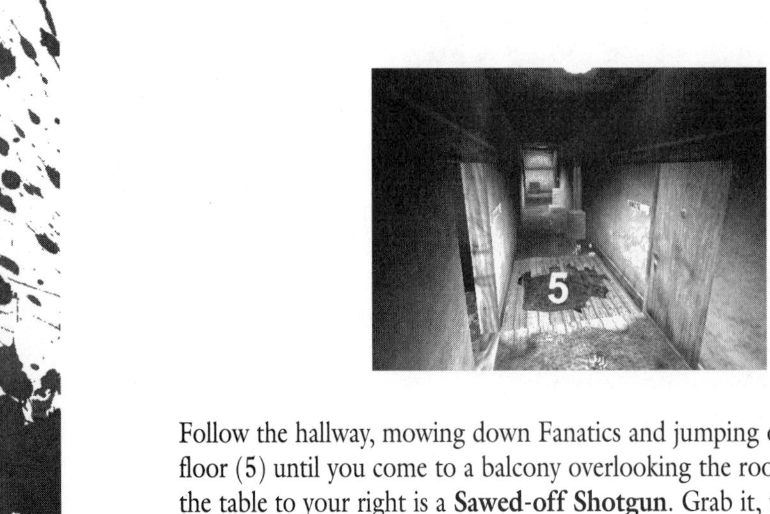

Follow the hallway, mowing down Fanatics and jumping over the gaping hole in the floor (5) until you come to a balcony overlooking the room with couches. Under the table to your right is a **Sawed-off Shotgun**. Grab it, then continue to follow the hallway until you come to another "Roof Access" door guarded by a Fanatic. Grab the nearby **Bug Spray** cans, then go through the door.

Fight your way up the concrete stairwell to the roof, where you will encounter Gideon and Ishmael will be raised from a rift. After that pansy Gideon makes his escape via helicopter, grab the **ammo** (6) nearby. You've got a feeling that things are about to get *really* ugly for you. You can hear the sounds from the streets below as the industrial sector is overrun by Otherworldly beasts. Time to backtrack through the building and see if you can find a safer place to be right now.

Go all the way back into the building to the lounge with couches and vending machines on the ground level. You'll have to battle otherworldly beasties all the way, as the industrial sector becomes overrun with them. Once you're back outside the building, an alleyway will be accessible to the left of the safehouse entrance (7). Take it.

Follow the graffiti-stained hallway to a doorway. Open it and gun down the pack of Soul Drudges standing on the other side. Go down the stairs to an area with crates. As always, break them open with the knife to see what you can find after clearing the area of Shikari. When you're done, go through the steel door (8) opposite the short stairway.

NOTE Another tribute to horror icons lies in the boiler room to the right after going through this steel door. Pinned to the wall is Freddy Krueger's glove.

After going through the steel door (8), fight off some Thieves and Soul Drudges. Then follow the hallway to your left and enter an area with a watery trench and two sets of stairs leading up to a platform. Grab the **Night Vision Goggles** and **ammo** in the room, then exit through the doorway on the left (9).

Follow the hallway and gun down a Drudge Lord guarding a short tube. Climb down the tube to an area with a trench filled with corrosive green sludge and a Shikari. Turn right from where you came in (10) and walk along the ledge to the doorway on your right (11). Go through and follow the graffiti-stained tunnel to an alcove with a **Flashlight** and a couple of **Time Bombs**. Then turn around and continue to follow the hall to a gaggle of Soul Drudges guarding the exit to the level. Wherever it leads it's got to be better than outside.

Level 12

SEWAGE TREATMENT PLANT

What is the deal with all the sewers? There are entirely too many sewers in this town. Better for people to just dump their waste out the window than cleanly and sanitarily dispose of it down the pipes so you have to sludge through just to get away from the hoards of Otherworld creatures. Even an immortal demigod gets grossed out by some of the things you see floating around down here. Well, if this is the only alternative to being on the surface, then it'll have to do. Gideon has run up quite a tab with you—and it's time to draw blood to pay the bill.

OBJECTIVES: .... Make it through alive and back to the surface.

ENEMIES: .... Shikari, Fanatics, Thieves

ITEMS: .... None

WEAPONS: .... Pistols, Howitzer

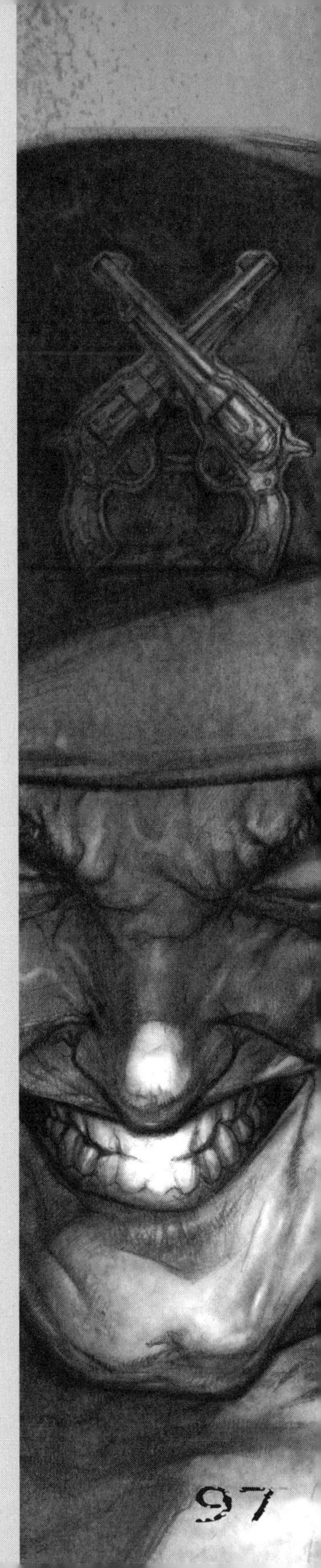

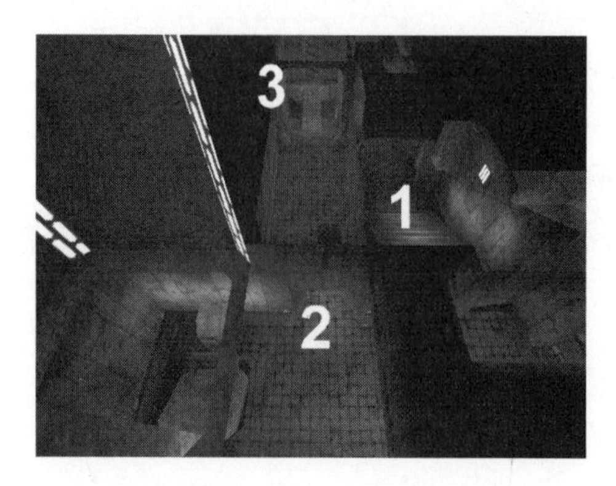

You'll immediately be greeted by two Shikari. Gun them down and follow the tunnel past the two grates and up the stairs (1). Well, great. The elevator has been broken and there's a Shikari with murder in its eyes waiting for you. Looks like you'll have to find another way to carry on. Turn right and go through the door (2) before the broken elevator. Gun down the Shikari, then peer over the edge (3) of the drop into the sewage below. Shoot anything that looks unfriendly. Then drop down.

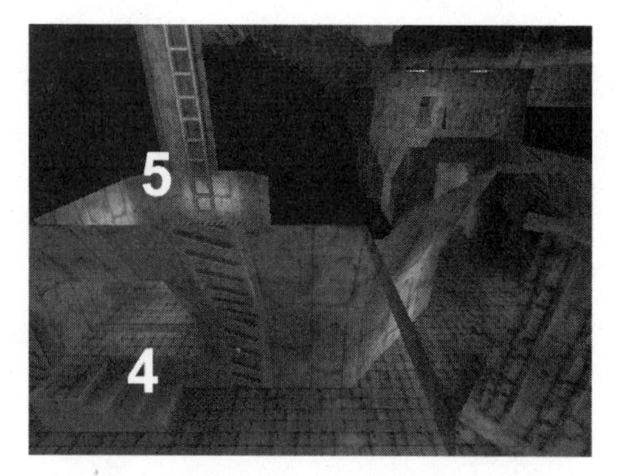

Take out any Soul Drudges or other baddies in the area. Wade through the crappy water until you come to a short set of stairs leading up out of it (4). Climb the stairs and then climb the ladder (5) up into the tube.

You will emerge in an area with a large pool of sewage guarded by Fanatics (they love their sewage and guard it jealously). Gun them down and trot along the catwalk running the circumference of the pool to the doorway on the other side (6), but watch out for the Thieves. Follow the hallway beyond, past some more Thieves, and take the lift at the end.

Follow the short hallway to a bridge spanning a giant fan. Gun down any Fanatics and Thieves in the area and run through the exit on the other side. Grab the Fanatic's Howitzer while you're at it.

WARNING

There's some really dangerous crossfire in this area from the Fanatics on the ledges all around you. Don't stop here to try to outshoot them; you'll loose.

Take the lift at the and of the hallway up to the grate bridge spanning the one you just ran over. Squish and Thieves in the area. Mow down another herd of Soul Drudges and a Drudge Lord, then climb the ladder (7) leading up out of this nasty place and on to the next level.

Level 13

MEAT-PACKING PLANT

The Cabal have their paws into just about everything, from drugs to gun-running to...meat-packing? Yes, meat-packing. This seems like as good a place as any to slaughter some more Cabal cattle and continue your chase. Maybe you can even pick up some of those complementary Grape-Flavored Ball Park Wieners you've seen advertised.

OBJECTIVES: . . . . Navigate the Meat-Packing Plant.

ENEMIES: . . . . Shikari, Zealots, Thieves, Bone Leeches, Soul Drudges, Fanatics, Cultists

ITEMS: . . . . None

WEAPONS: . . . . Pistols, Assault Rifles, SMG's

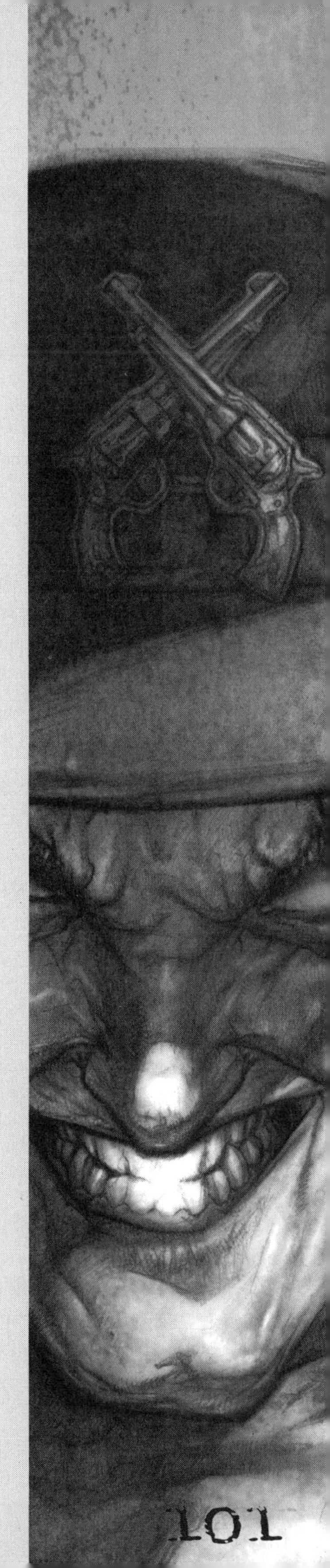

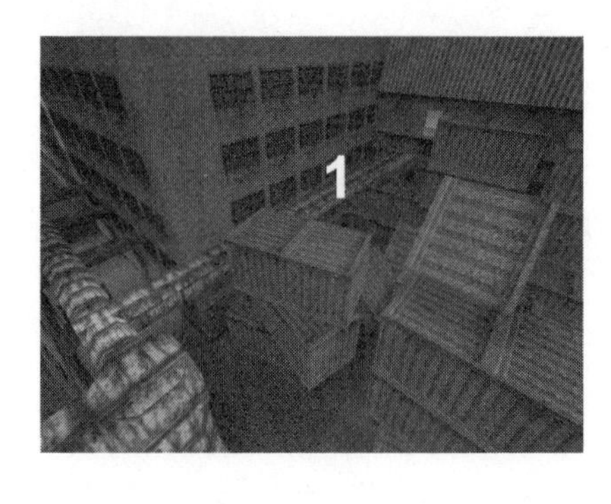

You start this level on the docking bay of the Cabalco Meat-Packing Plant ("Packing Meat for 20 Years"). Either gun down or run past the Zealots that warp in and head for the alley across from you. Follow it until you come to a jumble of giant crates stacked haphazardly. The crates form a sort of maze of narrow passages through which you need to wind, taking out any Thieves you encounter along the way. Toward the back, there is a crate that forms a ramp that you can climb onto the top of the others. From there, **jump over to the blood-stained pipe** (1). Walk along this pipe to the area on the other side of the giant crates.

TIP

You can walk the other way on the blood-stained pipe back toward the beginning of the level to score a number of items. It may call for some fancy jumping, though.

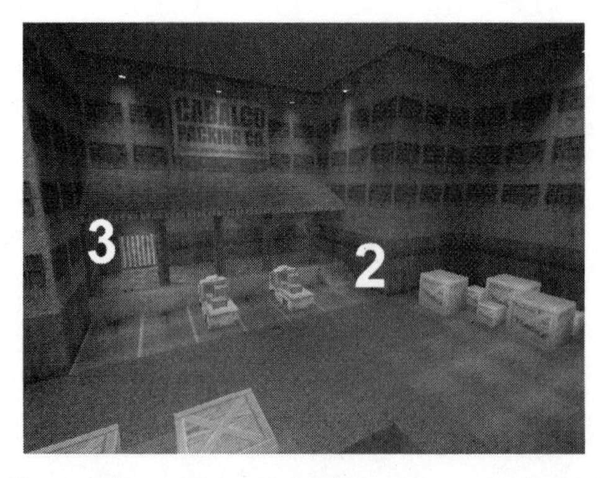

Follow the alley on the other side of the crates, gunning down Fanatics as you go. Eventually you will come to a large open area with a couple of Drudge Lords and Soul Drudges. Climb the stairs (2) to the loading dock and **open the docking door** (3) to gain entrance to the plant.

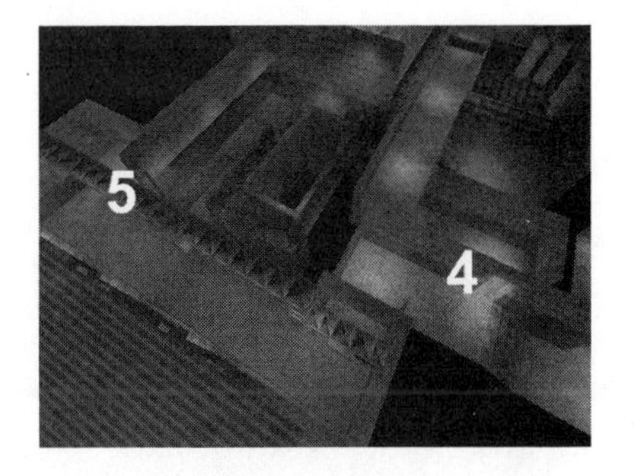

Clear the hallway of Cultists and follow it to another docking door. Open the door and gun down the Fanatics on the other side. Walk out into an area with the giant vats of viscous red goop and a grate catwalk overhead. Walk forward under the catwalk and go through the hallway opposite the door you came through. Walk past the "Flavor Room" (4) and continue following the hallway until you reach the door to the "Meat Room" (5).

NOTE

There is a security station nearby where you can find a lot of items.Make sure you clean it out.

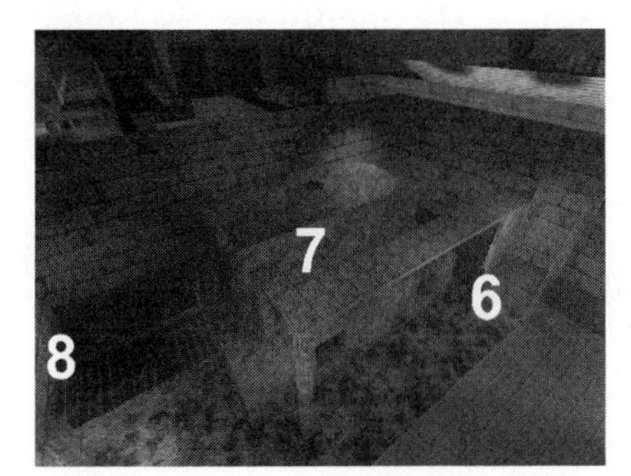

Go through and **hop on the lift** (6) to your right up to the catwalk. **Throw the lever** (7) to activate the grinding machine. Hop down onto the conveyor belt and ride it through the small door (8) into the rather bloody "Gristle Separating Room" beyond.

Clear the room of any Cabal agents, then take the stairway on your left up to the catwalk above. Follow the catwalk until you come to the room with the giant vats of red goop. Circle the vats on the catwalk and keep following it until you reach the "Processing Area."

WARNING

Don't bother going for a swim in those vats, no matter how appealing it looks. Nothing is in them and you may drown.

Follow the catwalk around until you come to an elevator (9). **Hit the button** and ride it down. Exit through the door on your left (10). Turn left and follow the hallway to the "Shipping" area. Watch out for the out-of-control truck as it comes barreling through the door, as well as the troops that come with it. When you're finished with them, exit the plant through the hole the truck made. The entrance to the next level, Harlock's Station, is on your left.

WARNING

Watch out for that truck. Ever since all the Meat-Packing Union leaders were mysteriously found floating face down in the swamp, the accident rate at these plants has skyrocketed. Don't let yourself become the next casualty.

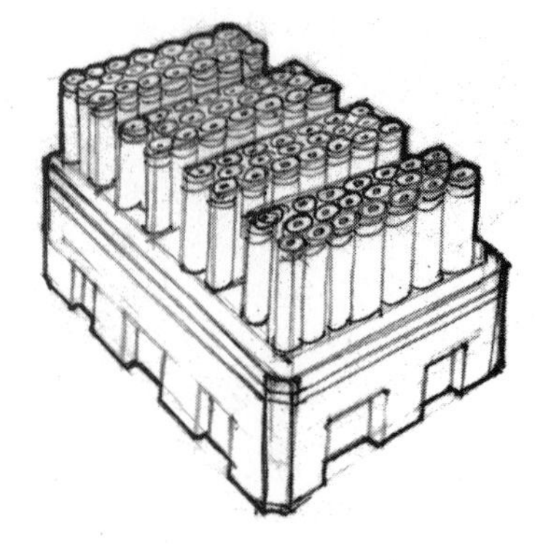

Level 14

HORLOCK'S STATION

Ugh—Trains. You're starting to really dislike trains. It's almost like Gideon knows it, too, because he's leading you right through the middle of a whole station full of them. This is a large level, and you've got a veritable army of Cabal agents and otherworld creatures to blast through. But hey, Gideon started this, and you're going to finish it one way or another. Time to pile up the bodies.

OBJECTIVES: .... Find your way into the train station and pursue Gideon.

ENEMIES: .... Bone Leeches, Shikari, Soul Drudges, Drudge Lords, Fanatics, Cultists, Zealots

ITEMS: .... Medkit, Binoculars, Remote Bombs, Proximity Bombs

WEAPONS: .... Pistols, Assault Rifles, SMG, Sniper Rifle, Voodoo Doll, Flare Guns

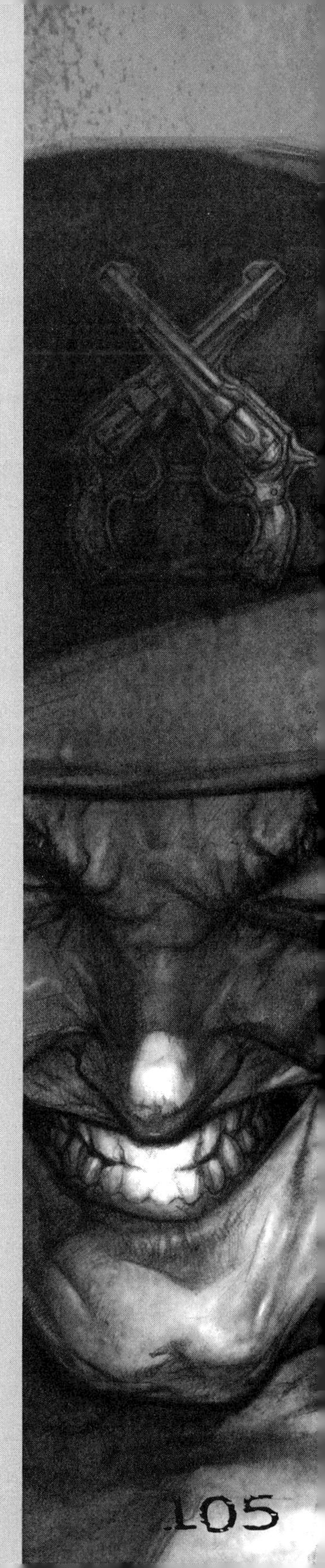

You start this level in an alley watching as really angry Shikari come at you full speed. Ignore them and let the train take them out. Follow the alley to an open area where a train periodically runs past on the tracks overhead. Take out the Soul Drudges and Drudge Lords that warp in to keep you busy. After that, you'll need to find a way up onto the train tracks. **Push the large metal crate** (1) up against the concrete ledge (2) across from where you entered the area. **Then push the small metal crate** (3) up against the large one. Hop up from crate to crate to ledge, then onto the track from the ledge. Just be sure to wait for the train to pass first, then run like a madman up the tracks the way the train was going.

TIP

Use the "grab" key to help you put the crates in position. Stand right up against the crate, press the key ("G" by default) and hold it down while you walk backwards. You should drag the crate along with you.

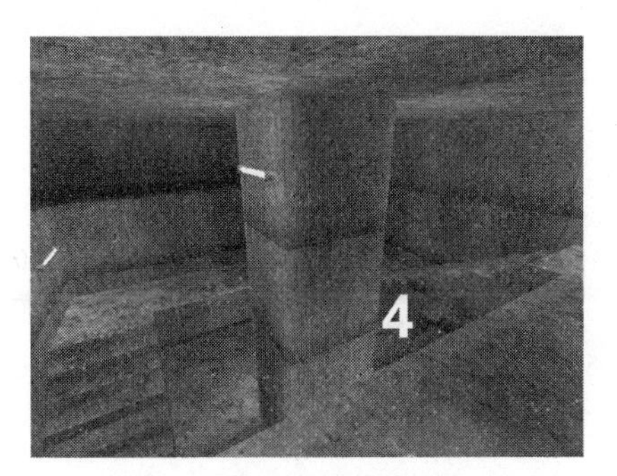

Run up the tracks to the short flight of stairs on your right. Quickly climb them before you're run down by the train, and take out any Shikari and Soul Drudges in your way. Follow the hallway to a room with a set of staircases running along its parameter. Take the stairs down, wipe out any Thieves in the area, and grab the **Flashlight** and **Proximity Bombs** lying nearby. Crouch and navigate in the crawlspace under the stairs (4). Grab the **Voodoo Doll** and come out in the middle of a pack of Soul Drudges

WARNING

Watch out for the exposed electrical rails on the subway tracks. If you try continuing your trek up the tracks, you'll get fried.

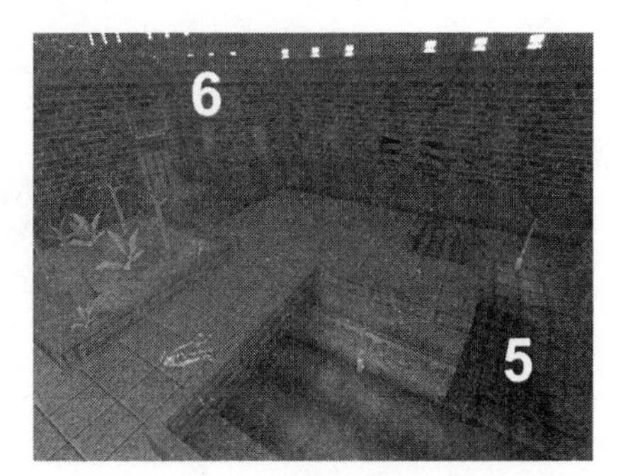

Run down the tunnel and climb the stairs (5) leading up to the courtyard before the Hotel Coral Essex. You remember spending a few nights here. Unfortunately, it seems the proprietor remembers as well, and he has tried to lock you out. Well, that won't do at all. After you've shot all the Otherworld beasties begging for your attention, **shoot out the window** (6) to the right of the doorway and let yourself in.

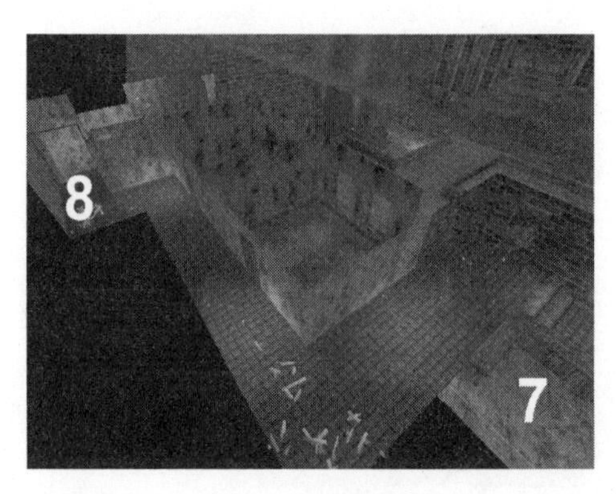

Relieve the rude desk clerk of his **Medkit** behind the counter (7) and follow the hallway down a flight of steps (8). At the bottom of the stairs, open the door to your left. It leads into a room chock full of Shikari. Clean the pests out.

TIP

Take a minute to search the rooms you pass along the way. Some, like the first one, hold items, including BINOCULARS and a SNIPER RIFLE.

Once the room is clear, shoot out the window and crawl out onto the fire escape (8). Hop down and go through the entrance opposite you (9). Follow the alley past "Tanya's Massage Parlor" (too bad they're closed) out into an open street area.

Shoot out the window (10) to "Schlegel's Choke n Puke Diner" and interrupt the group of Cultists out on their lunch break. Pepper them with gunfire and then pause to eat their "Deluxe Horse Burger with Bacon and Gouda Cheese." Grab any **Flare Pistols** or **SMG's** you can find amidst the carnage.

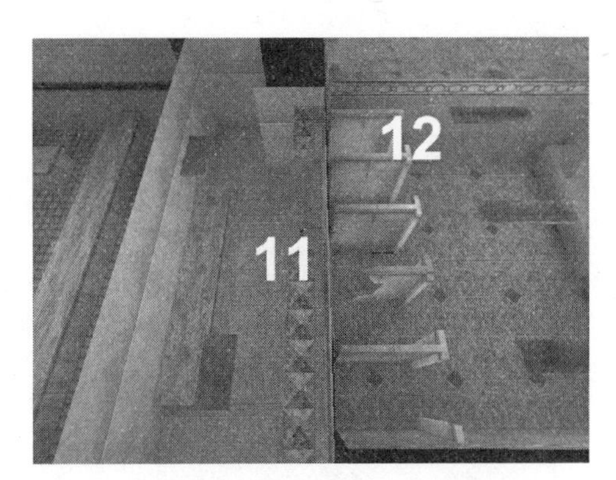

Go through the door to the kitchen and stomp out any Bone Leeches you find helping themselves to the Economy Size Barrel o' Horse Parts. Looks like Schlegel is done for the day—well done, by the looks of him. From a safe distance, **shoot the stove** (11) where poor Schlegel lays. This will rip a hole in the wall to the bathrooms next door. Go through and grab the **Anger powerup** from the right-most stall (12).

Quickly turn around, exit the bathrooms, and get medieval on the gang of Fanatics in the train station lobby before the triple damage wears off. Take the stairs (13) to the left of the ticket booth and follow the hallway to the left at the top.

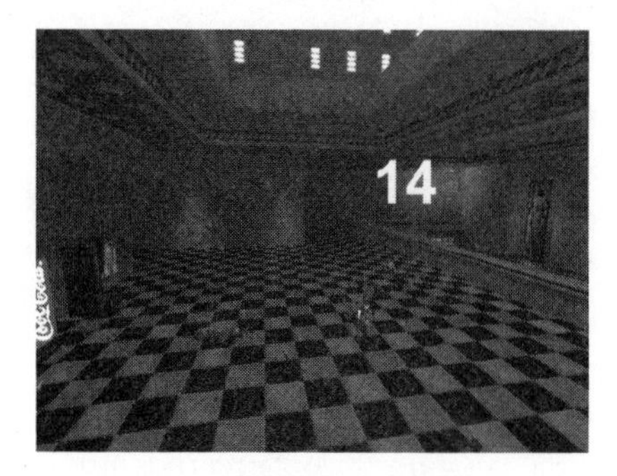

Come out into an open area with vending machines on the right and a sign (14) reading "Downtown Express Train Platform" over to the left. Gun down any Fanatics standing around and follow the sign to the Express platform and gun down those looser Fanatics waiting for the Uptown Express. Hop down onto the train tracks (usually not a good idea, but go with it this time around) and follow it to downtown.

Level 15

LOVE CANAL

Ahh, Downtown. The epicenter of culture, nightlife, industry, and wholesale massacre of pesky Cabal agents. The subway tracks from the train station have deposited you on the outskirts of Downtown, near the shipping harbor. Gideon may have come close to giving you the slip, but you're not beaten yet. Shot, bludgeoned, slashed, bitten, burnt, electrocuted, and gored, but not beaten. This is another fairly large map, and rest assured that you won't be short of targets as you continue your hunt for the leader of the Cabal.

OBJECTIVES: .... Navigate the water tunnels to gain access to the shipping locks and catch another subway train.

ENEMIES: .... Bone Leeches, Shikari, Soul Drudges, Drudge Lords, Zealots

ITEMS. .... None

WEAPONS: .... None

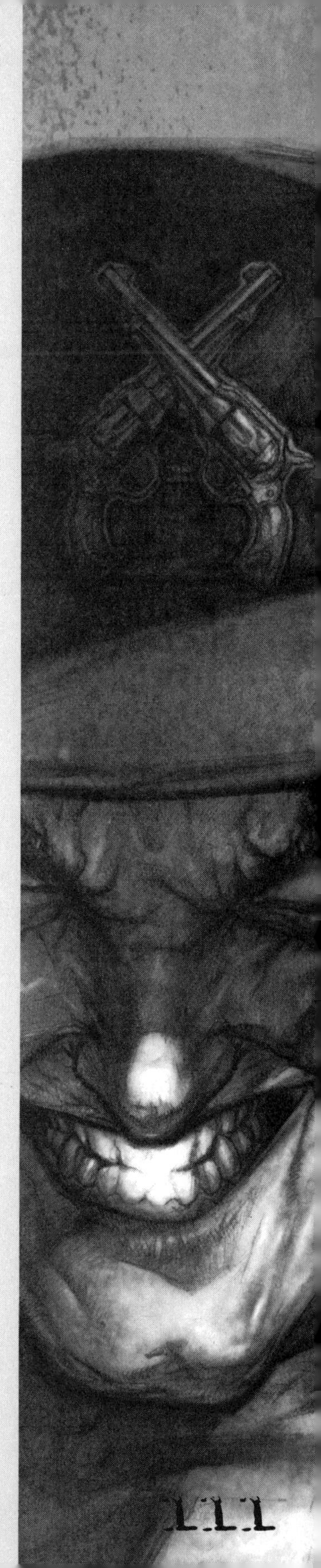

Don't be asleep at the keyboard when you start this level. Those two Soul Drudges are probably feeling pretty good about that look of terror in your eyes, but they won't live long enough to realize it's not them that's got you running for your life. Run forward and **dive over the side** of the rails to avoid getting smashed by the train. Follow the alley to your right to a large tank full of water and three drainage tubes. Dive in and swim through the half-submerged tube (1).

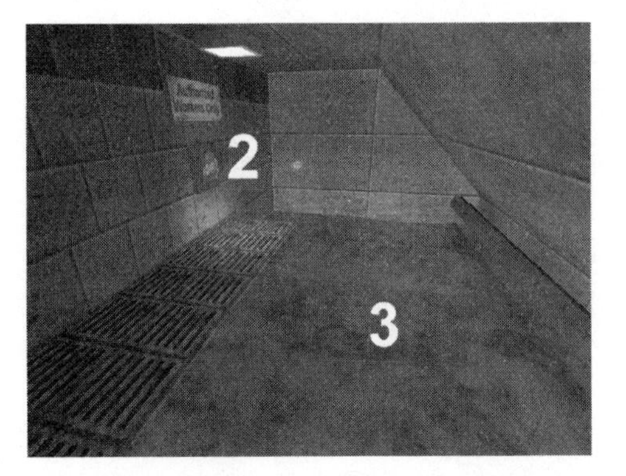

Slide down the waterfall and dive under the water. **Shoot out the bars** blocking the underwater tunnel and swim through. Climb up the ladder onto the ledge overlooking the pool and **turn the knob** (2) under the "Authorized Workers Only" sign. This will lower the bars (3) blocking another underwater tunnel. Dive back in and swim down the tunnel and down into a waterfall.

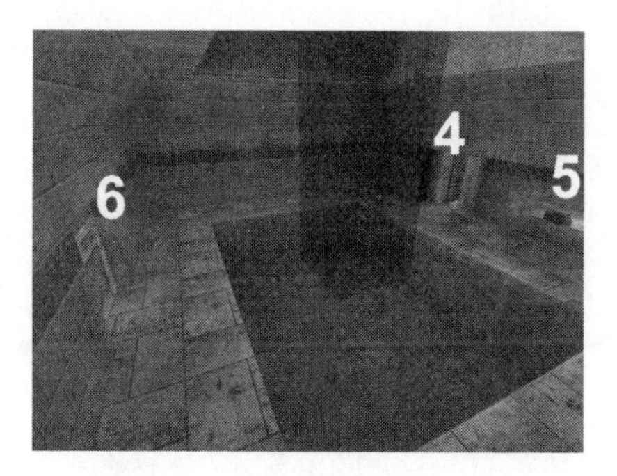

The waterfall deposits you in a square room with a control room opposite a locked security door. Go through the doorway next to the window (4) to get into the control room. Once inside, **activate the controls** (5) to open the door (6) on the other side of the pool. Go back out and go through the door.

NOTE There is another door next to the locked security door leading to a tall staircase. This staircase will take you back to the pool with the bars you lowered with the knob.

Follow the hallway through several watery cascades to a room with a water-filled trench and a stairway (7) against the far wall. Dispatch the Soul Drudges and Shikari guarding it, then climb the stairs and go through the opening (8) at the far end of the ledge.

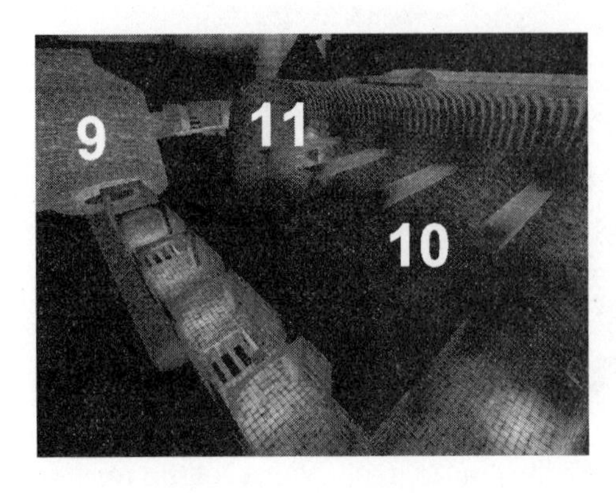

Continue following the hallways beyond, past several Soul Drudges and Shikari, until you come to a massive column of falling water (9). Walk around it to the right and follow the hallway until you come to a wide, dark hall (10). Be very careful here, because there are deep pits hidden in the shadows that will swallow you up. **Use your flashlight** if it has any juice left. Carefully skirt around the pits and climb the stairs (11) at the end of the hall.

TIP

If your flashlight is out of juice, you're in real danger here. You might look out for the pits by spraying the Insect-a-Cutioner's alt fire before you as you go.

Follow the short hallway until you come out to a wide hallway with a bottomless pit across from you and a catwalk suspended by chains above. Turn right and follow the ledge to the ladder (12) leading up. Climb it and walk along the catwalk until it feeds into another tunnel (13).

Follow this tunnel until you come to a bridge that actually runs *through* the massive column of running water you encountered earlier. Go through the water and follow the tunnels over rickety grates until you come out to a room full of Zealots with a very tall staircase running its parameter. Climb the stairs and go through the doorway at the top (14).

Follow the hallway beyond until you come to an outdoor area with canal locks guarded by a couple of Drudge Lords and Soul Drudges. Go through the doorway marked "B16" (15) and **activate the controls** inside. Run down the nearby stairs, following the hallways until you come to the barge. Jump aboard and drive the boat up into the next lock by **activating the boat's controls**. Climb up the ladder out of the water and return to the control room to lower the next lock gate. Repeat until the barge is in the first lock and the water is raised as high as it will go. Jump across the roof of the barge and go through the door (16) on the other side.

Follow the hallway beyond past a Drudge Lord, down some stairs, through some Shikari, past some more Drudge Lords, and down a ramp to the buss station. Cross the tracks and climb the stairs (17) to catch your next train.

Level 16

CABALCO TRANSIT SYSTEM 3

That rascally cult leader has pulled the double-back switch-a-roo on you. Time to head back to the train station you visited earlier. And the only way to do that is to take another subway. The big G must be keeping tabs on you, because this train just so happens to be overrun with Otherworld fiends and Cabal agents, too. Oh well, so much for the Transit System's safety record.

OBJECTIVES:........ Fight your way to the front of the train and get off at Horlock's Station.

ENEMIES: .... Shikari, Soul Drudges, Drudge Lords, Fanatics, Prophet

ITEMS............. NecroWard, Remote Bombs, Ward

WEAPONS:.......... Assault Rifles, Tesla Cannon

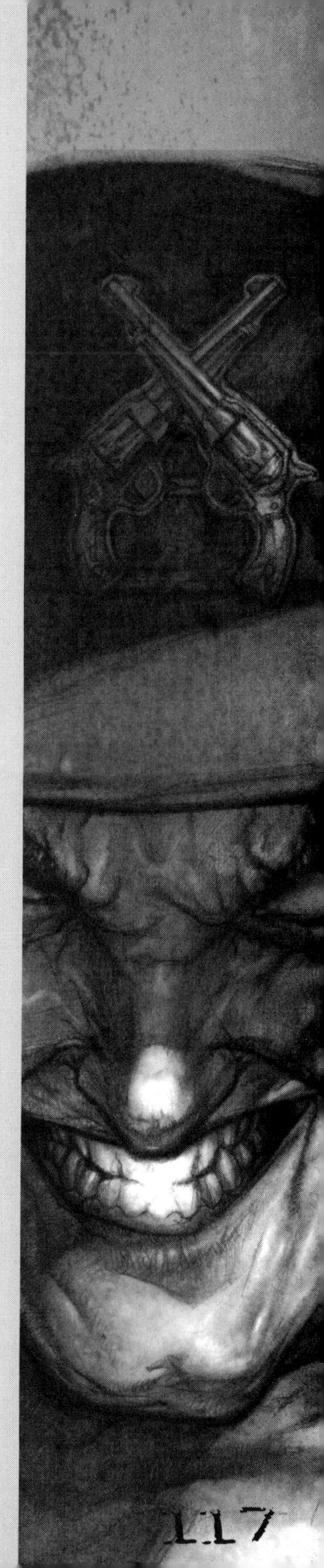

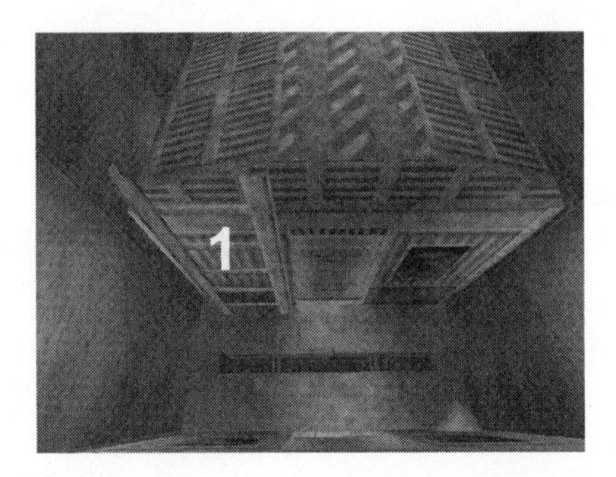

For the most part, this is just like the previous train rides: fight your way straight up the train to the front. However, at one point there will be a gap between the subway cars. Turn to your right and climb the ladder (1) to the roof of the train. Turn around and jump across to the roof of the next car. Run ahead and run down onto the ledge of car in front of that one. Continue marching up to the front car, where you will have to duel with a **Tesla Cannon**-wielding Prophet.

WARNING

When you have to go from the roof of one car to the ledge of another to get back in, fight the temptation to jump across the gap—just run off the edge and you'll fall into the right place. If you jump, you're likely to bonk you head on the ceiling and fall to your death.

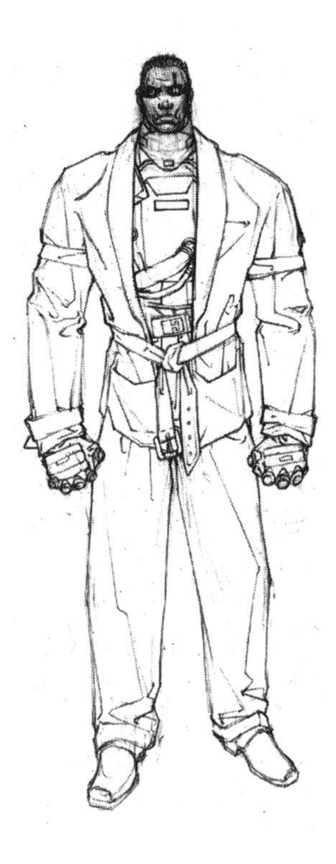

Level 17

RETURN TO HORLOCK'S STATION

If you see one more train, you're going to turn into a bloodthirsty evil demigod and slay everything in sight. Oh, wait...too late. Well, you're still peeved. Your assault on the Cabal has brought you back to the train station you just visited, but there are areas open to you that were barred before. And there are plenty of Cabal reinforcements, as well. This level is firefight from start to finish, so slap in a fresh clip and put on your hip waders, because things are going to get messy.

OBJECTIVES:......... Fight your way to the entrance to the Underground.

ENEMIES: .... Shikari, Soul Drudges, Drudge Lords, Fanatics, Cultists, Prophet

ITEMS. .... Ward

WEAPONS:........... Assault Rifles, SMG, Flare Gun, Howitzer, Tesla Cannon

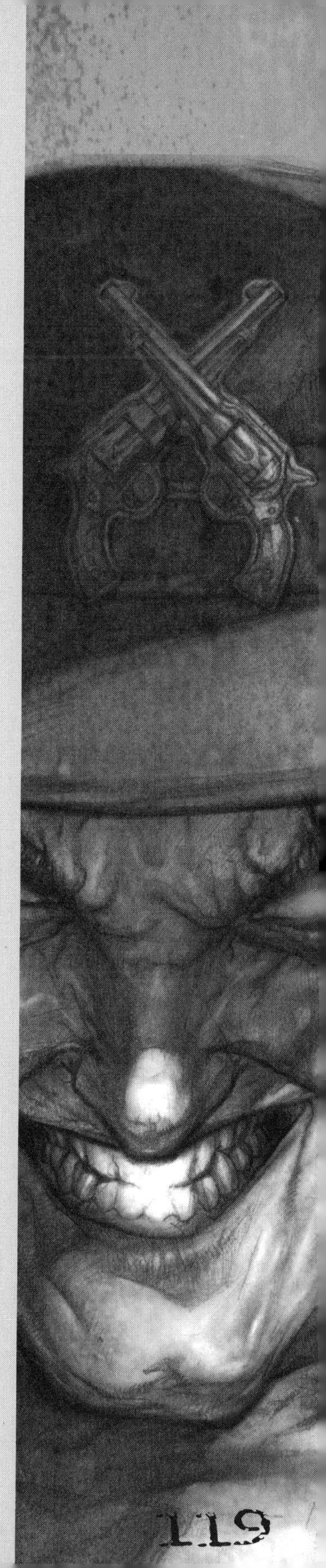

For once, you're actually able to step off the train and start a new level. Proceed to the stairs (1) at the end of the eastbound platform, mowing down Fanatics as you go. Watch out, though, because one of those maniacs is carrying a Napalm Cannon. Grab the **BMG ammo** while you're at it.

Continue blasting through the crowds of Fanatics until you come out to the train station lobby with its checkered floor. Follow it around to the left and continue following the hallway past (or rather through) Zealots, Fanatics, and Cultists. When you come to the main lobby with the ticket offices, drop down and walk under the balcony (2) toward the "Blue Line WestBound" platform. Give any Fanatics that try to stop you a facefull of buckshot.

Go down the escalators (3) and continue following the hallway with the blue and white tiles. You'll have to cut down hoards of Fanatics, so be careful and use the corners strategically to stay alive.

WARNING

One of the Fanatics just past the escalators actually managed to get a hold of a HOWITZER. Normally this weapon is great, but when it's being pointed at you it quickly looses its charm. Take him out as fast as you can, because he's a pretty good shot with that thing.

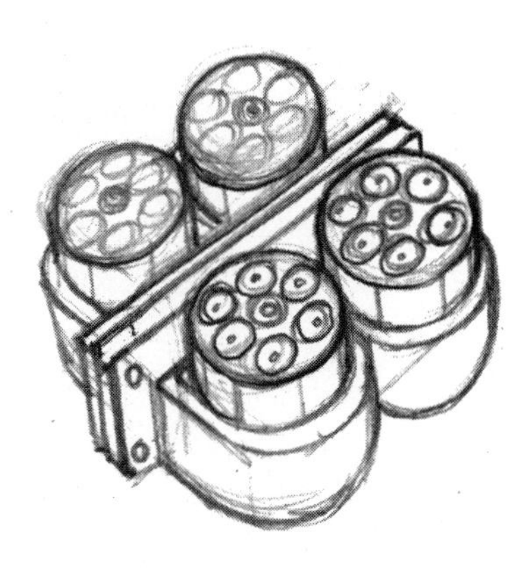

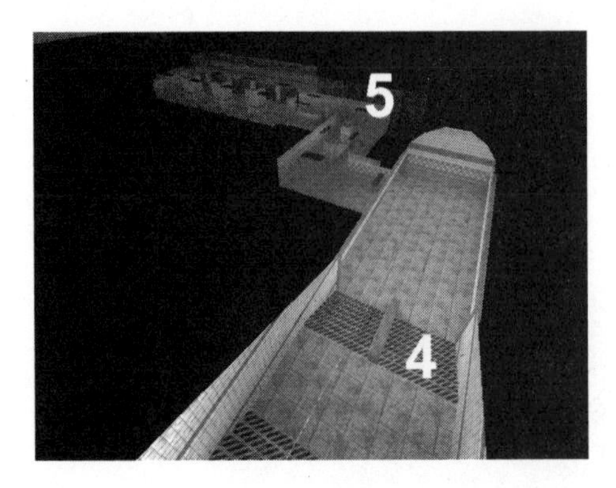

Continue following the hallway and the signs for the West Bound Blue Line. Go down a double flight of stairs (4) and duke it out with a Prophet wielding a **Tesla Cannon**. Be careful, though, because he can really put some hurt on you. Once you're done with him, proceed to the train platform. Since you don't really have time to stand around and wait for another subway car, go ahead and jump down onto the tracks and walk into the tunnel (5) to exit the level and continue on to the

TIP

Try running the Prophet out of ammo by running back and forth and dodging his shots. Best to use a corner for cover, though, because he can occasionally let loose with the Tesla Cannon's alt fire. Once he's out of cells, he'll switch to an Assault Rifle, but he should be near dead at that point.

Level 18

THE UNDERGROUND

Gideon's tracks have led you through the shadowy subway tunnels to a murky subterranean lair called the Underground. Kind of creepy, really. You've already died once, but that just makes this sort of place all the more uncomfortable to be in. You'll have to creep through this subterranean maze carefully, because there are lots of Otherworld creatures lying in ambush. Don't forget to check all quarters when entering each new area, and that includes looking up above you. The last thing you want is a really hacked-off Shikari dropping down on your noggin.

OBJECTIVES:........ Defeat the Behemoth to continue your hunt.

ENEMIES:........... Soul Drudges, Drudge Lords, Thieves, Hands, Shikari, Behemoth

ITEMS:............. Flashlight, Medkit, Night Vision Goggles

WEAPONS:........... None

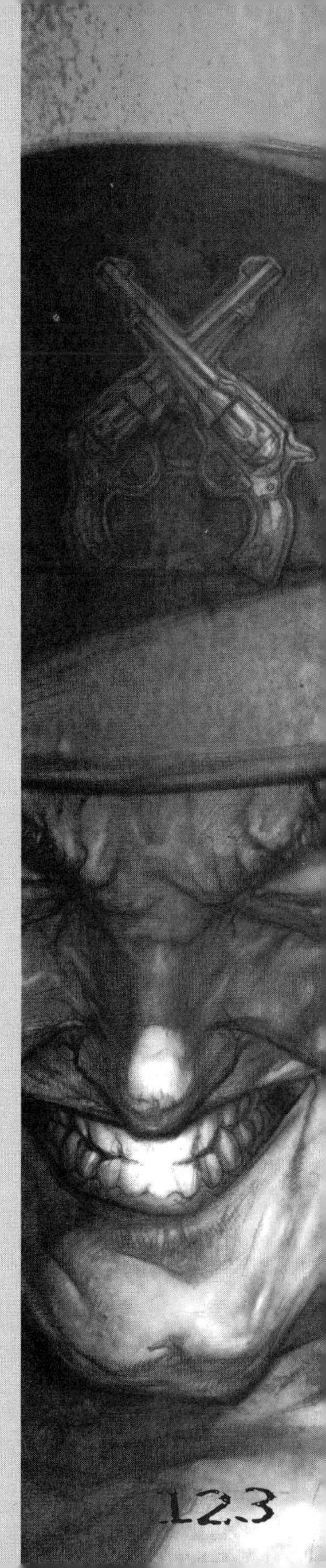

You start this level off looking down a long, dimly light hallway. Walk forward a few steps, and you'll find a chamber to your right (1)with a few Thieves, a **Flashlight,** and some **ammo.** After you've cleared it out, proceed down the hallway. Kill the Hands at the end and grab the **ammo** in the corner.

Take your first left and follow the hallway. A brick wall on your right picks an unfortunate time to collapse, revealing an entombed Drudge Lord (2). Blast him, grab the ammo from his lair, then walk through the spider web (3), proceeding down the corridor. Come to an opening in the wall on your right guarded by a pack of Soul Drudges. Blast past them and follow the hallway. Be ready for the two Shikari that warp in.

Walk through another spider web and take a right when the tunnel turns. You'll come to a fork (4) with stairways leading up to the right and left. Proceed carefully, because two Shikari are waiting for you directly overhead and a Drudge Lord is nearby. Don't let them drop in on your party uninvited.

Go up the stairway to the right and follow the hallway when it turns left. Go a short ways, and encounter a Drudge Lord knee deep in water guarding a pair of **Night Vision Goggles.** Do him in, then continue following the hallway until you climb over some rubble and through a spider web to face another Drudge Lord and a Shikari. When you're done with them, wipe out any Hands and Thieves nearby, then follow the tunnel until you come to the lair of the Behemoth (5). You'll have to fight a Drudge Lord along the way. Take the Behemoth out by either shooting and ducking for cover from the hallway above, or b y using the pillars in his lair for cover. Make sure you grab the **Medkit** in the corner and watch out for the Drudge Lords and Shikari that will warp in.

NOTE

The stone pillars in the Behemoth's lair can be destroyed. This might not be a good thing, since they afford you at least a little cover from the deadly attacks.

Level 19

FRANK COTTON MEMORIAL BRIDGE

You've had enough of waiting around for Gideon and his goons to come to you. It's time to storm the palace gates. Or drawbridge in this case. The road to the final confrontation with Gideon starts with your attempt to get past the most dreaded of security measures: the drawbridge of doom! Well, it's really not that bad.You've just got to fight your way to the controls and lower the darn thing.

OBJECTIVES:........ Lower the drawbridge to grant access to Security Checkpoint.

ENEMIES: .... Prophets, Fanatics, Shikari, Thieves Cultists, Drudge Priest, Bone Leech

ITEMS: .... Health

WEAPONS:.......... Assault Rifles, SMG, Sniper Rifle, Napalm Launcher

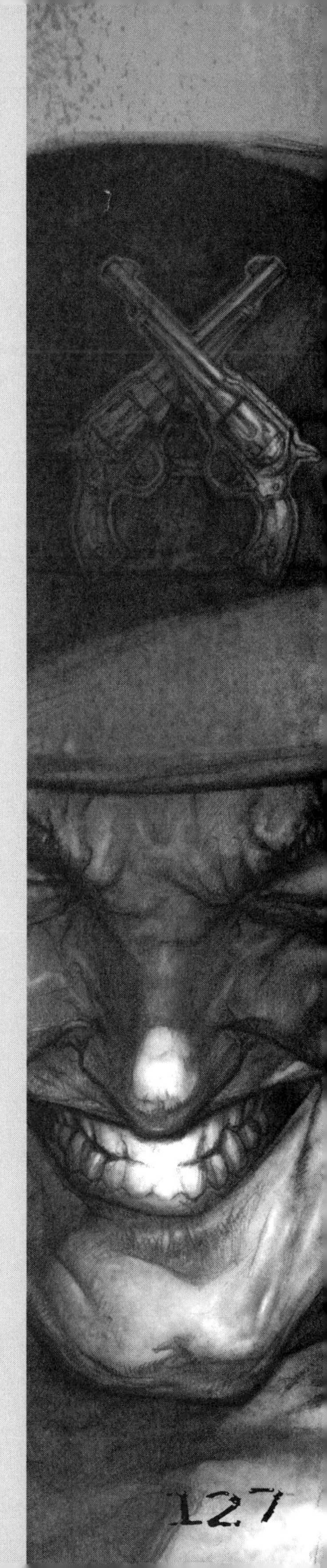

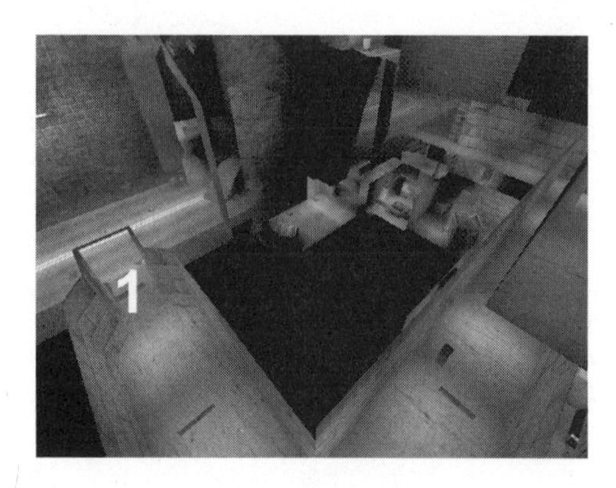

Gun down the Prophet, Shikari, and Fanatic that come out to greet you. Follow the collapsed tunnel and take the door to the right of the crash sight (1). Follow the short service hallway around to the other side of the blockage.

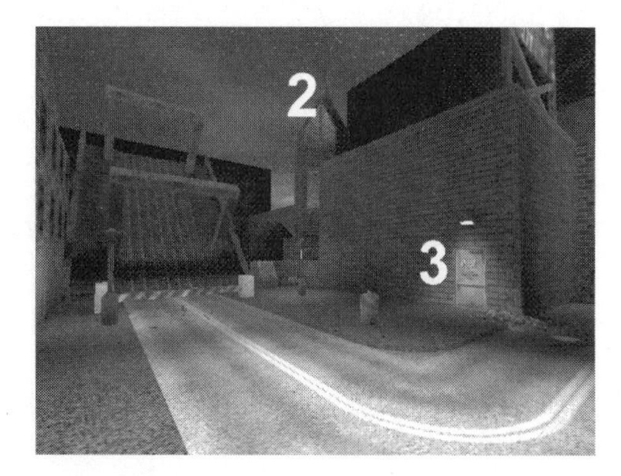

Yep, the bridge is up. Not only that, it's guarded by a horde of Fanatics. Blast them to Kingdom Come and pick up any **ammo** they drop and the **bug spray cans** nearby. You'll have to find the controls to lower the bridge. That control tower (2) looks like an obvious place to start but you'll have to find your way up there. Start by going through the door into the building nearby (3).

TIP

It's actually possible to jump across the gap between the two segments of the bridge. To do so, run along the green railing on the right or left side and jump at the absolute last second. It would be a shame to miss out on all the fun-filled carnage (or is it carnage-filled fun?) in this level, though.

A broken ladder on the other side of the door leads straight down. Gun down the Thieves below and carefully climb down to avoid taking full damage. Follow the hallway down some stairs guarded by a Shikari to a fork. Since the door to the right is locked, go left into a room with a Soul Drudge and a broken ladder leading up (4). Since the bottom two rungs of the ladder are broken, you'll have to **jump from the crate** (5) to climb it up to the control room.

Well, great. The bridge controls are broken. **Activate the Valve Access controls** (6) while you're here, though. They open a trap door back in the room below you. Climb back down the ladder and go through it.

Find yourself in a room with a few inches of standing sewage. Gun down any pesky Soul Drudges that come after you and then go through the door (7) before you into a furnace room. Grab the **ammo** nearby and then **open the garage door with the controls (8) on the wall**. Clean out the storage room beyond, then go through the door opposite the controls you used to open the garage door.

This room contains a steam pipe running up to the ceiling where a couple of Shikari chatter and scamper about. **Shoot out the grating** and climb up the ladder (9) on the other side of the pipe.

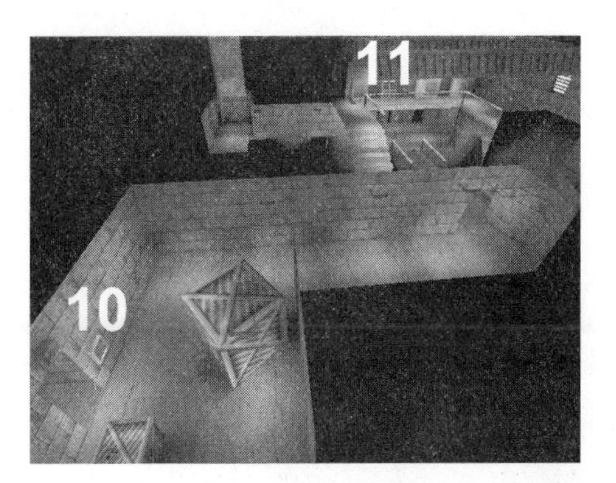

Kill any Soul Drudges, Thieves, and Shikari in the area. Then walk around the corner, past a door with a security panel (10), and around another corner to a room with a metal bridge spanning a trench filled with green goop. Climb the stairs to the left of the bridge and **activate the control panel** (11) on the balcony. This will lower the bridge outside. Drop back down and follow the hallway to the left under the balcony.

Follow the hallway until you come to a ladder leading up a large tube (12). Climb the ladder up to an abandoned city street. Follow the street past a police crime scene, a Café, and a Pool Hall. There are lots of **items** to be picked up along your way, and you'll have to fight off Shikari and Fanatics, as well.

NOTE

All of the shops you see on this street are closed for business, and they have those darn bullet-proof doors. You won't be able to break in and look around at this time.

WARNING

Watch out for the Prophet with the SNIPER RIFLE shortly after you pass the taped-off crime scene.He can put a bullet squarely between your eyes if you give him half a chance.

Follow the street until you come to a basketball court. Play a little game of "catch the bullet" with the Behemoth and Napalm Launcher-wielding Fanatic, then climb the short flight of stairs and go through the door (13) underneath the "Cabalco!" sign.

This will take you into a storage area with lots of wooden crates and a grated catwalk overhead. Gun down anything that moves (note: Fanatics move), then go through the short flight of stairs and doorway (14) at the other end of the room.

Come out into a wide alley with a trash dumpster, a ladder, and a door. Watch out above as a Drudge Priest tries to surprise you. Kill it and any Shikari hanging about. Go through the door (15) labeled "Keep out" (hey, you can never believe anything you read nowadays). Follow the hallway on the other side, climb the red ladder, and **shoot out the grate in the floor**. Drop down through the grate and find yourself in the access hall you went through at the beginning of the level. Follow the hallway back outside and cross the now lowered bridge.

NOTE

You can jump onto the trash dumpster in the alley with the Drudge Priest and climb the ladder to gain access to the ledges flanking the city street. You might find some fun stuff up there.

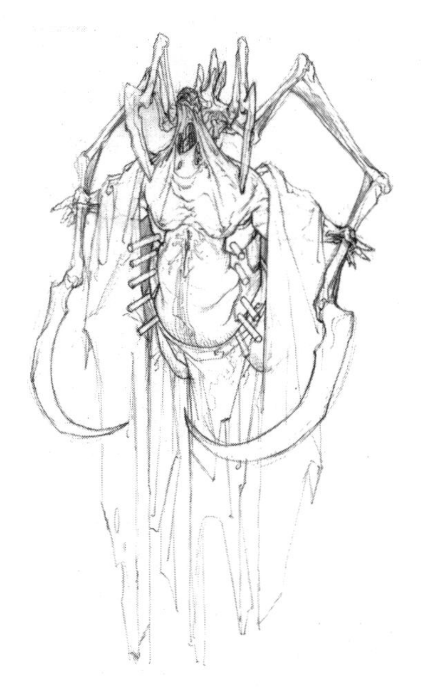

Level 20

SECURITY CHECKPOINT

You got past the drawbridge, but your assault on the Cabal headquarters has barely begun. There are severallayers of defense between Gideon and yourself, the next of which is the security check point. You'll face an army of Fanatics, with a few Prophets, Cultists, and even Otherworld creatures thrown in for flavor. A direct frontal assault on the Cabalco headquarters wouldn't be advisable, even for you, so you'll have to find a way to sneak in. Fortunately, you've heard about a secret entrance via an Old Town temple. Find the entrance to that temple, and you're one step closer to shoving a shotgun down Gideon's throat and letting go with both barrels.

OBJECTIVES:........ Infiltrate the security check point and find the entrance to the Temple of Poon.

ENEMIES:........... Prophets, Fanatics, Cultists, Zealot

ITEMS:............ Medkit

WEAPONS:........... Assault Rifles, Pistols, SMG's, Tesla Cannons, Howitzer, Minigun

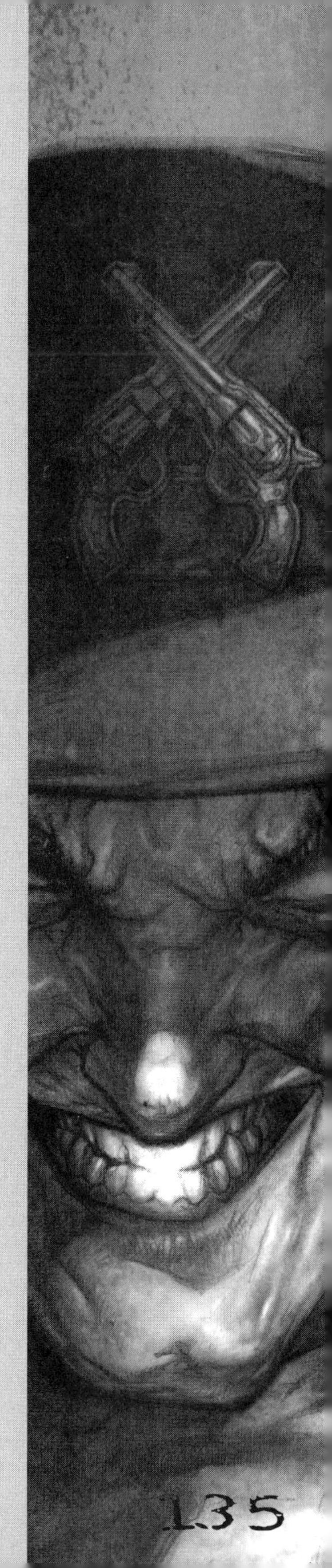

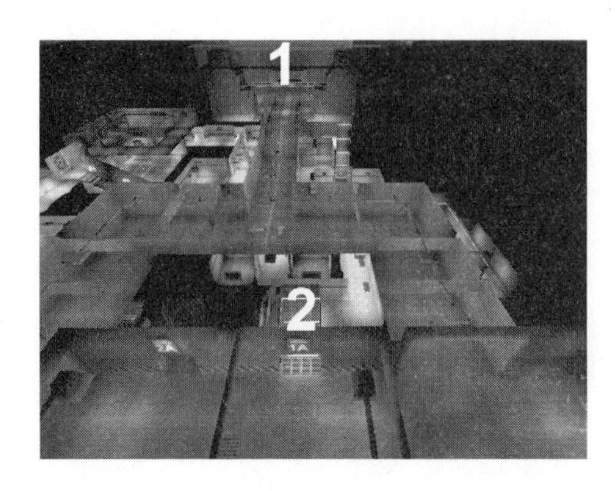

This is another level that's intense right from the start. As soon as you set foot in front of the security gate, you're ambushed by a pack of Fanatics and Cultists. One of the Fanatics on the balcony overhead is even wielding a Tesla Cannon. Quickly run forward under the balcony (1) into the parking garage. Follow the garage around to the left or right to an area with some parked cars and a set of elevators. Kill the cultists and the Prophet with the Minigun, then take the right-hand elevator marked "1A" (2).

The elevator will take you down into the complex. Follow the hallway to the right, past a control pad on the wall (3). **Activate the controls,** then go to the room and activate the controls at the bottom of the stairs. This opens a door outside the hall. Go back out to the hall and turn right. Follow the hall toward a window with an elevator on the other side (4). Gun down any Fanatics in the area, then walk around to the right and take the elevator up.

The elevator will take you into one of the guard shacks that flanked the parking garage entrance at the beginning of this level. Climbing the ladder next to the handprint control grants you access to the balcony. Gun down any remaining Fanatics and run across to the other shack. Drop in and grab the Cabalco **security pass** (5) on the shelf. Backtrack to the first guard hut and ride the elevator back down.

From the elevator, turn right and follow the hallway until it forks. Take a moment to clean out the barracks on the left (6). There's a lot of **ammo** and a **Medkit** hidden in the trunks you'll find within each room. After you're done, take the right fork (7). Your path will soon be blocked by a red force field (8), so turn right and **use the controls on the wall** to open the locked door (9) and proceed.

When the hallway forks again, go left (going right would take you to the Infirmary), then go through the first door you come to on your left. You'll find yourself in a shooting gallery. After grabbing the **Minigun** walk around to the right of the range and **climb on top of the crates** (10). **Shoot out the glass window** to your right and jump into the room overlooking the shooting gallery. Clean out the Cabal agents that come greet you.

NOTE Feel free to shoot the moron standing in front of the big target. You can then take shots at the paper target and check your aim by pressing the button down on your left.

Destroy the controls (11) to shut off the red force fields throughout the level. Then exit the room through the doorway opposite the controls and take the stairs down to another hallway. Turn left and follow the hallway until you find another door on your left. Activate the controls on the wall to open it.

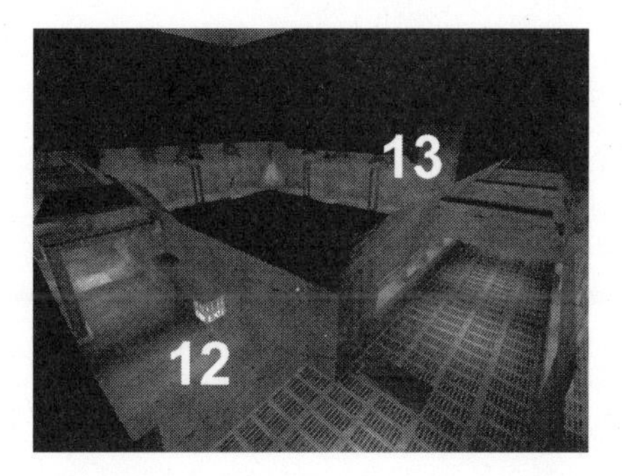

Hop down into the concrete tunnel and walk past a disturbing Biohazard sign. Take your first right (12) and follow the halls filled with puddles of glowing green goop. Watch out for the Zealot that ambushes you through a rift. Continue following the hallway until you come to a ladder (13). Take the ladder up to exit the level.

WARNING

Those green puddles are not good for your health. Don't try to take this opportunity to have a bath. Avoid taking damage by hugging the wall to the left or right of the puddles and creeping past them on the narrow ledge between the puddle and the wall.

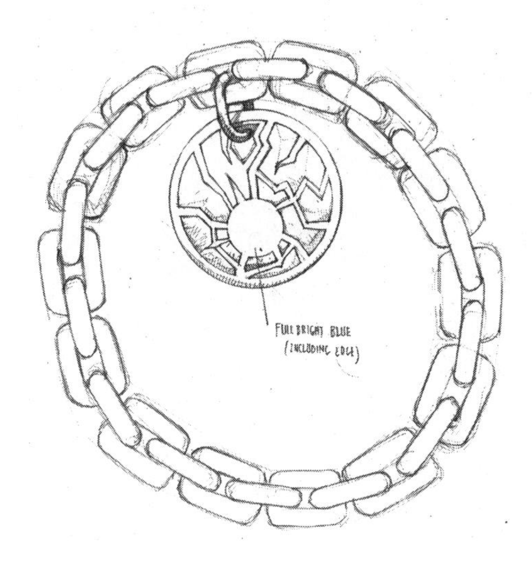

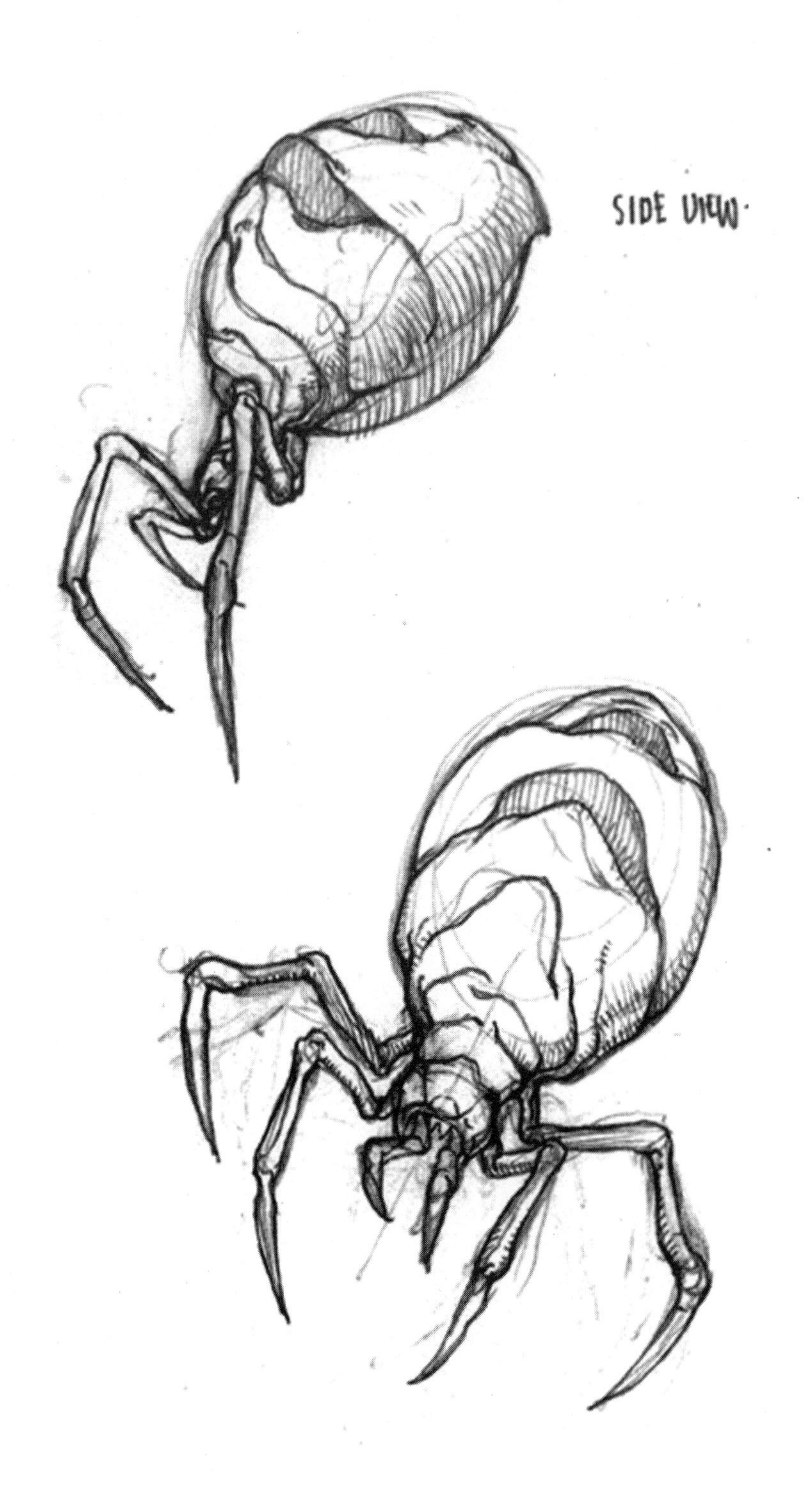
SIDE VIEW.

Level 21

TEMPLE OF POON

Super villains have a secret entrance to their lair. It's in their contract.In this case, the Temple of Poon (an ancient deity Brother to the Goddess "Tang") will provide you with that entrance. It's relatively unguarded, but you'll have to fight your way through a few nasty Otherworld creatures. It doesn't look like it matters a whole lot, though, since Gideon apparently knows you're coming. This level starts off with Ophelia being raised from a rift. Before you can get reacquainted with your old flame, however, Gideon whisks her away. Okay, now it's personal. Somebody's gonna bleed over this. A lot.

OBJECTIVES: .... Give chase to Gideon and find the secret entrance to the Cabal's headquarters.

ENEMIES: .... Shikari, Soul Drudges, Thieves, Drudge Lord, Drudge Priest, Bone Leeches

ITEMS: .... Life Seed

WEAPONS: .... Life Leech

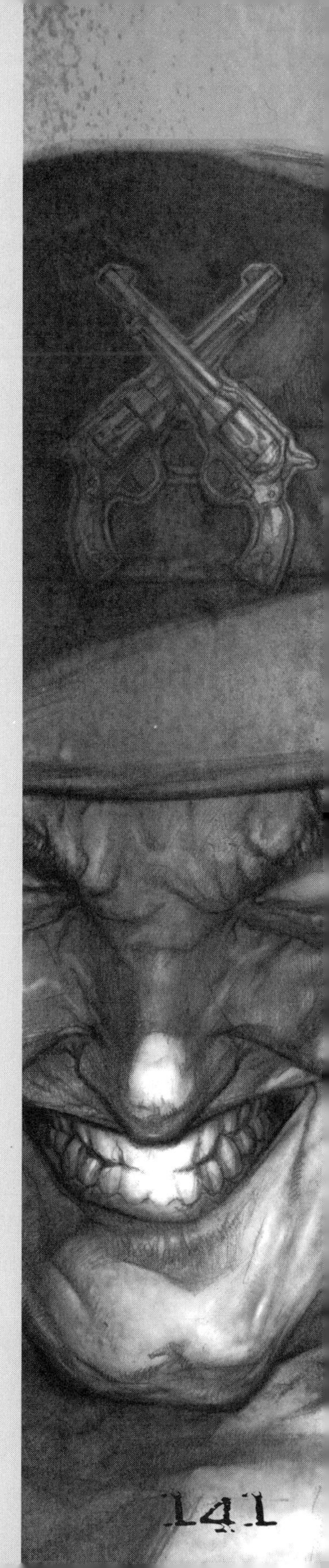

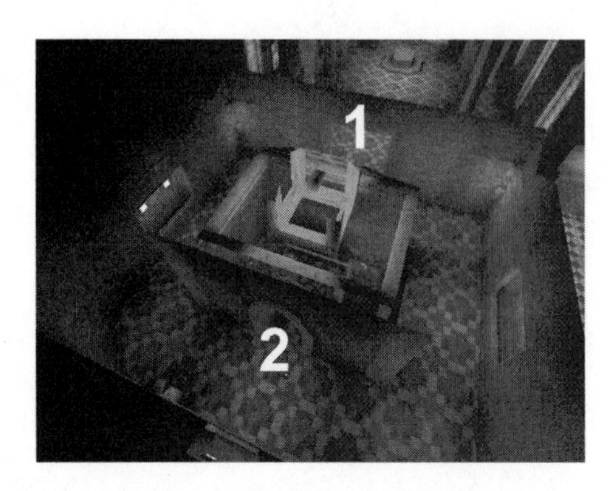

After you're done with your little encounter with Gideon and Ophelia, turn around and open the two massive doors (1) leading out of the antechamber. Kill the Shikari and Thieves that come after you. Walk around to the left or right and go through the archway (2) leading to the stairs. Kill all the Soul Drudges and Thieves guarding them, then go down the stairs.

After clearing out all the Shikari and Thieves waiting for you at the bottom of the stairs, turn left and follow the hallway. Keep following the hallway for quite a while, past a double set of wooden doors, until you come to an archway and a staircase leading up.

NOTE

The double wooden doors you encounter along the hallway after the first set of stairs leads to a large chamber. You can stop in there to grab the LIFE LEECH if you like.

Fight off the Soul Drudges and the Shikari in the area. Ascend the stairway and come to a set of double arches (3). Go through the arches into the room beyond, and then through another archway to a two-way fork.

WARNING

Don't dally in the room before the double arches. There are several Thieves that can drop down from the stained glass above and grab you.

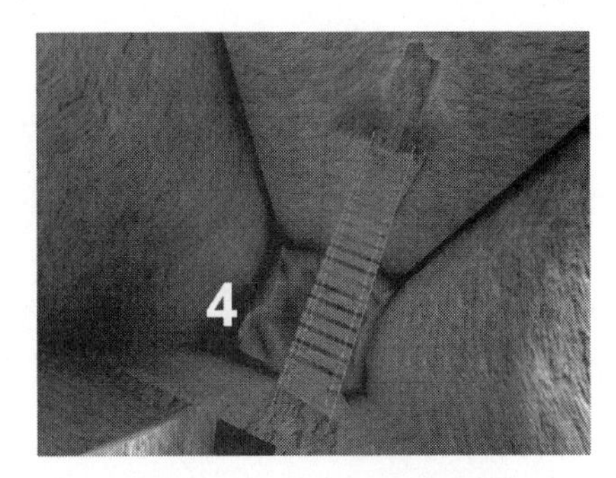

Turn right and follow the hallway until you come to a rickety bridge of planks spanning a great chasm (4). If you look up you can see the towering...um...towers of the Cabalco headquarters. That's where you want to end up. Crossing this old, rotting, dangerous looking, non-too-safe collection of twine and splintered boards seems like a good next step. Ooops. You're falling. Still falling. Continuing to fall. Splash! Well, you're not dead, just slimy. Swim out of the green water and go through the tunnel on the left (5).

NOTE

If you have a speed of 5, it's actually possible to make it across the bridge. Run and jump at the last instant. Keep hitting the jump button to clamber up the last bit of the fallen bridge.

The short tunnel leads into a construction area with a wheelbarrow, some crates, a Drudge Lord, a Drudge Priest, some Bone Leeches, and a lift on the left. Clear out the room, then ride the lift back up. At the top, turn around and follow the hallway around a couple of turns and through another room with some crates. Just past this room, find another lift (6) on your left that leads up to the next level.

TIP

Before taking the lift that exits the level, follow the hallway to the other side of the bridge that collapsed on you. Grab the LIFE SEED from the ledge.

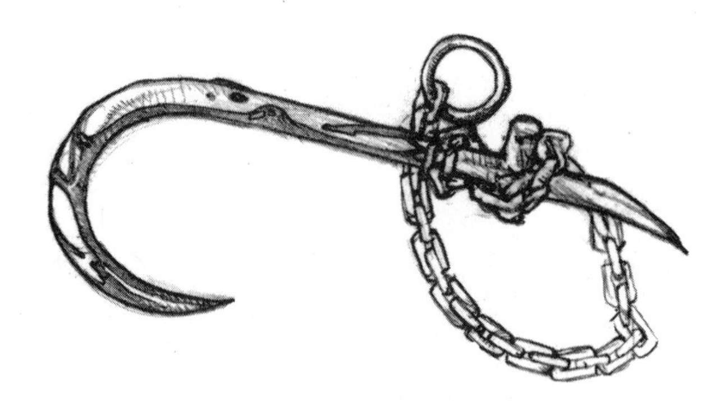

Level 22

CABALCO ENTERPRISES

Ahhh...at last. The very heart of all the evil. Well, all the evil besides yourself. You kind of expected something different, though. Maybe a dreary castle filled with chanting, knife-wielding monks, deadly traps, and oppressed peasants. Instead you find a modern high rise skyscraper filled with coffee machines, break rooms, and employees with a pretty good pension plan. Weird. Well, at least there is one thing you did expect: a bunch of really ticked off Cabal agents trying to kill you so fast you'll be dead last week. Good. Just the way you like it.

OBJECTIVES: . . . . Find the entrance to the Power Station.

ENEMIES: . . . . Cultists, Fanatics, Prophets, Shikari, Drudge Preists, Bone Leeches

ITEMS: . . . . None

WEAPONS: . . . . Pistols, Assault Rifles, SMG's, Flare Pistol, Sniper Rifle, Tesla Cannon, Minigun

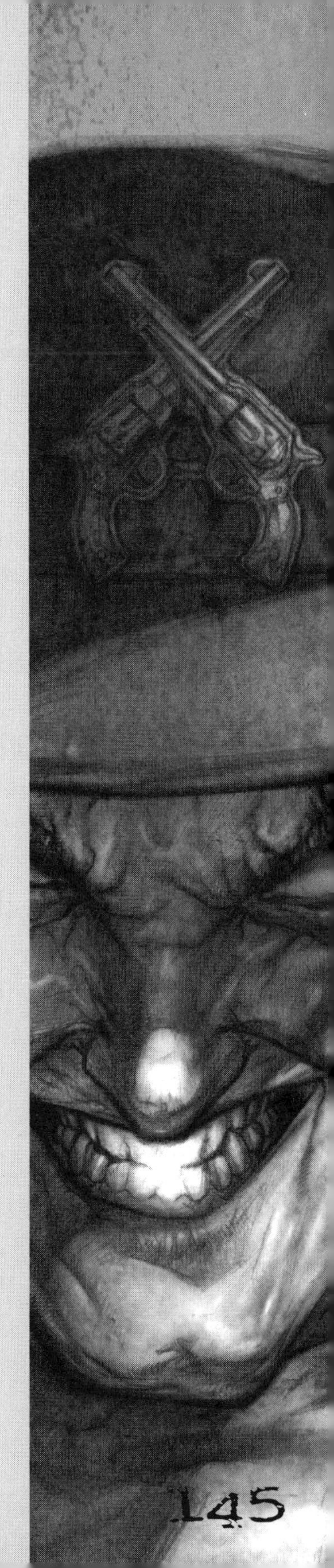

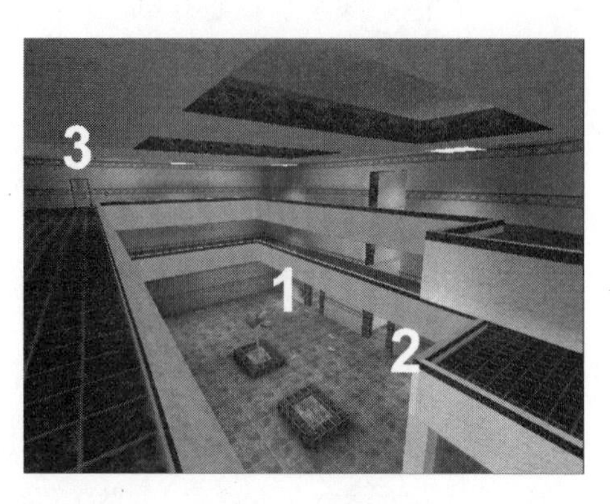

Walk down the short hallway and open the secret door. You'll come out into the main Cabalco lobby. Take the Fanatics and Cultists out however you like. One of the exits from the area will be blocked by security lasers (1). Take the exit next to it (2), follow the passage, and climb the stairs until you reach the third terrace level overlooking the main lobby. Turn right and follow the walkway until you come to a door (3).Go through the door and find yourself in the security control room with a couple of Cultists. **Activate the panels** to shut off the security lasers blocking the first doorway (1) on the lobby ground level.

Retrace your steps down to the first floor of the lobby. Go through the unblocked entrance on the left (1) and follow the passageway, past some posters, until you come to an open area with some broken elevators and restrooms. Gun down any Fanatics and the Drudge Priest in the area, then take the functional elevator (4) between the restrooms. Aigh! The horror! The horror! Elevator music has always terrified you.

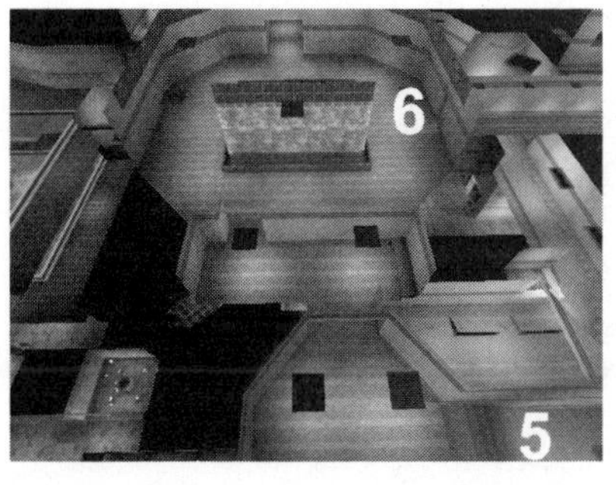

You will now be in an area with hardwood floors and a blue runner carpet. Follow the carpet and turn right when it forks at the mural. Keep following it, mowing down Fanatics and a Prophet as you go, until you find a stairway leading up on your left near a soda machine. Take the stairway up to another level with hardwood floors. Go through the passage on your right (5) and come into a room with water streaming down a huge marble block in the middle. Find the doorway to the right leading out of the room (6) and take it after cutting down the Fanatics (make sure to grab the **ammo** and **Sniper Rifle** that they drop).

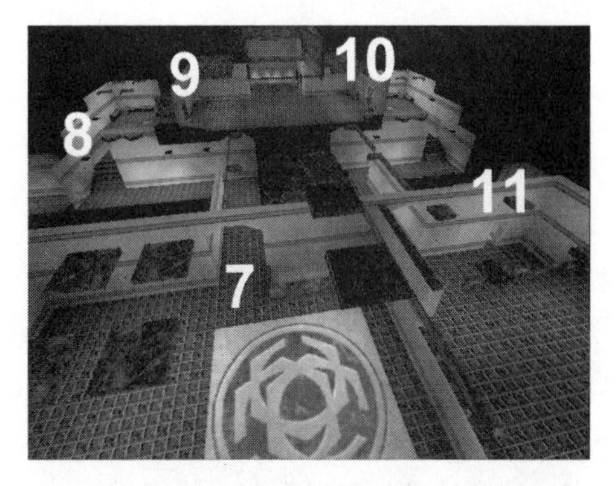

Follow the hallway to the top of a short flight of stairs leading down into a large open area with a Cabalco mural on the floor. Go down the short flight of stairs and through the archway opposite them (7). Continue following the hallway to a short flight of stairs to the right of a locked door (8). Climb them, then go through the doorway on your right (9). Cross the large room with Fanatics and a Behemoth, go through the door (10) opposite the one you just came through, then down another short flight of stairs. You'll have to fight Fanatics, Cultists, and Prophets the whole way. Keep following the hallway until you come to a ledge overlooking the room with the giant Cabalco mural on the floor. Go through the door behind you (11) and take the elevator to the Power Station.

Grab the LIFE SEED under the stairs in the room with the floor mural.

Level 23

POWER STATION

Time to pull the plug on the Cabalco security systems. A giant mega-corporation needs power to run, and since they *are* the power company, this usually isn't a problem. Well, time to make it a problem. You'll need to navigate the treacherous environment of the Cabalco Power Station to knock out key breaker boxes. You'll then return to the Cabalco headquarters for the next leg of your journey.

OBJECTIVES:........ Deactivate the power so you can continue your assault.

ENEMIES: .... Prophets, Fanatics, Shikari, Cultists, Hands

ITEMS: .... Ward

WEAPONS:........... Pistols, Assault Rifles, SMG's, Tesla Cannon, Howitzer, Flare Pistol, Napalm Launcher

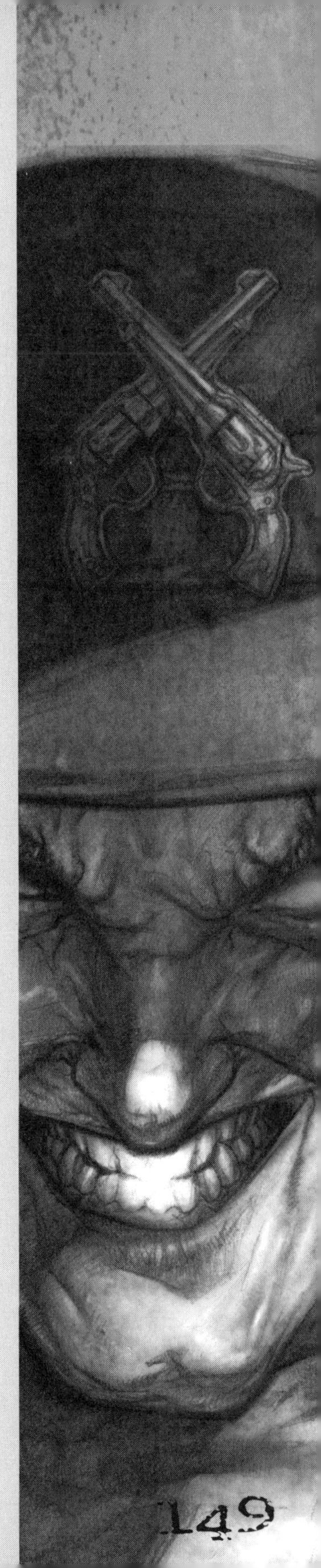

You start out on a balcony overlooking a square room with two doors. Clear out the Prophet and Fanatics below, then jump over the railing into the room. Go through the door (1) to the right of the ladder leading back up to the catwalk. This leads to a hallway surrounding the room you were just in. Kill off the Fanatics, then go through the door opposite the one you just came through.

Follow the hallway until you come to a partially flooded room with a Flare Pistol-wielding Cultist. Be careful here, because that water is full of electricity. It'll hard boil you in a second. From the stairs (2), jump onto the platform on your right (3), then onto the ledge to the right of that (4). Exit the room through the passageway across from the stairs.

Follow the hall until it forks to the left and right. Kill off the Fanatics, then follow the fork to the right. Gun down any Fanatics you encounter, walk past a large yellow sign reading "Sector 1", and shoot out the **breaker boxes** along the left-hand wall (5). Then continue following the hallway until you come to another door on your right.

Go through the door, follow the short hallway, then go through another similar door. You will now find yourself in another square room with two handprint controls and a stairway leading down into a square pit. Gun down the Fanatics and Cultists in the area, as well as the Shikari that warp in. When you're done, go down into the pit and through the small hallway (6) under the "Sector 2" sign. In there, you will find some ammo, a couple of hands and a handprint control pad. **Activate the control pad** to unlock the door outside, then return to the pit, grab the **Ward** from under the stairs, climb the stairs, and exit the room through the now unlocked door opposite the one you came through.

Run along the catwalk over the sizzling raw electricity until you come out into a large room with a platform in front of you. Clear the room of Fanatics and Shikari, then **find the breaker boxes (7) and destroy them**. Exit through the doorway under the "Sector 3" sign (8).

WARNING

After you leave this room, a section of the catwalk is weakened and will collapse as you approach it. Luckily for you, some day dreaming Cultists happened to be standing in it.Jump the gap and continue on...

Follow the hallway and the grated catwalk beyond to the last large room of this level. Gun down the Fanatic on the catwalk above and the Death Shroud below, then take the lift (9) up. Activate the handprint control on the wall to open the gate (10) and exit the level.

Level 24

RETURN TO CABALCO INDUSTRIES

Now that you've messed with the Cabal's power supply, the door blocking your path to the Research and Development lab is unlocked. Your next step is easy: find the entrance to the lab.

OBJECTIVES:........ Find the entrance to the Research and Development Lab.

ENEMIES: .... Prophets, Fanatics, Shikari

ITEMS: .... Life Seed

WEAPONS:........... Assault Rifles, SMG's

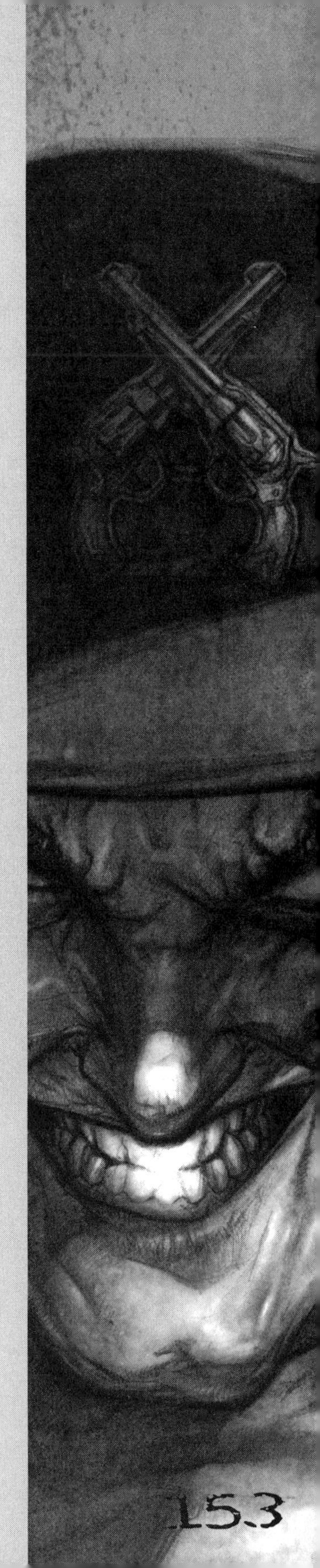

From the door leading to the power station (1), go up the short flight of stairs in front of you. Hop over the ledge to the lobby with the giant Cabalco logo on the floor, then go through the archway on the right (2) after clearing the area of Fanatics and a Prophet. Follow the hall to the previously locked door to the left of the stairs (3). Go through, follow the hallway, go through another door, then go through the entrance to the Research and Development Lab (4).

TIP

Don't forget to grab the LIFE SEED under the stairs in the lobby.

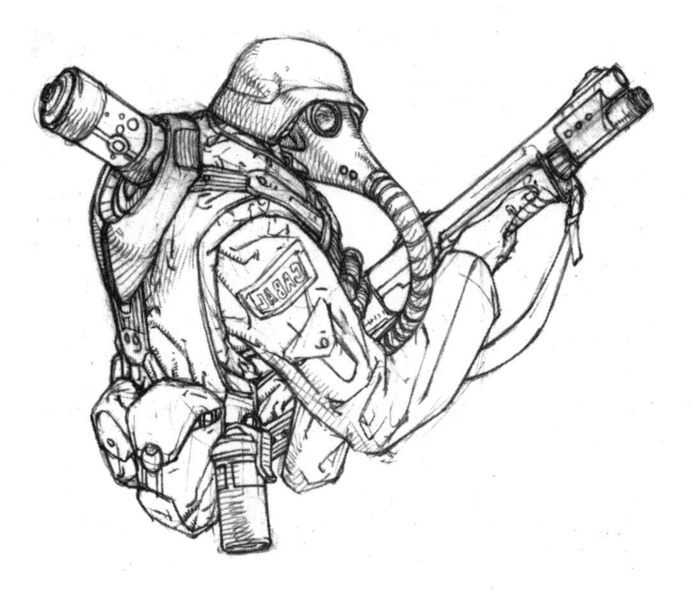

Level 25

RESEARCH AND DEVELOPMENT

Somebody is keeping you from going on to the offices above the lobby. That somebody must be gunned down in a blazing flurry of bullets. The Research and Development Lab seems to be the next best place to look for him. This is quite an interesting level, as it appears that the Cabal has been behind the appearance of all these Otherworld creatures after all. Not only are they responsible, they're conducting all kinds of strange experiments on them. Time to introduce Caleb's First Law of Physics: "A body at rest has most likely just been shot to death."

OBJECTIVES:........ Track down and kill the Mad Scientist.

ENEMIES:.......... Shikari, Bone Leeches, Thieves, Soul Drudges, The Hands, Fanatics, Cultists, Mad Scientist

ITEMS:........... None

WEAPONS:.......... Pistols, Singularity Generator

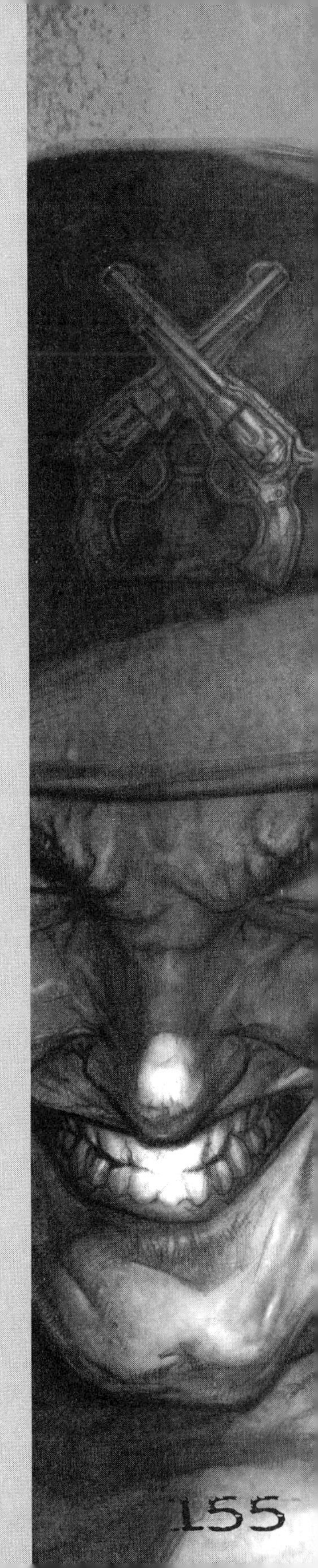

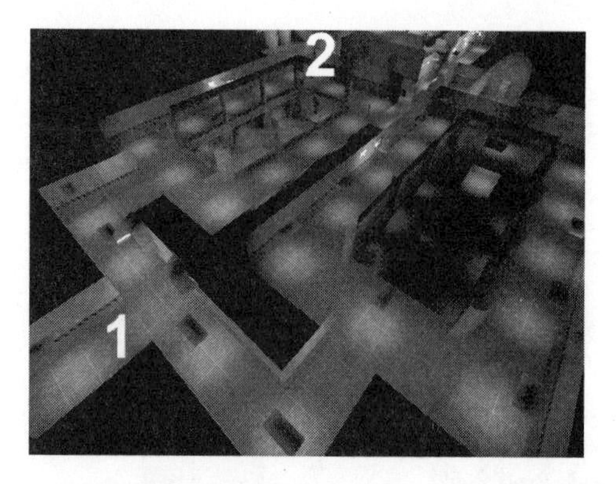

From the hallway you start out in (1), follow the fork to the right into the first biosphere. You'll run into a Shikari and a Cabalco Scientist. KIll them both and take the scientist's security pass. Climb up the fallen beam out of the biosphere and follow the hallway around to the security door. Open it and enter the second biosphere. Walk along the left wall and take the elevator (2) down after clearing the hallway of Thieves.

One of the Cabal scientists is hiding somewhere in this level with a security pass you need to proceed. You need to track him down and find a way to get at him. From the first elevator, turn right and follow the hall until you come to a couple of explosive barrels. Look up at the ceiling and notice that there is a hole covered by a grate (3). **Shoot the grate** and climb up the short ladder to the crawlspace above.

Follow the crawlspace until you come to another grate (4) directly over a small laboratory with a scientist and a security pass (5). **Shoot out the grate, grab the Security Pass,** and **then activate the controls on the wall** (6) to shut off the force field.

NOTE There are a lot of interesting things to see and kill on this level that aren't necessary to move on to the next. Feel free to look around, but try to keep your bearings so you can return and follow this walkthrough if you need to.

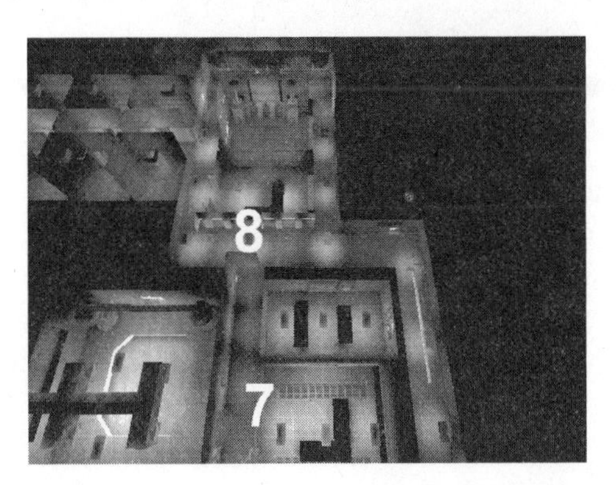

Exit the lab through the door on the left (7), then turn right and go through the door at the end of the hall (8). Take the first door on your left into the mental asylum wing. Walk all the way past the padded cells to the door at the end of the hall. Enter the lab full of Soul Drudges and Hands, then retrieve the **Security Pass** from the counter. Backtrack past the padded cells to the outer hallway, turn left, and follow the hall until it forks again. Take the fork to the left and follow the hallway past several doors, until you come to a door labeled "Restricted Area Authorized Personnel Only." Your gun is all the authorization you need, so let yourself in and gun down the Shikari on the other side.

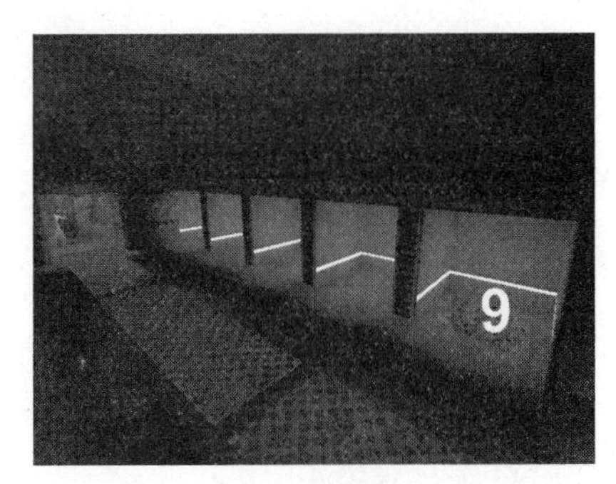

You will now be in a long room with a hole in the floor to your right (9) and bullet-proof glass straight ahead. **Drop down through the hole** into a watery tunnel with some Soul Drudges and Bone Leeches. Gun them down, then follow the tunnel until it terminates in a ladder. Shoot out the grate overhead and climb up the ladder. You'll now be able to stick it to that annoying Mad Scientist.

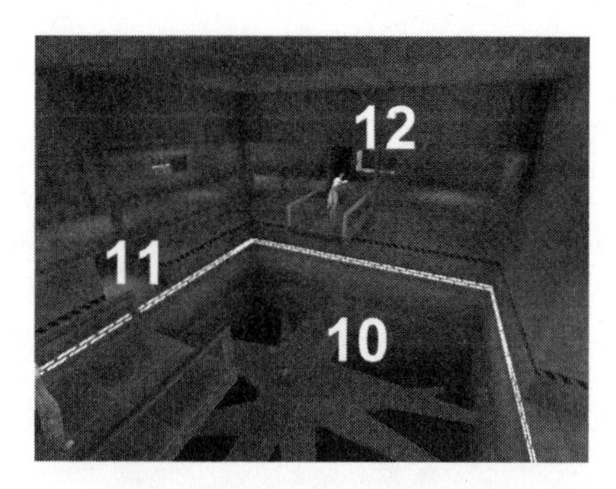

Take the elevator in front of the hole you came up through. This will take you to the lair of "Doctor", the Mad Scientist. Getting to him is going to be really tricky. You'll have to jump across a great pit onto three spinning steel crosses (10). It'll make you sicker than the Tilt-A-Whirl at the state fair as you spin around, trying to jump to the ledge opposite the one you came on (11). Once you do, however, take the short lift up to the upper balcony, gun down the Mad Scientist, and grab the **Security Pass** (12). Then you're going to have to jump back again to retrace your steps and exit the level.

TIP

Now would be a good time to save your game. It's probably going to take you a few attempts to make it across those whirling crosses. Wait until a long end of the blade swings around to you, jump on it, and don't stop running.Jump again across to the other side.

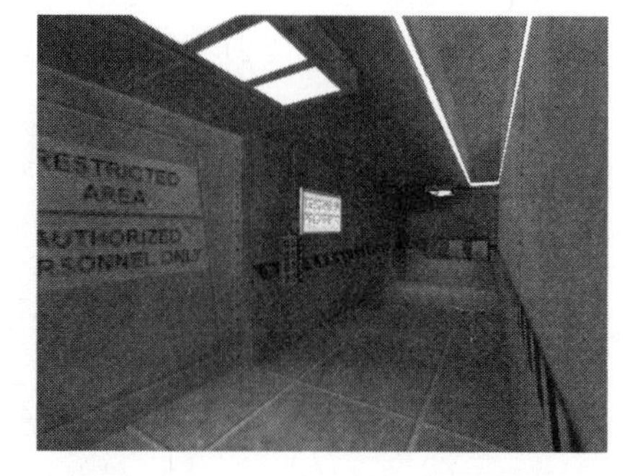

Backtrack to the elevator where you took the lift up to the Mad Scientist's lair. **Activate the controls on the wall** to lower the bullet-proof glass, then walk over the grated floor and through the door. Turn left and follow the hallway until you come to a door next to a white sign that reads "Testing In Progress." Watch out, though, because the scientist on the other side of the glass doesn't like the looks of you and is pretty likely to let loose with that Singularity Generator he's carrying. Go through the door, kill the scientist, take the weapon, go through the two doors beyond the testing chamber, then exit the level.

Level 26

RETURN TO CABALCO OFFICES (AGAIN)

Things couldn't be easier. All you've got to do here is return to the elevators that were not functioning before and ride them up to the offices at the top of the headquarters building. You'll notice that while you were in the Research and Development Lab some Cabal reinforcements have shown up. Even better, more otherworld creatures have warped in.

OBJECTIVES: .... Enter the elevators leading to the offices

ENEMIES: .... Fanatics, Behemoth, Drudge Lord, Death Shroud

ITEMS: .... Wards, The Anger

WEAPONS: .... Assault Rifles

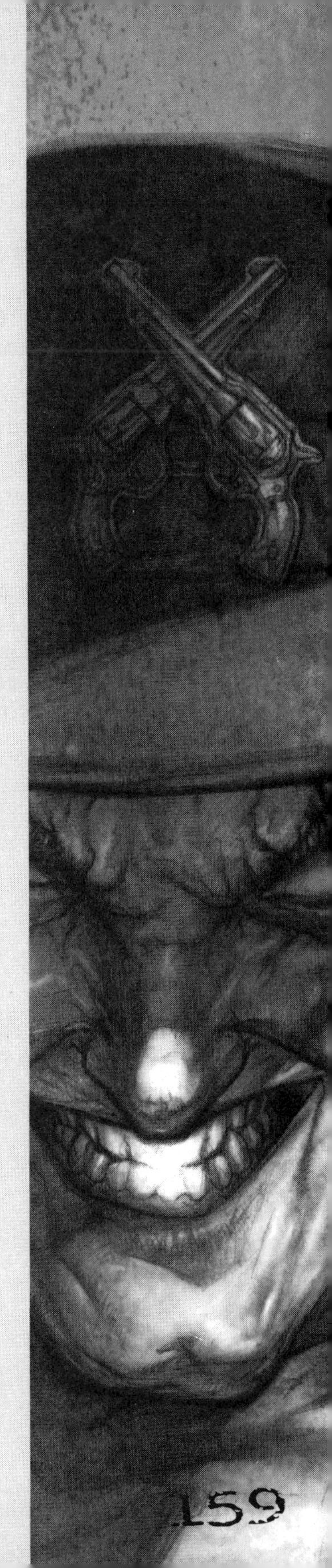

From the entrance to the Research and Development level (1), turn left and go through the door, through another door, then take the stairs (2) on your left. Gun down any Drudge Lords or Fanatics you encounter. Follow the hall through a set of double doors to a large room with elevators (3) on your left. Oh, and don't forget to notice the Death Shroud and the pack of Shikari waiting in the elevator lobby for you. You're in for a really tough fight here. Use the Singularity Generator to take out the Shikari, then gun down the Death Shroud. Make sure you grab the **Anger** powerup in the flower bed to make things a lot easier. Once you're done, **activate the controls** on the wall to open one of the elevators. Ride it to the next level.

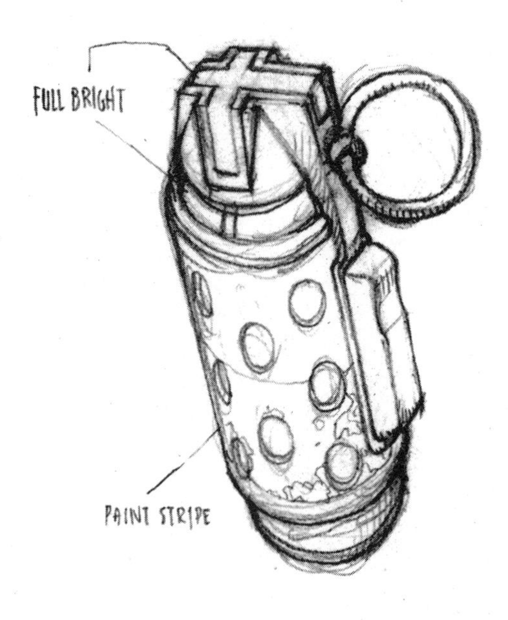

Level 27

CABALCO OFFICES

Nothing has been able to stop you so far, and Gideon is running out of places to hide.It's time to tear through the Cabalco corporate offices, blasting whatever gets in your way.It's so close, you can almost taste it.This level can be a relatively short trek if you want it to be, or you can detour and slaughter a few more Cabal agents just for fun.Either way, you'll eventually have to find the secret elevator leading to the rooftops, where the Caballeader has taken his final refuge.

OBJECTIVES: . . . . Find the secret rooftop elevator.

ENEMIES: . . . . Fanatics, Cultists, Prophets, Zealots, Shikari, Bone Leeches

ITEMS: . . . . None

WEAPONS: . . . . Assault Rilfes, SMG's, Tesla Cannons, Flare Pistol

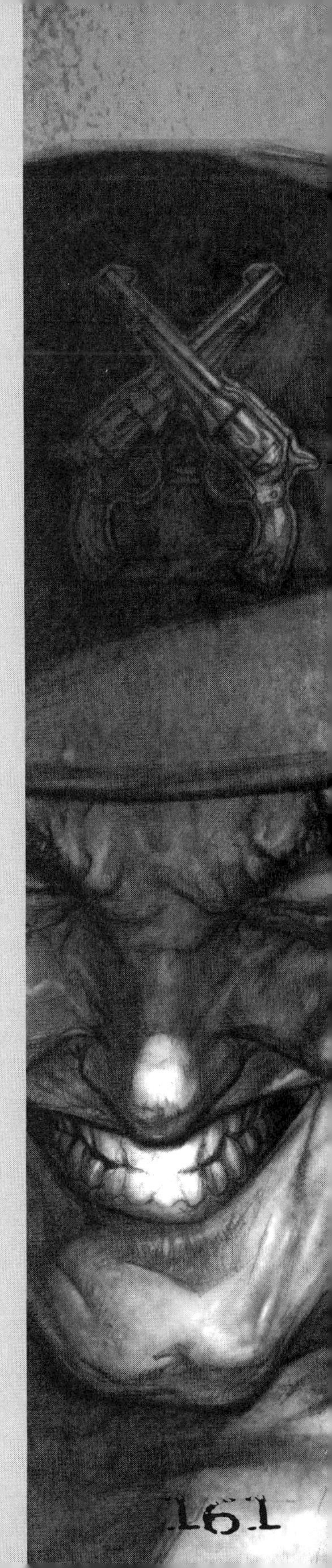

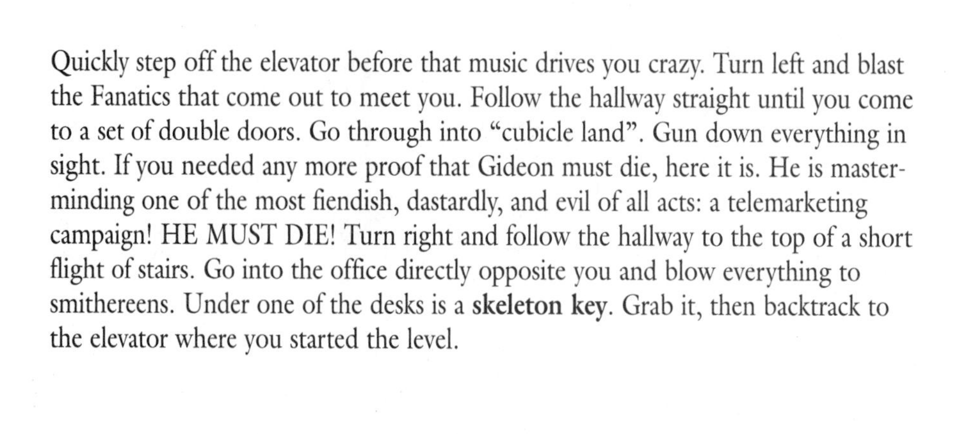

Quickly step off the elevator before that music drives you crazy. Turn left and blast the Fanatics that come out to meet you. Follow the hallway straight until you come to a set of double doors. Go through into "cubicle land". Gun down everything in sight. If you needed any more proof that Gideon must die, here it is. He is masterminding one of the most fiendish, dastardly, and evil of all acts: a telemarketing campaign! HE MUST DIE! Turn right and follow the hallway to the top of a short flight of stairs. Go into the office directly opposite you and blow everything to smithereens. Under one of the desks is a **skeleton key**. Grab it, then backtrack to the elevator where you started the level.

Go straight past the elevator and follow the hallway, gunning down any Fanatics that stop to say hello. When you come to a room with a large Cabalco logo on the floor and cubicles on your right, head to the right and go through the door (1) behind the cubicles. Just watch out for the Shikari that drop out of rifts to ambush you.

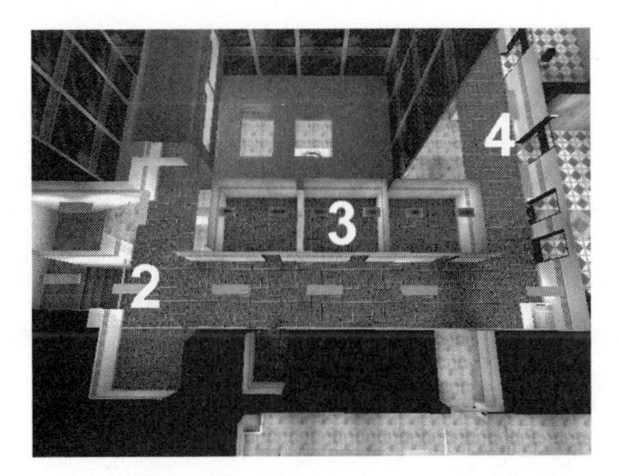

Follow the stairs beyond the double doors all the way to the top (2). Turn right, then clear out the small offices and janitor's closets on your left (3)—they each contain either **ammo** or **health**. Once you have the goodies, enter the large office (4) with the two windows inhabited by a couple of cultists. Gun them down.

In this office there is a small control panel on the floor underneath the desk (5). **Activate the panel** to open a secret passage behind you, leading to the rooftop elevator.

Level 28

ROOFTOPS

Finally! That geek Gideon has run out of hidey holes, and there's not a subway train in sight. Just him, you, and the open sky. Time for a good old-fashioned shoot-out. Funny, though, you don't ever remember seeing him drenched in blood and flying around like a hummingbird on too much caffeine. And he appears to be throwing very painful blasts of dark magic in your general direction. Better make him stop that, and something tells you that polite conversation isn't going to work.

OBJECTIVES: . . . . Battle Gideon and survive.

ENEMIES: . . . . Enhanced Gideon

ITEMS: . . . . The Anger, Life Seed

WEAPONS: . . . . None

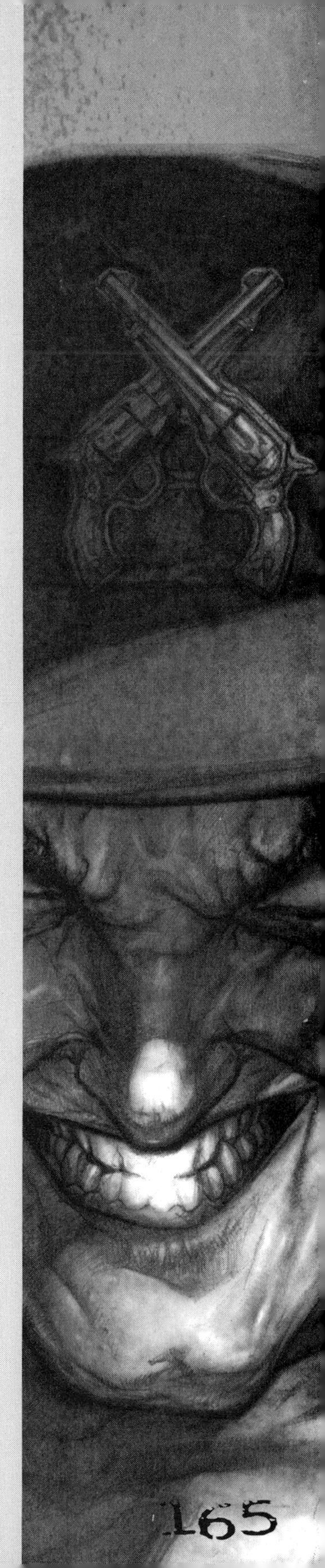

Gideon is fast, and he hurls magic at you quickly, as well. Keep moving at all costs, and switch to your most powerful weapon. Don't waste ammo by firing at him when he's flying about. Instead, wait patiently for him to stop moving for a second, then let him have it. Also, Gideon will teleport around to avoid your fire and get behind you, so try to stand with your back against a wall so he can't tag you from behind. If you want to try for it, there's an **Anger powerup** (1) that you can reach through a tricky jump from the ledge underneath the neon Cabalco sign. Also, there is a **Life Seed** hidden on the window washing platform (2). However, trying to grab either one will likely give Gideon a few free shots at you. Make sure to try and stay away from the building ledges since Gideon will try to knock you over. Once you've worn the Cabal leader down, he'll pick up his skirts and run for it, though, at which point you can give pursuit and move on to the next level.

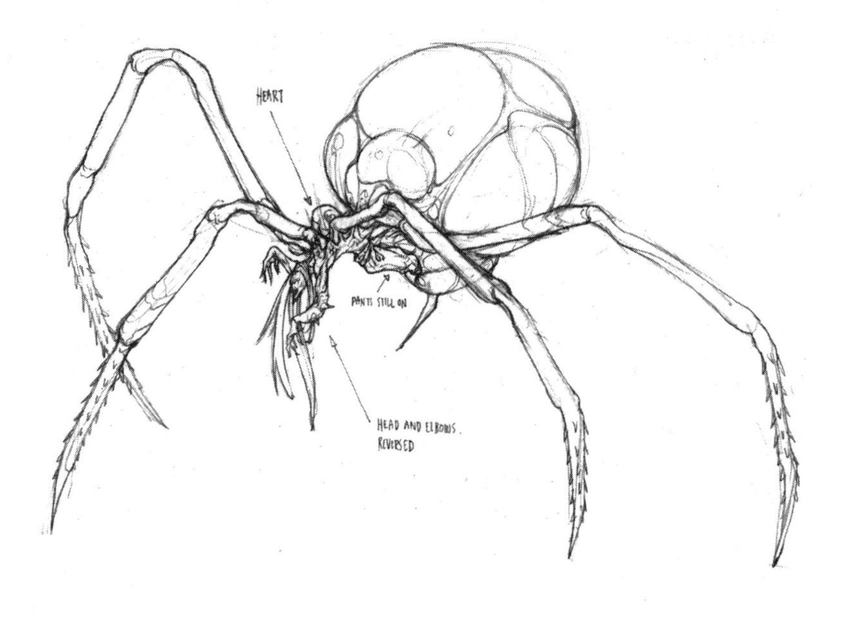

Level 29

ANCIENT CITY

Man, some people just can't take a hint. You fill them full of lead, magic, napalm, and everything else you can find, and they just refuse to die politely. Looks like you're going to have to do this the hard way and follow Gideon to the ancient city that's the source of his fell magic.It's time for your final showdown with the CEO of Cabalco and Cultist Quarterly's Maniacal Man of the Century—Gideon. This time it's for good.Yet, should you survive your confrontation, something else even worse maybe waiting in the background. Only one way to find out.

OBJECTIVES:........ Defeat Undead Gideon, defeat the other Chosen, then confront the Ancient One.

ENEMIES:........... Undead Gideon, Behemoth, Naga, Drudge Lords, Soul Drudges, Shikari, Drudge Priests, Fanatics, Death Shroud

ITEMS:............ Willpower, Remote Bombs, Medkit

WEAPONS:.......... Pistol, Shotgun

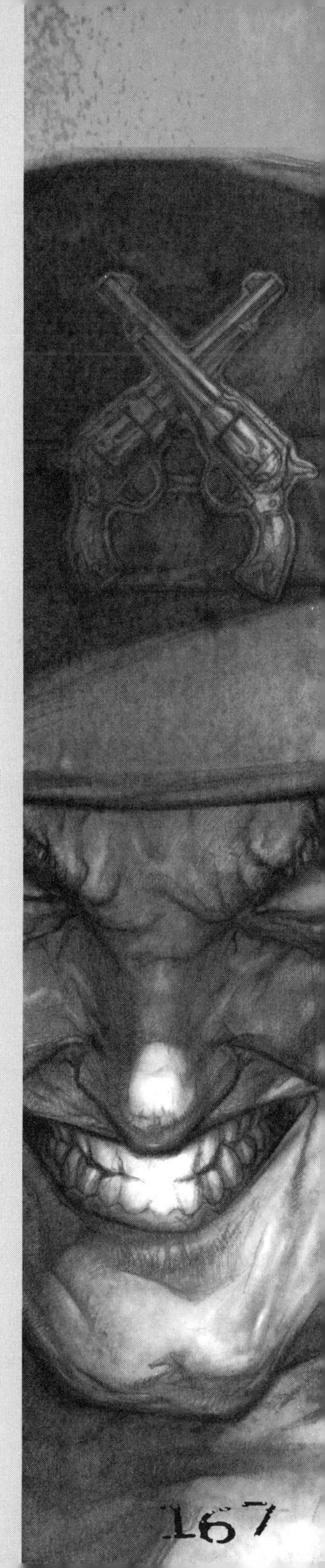

You start this level in a foggy desert area amid jumbles of broken rocks. There's a Behemoth nearby, as well as a couple of Fanatical members of the Cabalco Expekitions Team.Deal with them both and grab the **ammo** from the crates the Expedition Team. Then follow the tunnel (1) out of the area.

Follow the tunnel until you come to the entrance to an ancient fortified city. Walk past the twitching bodies on spears and open the main door. Gideon awaits you on the other side. Once you greet him, he changes into something really, really unpleasant. Hope you don't suffer from arachnophobia. There isn't any real secret to slaying the Undead Gideon. The courtyard you battle him in is tight, but do your best to keep moving and try to stay behind him where he has a harder time attacking you. Also, attacks to Gideon's appendages will do little damage; concentrate on his body and head to take him down faster. Be careful with area effect weapons here, since you're battling in such confined spaces. It may take you a couple of tries, but eventually you should be able to wear him down and beat him. And it's not over yet.

Make no mistake, killing the Undead Gideon will be difficult. When you fight him, hits to his appendages will only cause a small bit of damage.You need to concentrate on the main body of this creature to make your shots count.

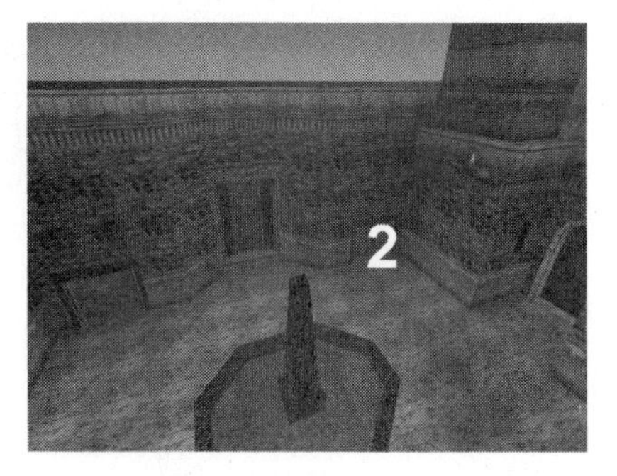

Once Gideon is slain, two doors open on either side of the one you came through. Kill the Shikari that rush out to engage you, then go through the one on the right (2).

TIP

If you can, run from trouble for the remainder of this level. Soul Drudges and Drudge Lords are particularly easy to avoid, so do so. This will save the last of your health for the final confrontations.

Jump through the hole on the right-hand wall (3) of the blood-stained room, then **throw the switch** (4) in the short hallway beyond. This will open two more large doors out in the courtyard where you battled Gideon. Make sure you kill any Shikari in the area and grab the **ammo** and **health** nearby.

Go back through the hole in the wall to the blood-stained room. Go back to the courtyard where you battled Gideon, then take the large doorway to your right. Follow the alley until you come to a Drudge Lord mauling another party from the Cabalco Expedition Team. Climb up the ramp to your right (5) to get some **ammo.** Then conmtinue following the hallway until you confront a Soul Drudge, a Shikari, and a Drudge Priest.

Enter the first narrow alley you come to (7). It holds a **Willpower** powerup and a Remote Bomb guarded by a Soul Drudge and a Thief. Take them out, then grab the powerup. Quickly turn around and go back into the larger alley. Follow it a few steps to the left, then go through a larger alley on your left again (8). Don't dawdle, since your Willpower will be running out and you'll need it for the battle around the corner. Turn the corner and come to a large bridge spanning a river. Before the Willpower runs out, mow down the Death Shroud that gets in your way.

TIP

As you go toward the bridge, there is a breach in the wall to your right with some HEALTH in it. Don't bother with it now, since the time on your Willpower is ticking down. Rather, return here after the battle to refresh yourself.

Once the Death Shroud that was guarding the bridge is dead, cross the bridge and go through the door at the other end (9). Continue to follow the alley until it forks.

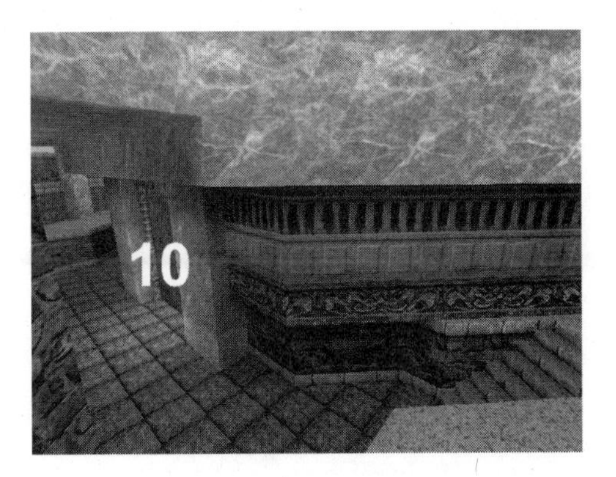

Take either the left- or right-hand path down a short flight of steps. Walk past the wall with the fountain, then through the large stone doorway (10) behind it. You are now in the Arena of the Chosen.

TIP

A walkway runs the parameter of the arena.It is accessible by stairs to the left or right of the doorway.You'll encounter a few baddies here.However, it's not necessary to fight them, and will probably cost you more health and ammo than it's worth.

NOTE

The map will change when you enter the Chosen Arena.

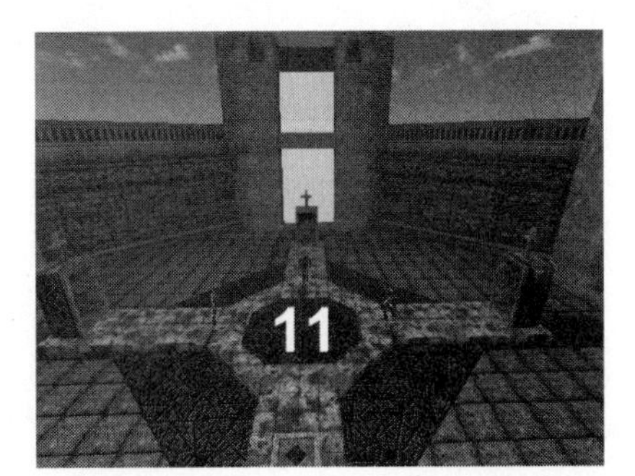

Once you enter the Arena, you're treated to a heartfelt reunion with the other Chosen. It warms the cockles of your heart to be among old friends again. Too bad they have to die. At least you only have to fight them one at a time, but it's still tough. Grab all the powerups in the arena, and the **Life Seeds** the slain Chosen leave behind. Use the sarcophagi for cover, and keep moving. Once the other Chosen are dead (again), the stone in the center of the Arena (11) opens, revealing the biggest rift you've ever seen. Ah, the burdens of responsibility. You could just go home and read some back issues of *Guns and Ammo and Liquor and Wild Shooting Sprees Weekly*, or you could jump down and keep the unholy terror down there from ripping this world apart. Decisions, decisions. What the heck. Jump on in and enter the next level.

Level 30

THE ANCIENT ONE

No tunnels. No hallways. No elevators. No levers. No doorways. No ladders. No bridges. No computer controls. No stairways. No mercy. Just you, the Ancient One, and a WHOLE LOT OF BLOOD.

OBJECTIVES: .... Kill the Ancient One (like you couldn't guess that).

ENEMIES: .... The Ancient One

ITEMS: .... Willpower, The Anger, Life Seed, Necroward

WEAPONS: .... None

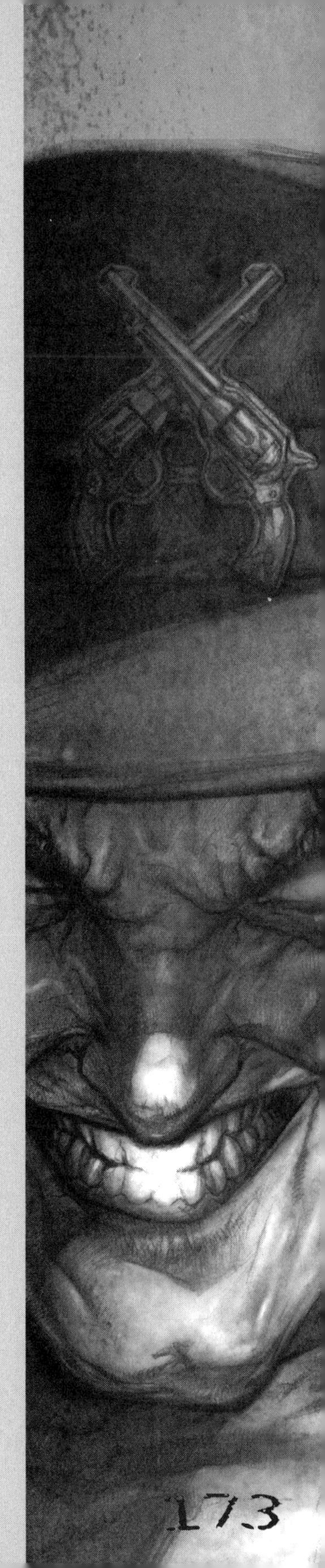

Man, this thing is ugly. Not only that, it wants to kick your butt so hard your grandma will feel it. It's showtime, boys and girls. Today on Caleb's Happy Fun Hour. The Ancient One buys the farm! You've got more room to maneuver here than you did in your last showdown with Gideon, but this guy is a lot tougher. Grab every powerup you can, and don't hold back. Make sure to grab the **Anger** (1), **Life Seed** (2), **Resistance**, (3), and **Necroward** (4) powerups. Try to use your high-powered long range weapons to take him out. If you die, then reload and try again. It the Ancient One dies, then congratulations! You've saved the world!

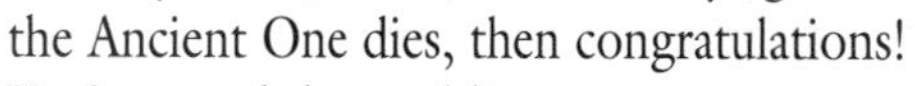

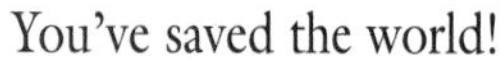

Part III

MULTIPLAYER BLOODBATH

Do Fanatics just not make you break a sweat anymore? Entire gangs of Cultists make you yawn? Do even Prophets armed with dual Tesla Cannons just not cut it? If you answered yes to all of the above, then you're ready for a good Bloodbath against your fellow humans. This part of the book will arm you with all the basic information you need to set up or join a Bloodbath game. Also included are basic and advanced tips for multiplayer *Blood II*, as well as brief descriptions and tips for each of the Bloodbath levels that shipped with the game.

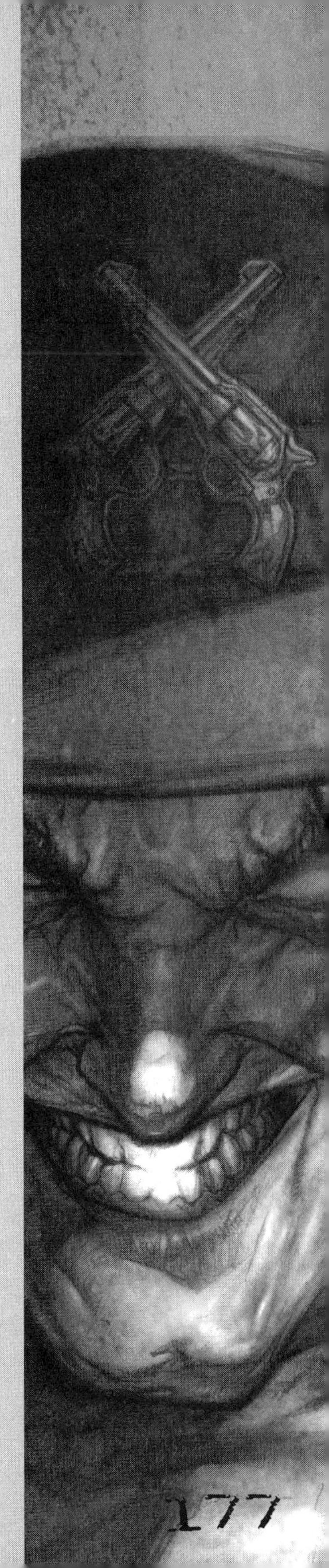

BLOODBATH BASICS

If you thought things were intense before, you haven't seen anything yet. Even the most advanced AI can be outsmarted, but trying to corner and frag a human opponent is an entirely different game. *Blood II* has many options for engaging in online mayhem, including TCP/IP connections to the Internet, modem-to-modem connections, and of course direct connections via serial Cabals...er...cables or a LAN. There's a lot of ground to cover in this chapter, so the information will be grouped into four categories:

- **SETTING UP YOUR GAME**—Describes how to set up a Bloodbath game
- **JOINING A GAME**—Describes how to find and join games in progress
- **CUSTOMIZING YOUR CHARACTER**—How to customize your player character and get the most out of it
- **BASIC TACTICS AND TIPS**—From the obvious to the insightful, these survival tips will keep you in the game longer and keep your frag count climbing

SETTING UP YOUR GAME

Technology is amazing. It makes simple things like splitting an atom or creating a game of multiplayer *Blood II* easy. The designers have set up an easy-to-use wizard for setting up or joining Bloodbath games. To access the wizard, you can either select MULTIPLAYER from the *Blood II* launcher or from the in-game menu itself after it has been started.

The first thing the wizard will ask you is what networking service you are using: TCP/IP internet connection, modem-to-modem, or serial connection/LAN. Select the appropriate one.

The next selection you'll have to make is whether you want to host a gaming session or join an existing one. Joining is covered in the next section of this book, so skip ahead if that's what you want to do. To create your own session, select HOST A NEW SESSION and click NEXT.

The next screen enables you to customize your player. This is so important that it has been given its own section later in this chapter.

After you have customized your player, the next three screens ask for several game settings:

- **Session Name**—Type in a descriptive name for your gaming session.
- **Level Ending Triggers**—These boxes enable you to specify what will cause a level to end. Set the maximum number of frags and/or the maximum length of the level in minutes.
- **Max Number of Players**—This enables you to cap the number of players that will be allowed to join your game. Depending on what maps you're running and how powerful your hardware is, you may want to limit this.
- **Amount of Ammo**—Allows you to set the amount of ammunition the player starts with and how quickly it respawns. "Insane" gives everyone unlimited ammunition.
- **Amount of Health**—Allows you to set how much health everyone starts with and how quickly it respawns.
- **Amount of Armor**—Allows you to set how much armor everyone starts with and how quickly it respawns.
- **Amount of Powerups**—Allows you to set how many powerups are in the game and how quickly they respawn.

- **Allow Falling Damage**—Lets you decide if falling from great heights hurts. It's actually not the fall that hurts, but rather hitting the ground at the end.
- **Healing Rate**—Lets you decide if you want healing to occur, and how quickly.

The next screen asks you to select which maps you want in this gaming session. Select them from the list on the left and add them to the one on the right. There's even a separate list for custom levels that you or others have designed yourselves. Once you've completed your list, hit FINISHED and you're set!

NOTE Once you've played through the last map on the list, the game will cycle back through.

JOINING A GAME

Joining an existing game is equally easy. Just Select MULTIPLAYER from the *Blood II* launcher or the in-game menu. From there, highlight your network service (TCP/IP for internet connection, modem-to-modem, or serial/LAN connection) and then select JOIN AN EXISTING SESSION.

The next screen asks you to customize your player. Since this is such an important element of Bloodbath, we gave it its own section below.

After you've customized your player, you can now access or search for new games. If you know the address of the game you want to join, you can type it into the provided field. If you just want to look around for games, leave the field blank and click OK. The computer will now search for games on your network (or on the Internet if you are connected) and provide you with summary information. Double-click on the game you want, draw your weapons, and join the mayhem!

TIP

Blood II has also shipped with support for the shareware utility *GameSpy*, which helps you find and connect to Bloodbath games. If you don't have *GameSpy*, you'll be happy to find out that the latest version comes bundled with your copy of *Blood II*. Look for it on the game CD. You can also find out more at www.gamespy.com.

CUSTOMIZING YOUR CHARACTER

Blood II: The Chosen breaks new multiplayer ground by allowing you to customize your player character. This adds new depth and strategy to the game, and allows for a variety of ways to play the game. Much of this stuff is a matter of style and preference, since the folks at Monolith have playtested and made sure no one setup will dominate others. Still, there are some general tips and advice that can help you get the most out of your choices. This section deals with the three ways in which you can customize your player: weapons, abilities, and special powers.

Choosing Weapons

Just like in the single-player game, Bloodbath players can only carry 10 weapons at a time. Before you join a game, you are asked to select which weapons you will use for that gaming session. Since there are so many means of destruction, this leaves many weapons out of an individual game, but that gives you plenty of reason to mix things up the next time. Here are a few things to keep in mind when shopping for armaments:

- **Go for variety**—Make sure you have a good mix of instant damage, accurate weapons (for example, SMG, Assault Rifle, Shotgun, Minigun), as well as area effect weapons (for example, Napalm Launcher, Howitzer, Singularity Generator). You'll want to switch between these types of weapons in different situations.
- **Give yourself a backup**—Don't just load up on all the most powerful weapons. The ammunition for these monsters is rarer, and you don't want to find yourself unable to return fire. Make sure you have some lower-level options in your arsenal, such as the SMG or Flare Gun.
- **Take advantage of ammo**—Don't just stock up on weapons that use only one type of ammo, like bullets or chemical batteries. You'll run out fast. Instead, make sure you have a weapon that uses every type of ammunition for maximum versatility. This includes magic weapons, which brings us to the next point.
- **Don't neglect magic**—Even if you have a magic ability rating of 1, keep at least one magic weapon in your arsenal. This is because Focus regenerates automatically, and can serve as an emergency reserve if you need it. For example, the alt fire on the Voodoo Doll makes for a great last line of defense.
- **Capitalize on game settings**—Choose your weapons according to specific game settings, particularly amount of ammo. If you notice a game is running on the "half ammo" setting, the Minigun or Death Ray probably aren't good choices, since they eat bullets and batteries so fast. However, join a game with unlimited ammo, and you may not need any other weapons!

Choosing Your Abilities

Bloodbath games also allow you to customize your individual abilities settings, which adds to the variety substantially. There are four abilities: strength, speed, resistance, and magic. Before you join a game you are allowed a total of 12 points, up to a maximum of 5 points for any one ability. Each of the abilities will be described in turn.

STRENGTH

Strength affects how much ammo you can carry and how much health you can accumulate. Choose carefully here, because if ammunition is scarce, you don't need a lot of strength and you may be better off allotting points to other abilities. If, however, ammunition in your game is plentiful, higher strengths may pay off. Table III-1 presents the ammo capacities for each of the 5 strength levels.

TABLE III-1. Ammo Capacities for Firearms, Demolitions, and Energy Weapons

STRENGTH	1	2	3	4	5
Bullets	100	200	300	400	500
Shells	50	75	100	125	150
Howitzer Rockets	20	40	60	80	100
Bug Spray Cans	10	20	30	40	50
Flares	20	40	60	80	100
Napalm Fuel	25	25	50	75	100
BMG (Sniper Ammo)	20	40	60	80	100
Batteries	100	200	300	400	500

Strength also affects how much health you can accumulate. Again, pay attention to the game's settings. If the maximum health setting is at "half," then strength isn't as important for this because health isn't as plentiful. If, however, double max health or regeneration is present on your server, high strength ratings are a boon. Table III-2 presents the maximum health for each of the levels of strength.

TABLE III-2. Maximum Health by Strength Level

STRENGTH	1	2	3	4	5
Max Health	100	150	200	250	300

SPEED

Speed affects how fast you can run, which has implications for running away from enemies, or keeping on their tail as they try to run from you. Faster players are harder to hit, and have the advantage of being able to get to places more quickly than slower players. This is especially critical at the beginning of a level when all the ammo and power-ups are up for grabs.

RESISTANCE

Resistance affects how much damage you can soak up. Players with more of this ability are tougher.

MAGIC

Finally, magic affects three things. First, it affects how much focus you can stockpile to be used as ammunition for magic weapons. The limitation to having tons of Focus is that there are relatively few magic weapons compared to other types. Second, the magic ability affects how quickly Focus regenerates after it has been used. Third, magic affects the maximum armor rating you can achieve from picking up Wards and Necrowards. Table III-3 presents maximum Focus capacity, regeneration rates, and armor levels for each level of magic ability.

TABLE III-3. Focus Capacity, Regeneration Rates, and Armor for Magic Ability

MAGIC	1	2	3	4	5
Max Focus	100	200	300	400	500
Regeneration Rate	1/sec.	2/sec.	3/sec.	4/sec.	5/sec.
Max Armor	100	150	200	250	300

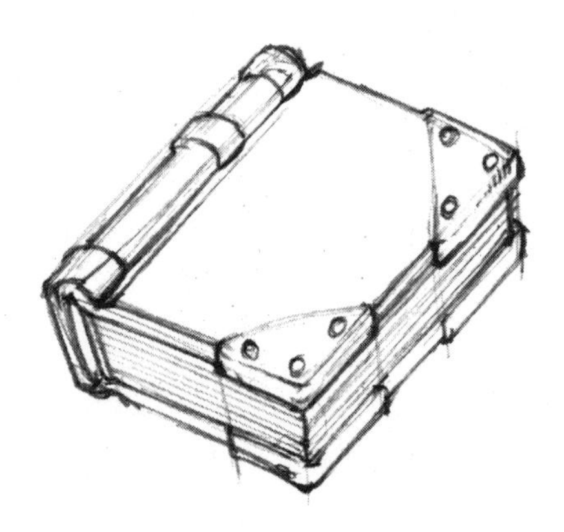

Special Abilities

There are also four special abilities that you can choose from in Bloodbath games. Each of them is unique, and which one you choose is largely a matter of style. Each one will be briefly described below.

BLOODLUST

This fits in with Caleb's personality the best, but any player can select it in Bloodbath. This special ability enables you to increase your bloodlust meter with every kill you make. The meter will slowly run down if the kills don't come quickly enough, so this ability works best in the more crowded, faster-paced levels. Once the meter is full, you get ten seconds of bloodlust in which you are resistant to 95 percent of damage (the same effect as the Willpower powerup). You can also extend the duration of his bloodlust by slaying more foes—every additional kill adds two seconds, up to a maximum of ten additional seconds.

STEALTH

This ability was devised with Ophelia in mind. If you select this ability, you will be able to become completely invisible by standing perfectly still for two full seconds. This is a great ability if you want to wait undetected for a major powerup to respawn, or to watch for someone to step into your remote bomb trap. This can also be used to ambush someone in a tight hallway with a double facefull of sawed-off shotgun shells at point blank range. Definitely do not underestimate this ability. The only drawback is that in more populated, fast-paced games, it's sometimes hard to stand still for two seconds without getting shot at.

SHIELD

This one has Ishmael written all over it, but as with all the abilities, it is open to any player in Bloodbath. This magical shield will protect you from up to 100 points of damage, but will be disrupted by any attack doing at least one point of damage. Thus, the shield will protect from an attack doing one point of damage or a hundred, but either attack will shatter it. If an attack does massive amounts of damage, the shield will absorb the first one hundred points. Once down, the shield slowly regenerates itself, leaving you defenseless until it is fully restored. This ability is excellent for small duels, but it can be difficult to keep the shield up in more frenzied battles. Still, the satisfaction you get from running right up into some Napalm Launcher-wielding zealot's face and watching him blow himself up by firing it at point blank range while you walk away unscathed is unparalleled.

OVERKILL

If you're like Gabriella, you just want to hurt your opponents. Badly. Is that so much to ask? Well, hurting them is even easier with the Overkill ability. If you have this power, each attack you make has a five percent chance of doing double damage. Double damage from the Howitzer, Sawed-Off Shotgun, or Napalm Launcher is quite impressive. Also, rapid-fire weapons like the M16 Assault Rifle or the Minigun quickly raise your chances of getting in at least a few critical hits.

BASIC TACTICS AND TIPS

Multiplayer is a completely different game. While most of the advice I gave you on the single-player game is still valid, there are a few new tricks to learn for the multiplayer game. This isn't really an exhaustive list, since Bloodbath is easy to learn; however, it takes much more time to master. With that in mind, here are some basic tips to get you started on the road to complete domination over your opponents.

- **Use the mouse!**—This has been said before, but it's so supremely important that it bears repeating. Learn to use the mouse-keyboard combination if you don't already. Using the keyboard to turn is just too slow, and it's practically impossible to accurately aim up/down or track a moving target without using the mouse to aim. Use it and your frag count *will* improve.

- **Know the level**—This is probably the thing that will increase your score the most after using the mouse to aim. Know the location of every item, health, ammo, secret location, and powerup on each level. This comes mainly from experience, but you can get a head start by loading up a Bloodbath level on your own and playing just by yourself.

- **Run patterns**—Once you know a level by heart, develop a pattern that will take you to all the ammo, items, and powerups. This will enable you to quickly equip yourself and dominate. You should also know the quickest way to get to any ammo or powerup from every respawn location. Again, this comes mainly from experience, but you can quicken things up by paying attention and playing the levels on your own to practice.

- **Never stand still**—Never stop moving. Ever. This is important for single-player games, and it goes triple for Bloodbath. A stationary target is an easy target, and an easy target is a dead target. Even if you're waiting for an elevator to come down, run around in circles until it arrives just in case somebody is watching with a Sniper Rifle. Also, make sure you have the "always run" option selected so you move about more quickly.

- **Be wasteful**—First off, grab every piece of ammo you can, even if you don't need it. Even if you don't have a Flare Gun, you can grab those flares to keep your opponents from using them against you. Second, if you're at full health or armor and see a Megahealth or Necroward, do a little damage to yourself (by, for example, pointing the Howitzer or Tesla Cannon at your feet and firing) so you can grab it. You'll be at full capacity again afterwards, and it will keep your opponents from acquiring the added protection.

- **Be a scavenger**—There is no honor in this game. Scavenge for kills whenever you can. If you see two guys duking it out, take them both out from a distance with a napalm rocket or the Tesla Cannon's alt fire while they're preoccupied with each other. Also, large area attacks like the alt fires on the Life Leech or the Voodoo Doll are great for picking off several weakened combatants at a time.

- **Be aggressive**—This game does not favor those that camp out in one spot and wait for opportunities to ambush. This isn't a statement about the morality or sportsmanship of such tactics. It's just a proven fact that such tactics result in fewer kills than actively going out and getting in people's faces. The only way you're going to score frags is by going after them as aggressively as you can. If (or rather, when) you die, you respawn and try again.

- **Cover your tracks**—Still, there are some times when you just want to run away, screaming like a little girl. This most often happens when you're low on ammo or there's some guy coming after you with The Anger and a Minigun. When running from an opponent, there are a few things you can do to shake them, maybe permanently. Dropping a Bug Spray can grenade with the Assault rifle's alt fire will make people think twice about following you. Also, the more fleet-footed can use run backwards and use the alt fire from the Insect-a-Cutioner to lay down a barrier of flame for their pursuers.

- **Pay attention to sounds**—The sounds from doors opening, lifts activating, and players jumping can often serve as important clues for your survival. If you hear someone coming around the corner, be ready for them. Likewise, try to keep as quiet as you can and use sounds to serve as decoys. This is less important in crowded, fast-paced games, but critical in smaller groups or duels.

- **Lay traps**—Most people make a bee line for ammo or powerups when they see them. Take advantage of this by either placing a bomb in their path, or aiming ahead with an area effect weapon like the Howitzer. A Proximity Bomb on the other side of a door is another effective trap. They may never see what hit them.

BLOODBATH MAPS

This section contains brief descriptions of all the Bloodbath levels that shipped with the game. The aim here isn't to provide an in-depth description of every location on the map. Rather, the aim of this chapter is to familiarize you with the maps and let you know what to expect. Some tips are given, such as what weapons you may find most effective, but you should really load up these maps to practice and explore them by yourself. This will give you an edge over someone unfamiliar with them.

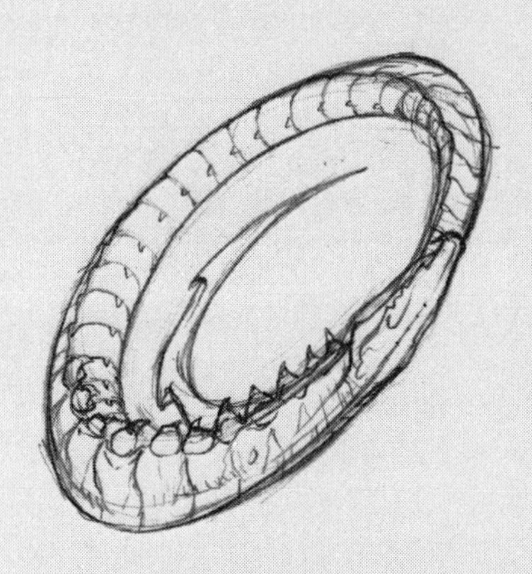

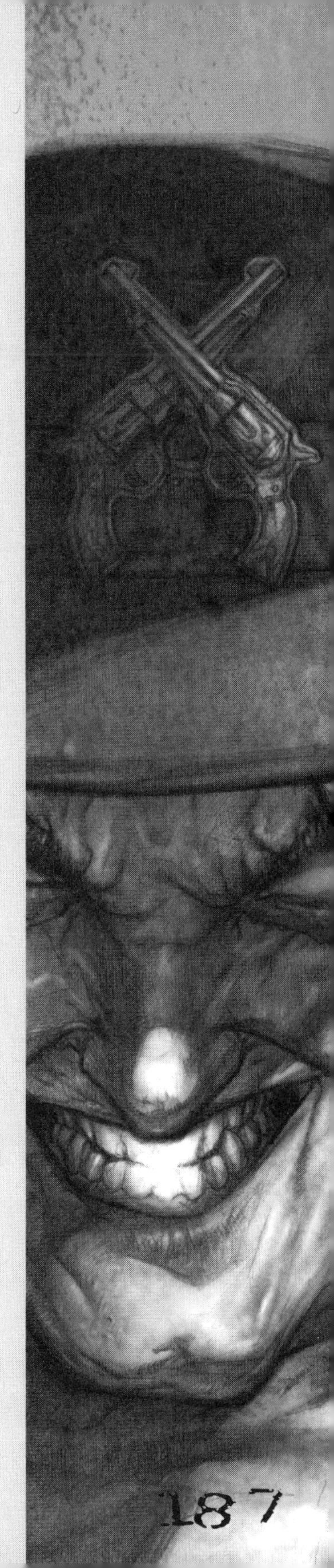

BLOOD ARENA

Number of players: 10 and above

Big map, with lots of open spaces. However, most of this map is also multileveled, so that you have to be right on top of somebody to keep a bead on them for longer than a second. Still, a player that gains the high ground could conceivably make things very unpleasant for those below by chucking grenades and napalm rockets down. The Singularity Generator is also a good choice in the open areas. Ramps lead down to a basement area containing an Anger powerup, and a lift grants access to an indoor area with a Stealth powerup and a Medkit. A player with a good pattern and the right timing can dominate all three powerups by dropping down from the Stealth and Medkit to the Anger. This map is best for crowds. With only a couple of players, the frags will be weeks apart.

A15

Number of players: 6 to 10

This is a foggy indoor area with lots of confined spaces. You'll want to make sure you're armed with some good close-range weapons like the Sawed-Off Shotguns or the Insect-a-Cutioner. Also, use of area effect weapons like the Howitzer or the Napalm Cannon can be dangerous here, so be careful. There's adequate ammunition spread throughout the level, as well as all the powerups (Medkit). Lifts offer access to the upper ridges, where you can rain destruction down on those below. With larger crowds, this level gets very intense very quickly, with non-stop frags. Many of these will come from less powerful weapons, since you won't be alive long enough to grab the ammo for the heavy artillery.

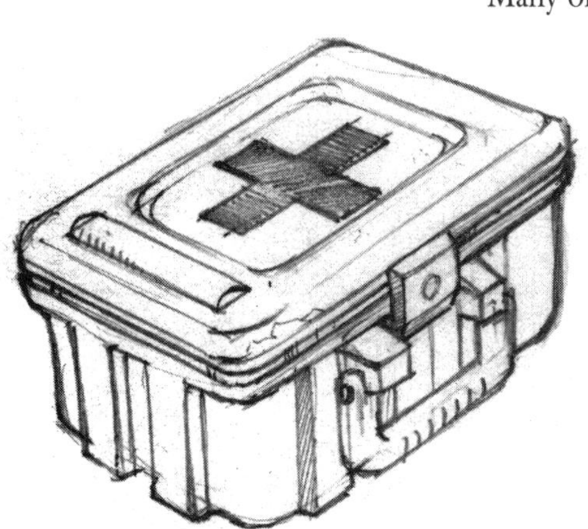

BLOODKEEP

Number of players: 2 to 6

This is a very small, castle-like level. There's nowhere to hide on this one, so get ready to crank up the intensity. There are also absolutely no open areas, so make sure you have your close-range weapons ready. The Insect-a-Cutioner is great on this level since you can line the tight hallways with flames, using its alternative fire. Weapons of mass destruction won't serve you as well on this level, as you'll end up taking yourself out most of the time, too. The indoor area contains an Anger and a Life Seed powerups, and the catacombs beneath contain the All-Seeing Eye. The Eye can be used to lay and detonate some clever bomb traps. This level is really ideal for duels or very small Bloodbaths. Too many people and there's not enough ammo and not enough room.

BODIES

Number of players: 6 to 10

This map is in an industrial setting with lots of ramps, hallways, and a few open areas. There is a Willpower and an Anger present, but you'll have to rocket jump or bomb jump to get to the latter if you don't respawn next to it. Both close-range weapons and area effect weapons will serve you well here. This map is good for medium to large groups of players, but is a bit large for duels or small groups.

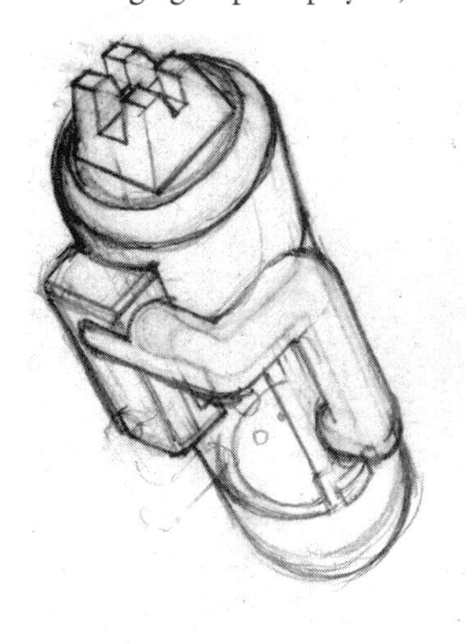

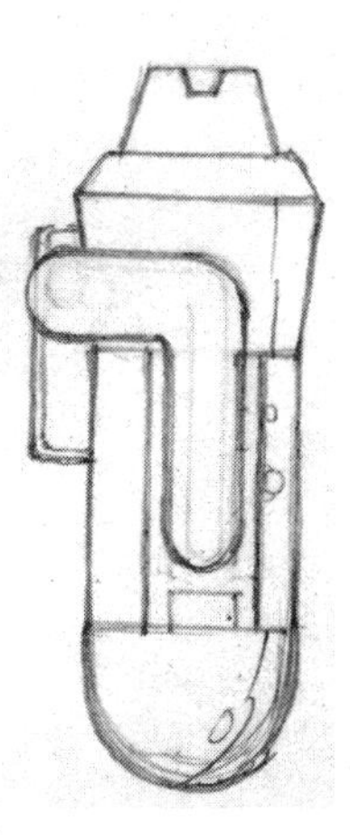

BROWNSTAR

Number of players: 2 to 6

This is a multilevel map based on the Ancient City theme. There's plenty of room to move around, but you'll want to be constantly looking out above you on this one. There is a wealth of ammo and armor at the top of the central column, but controlling it will be difficult since it is accessible by either a lift or a spiral staircase. Ramps offer access to a catwalk that runs the parameter of most of the map. A variety of weapons will be useful here, but area effect ones are more useful than close range ones. The Howitzer is useful, as is the Minigun. However, the Shotgun or the Barettas are not as useful, as there are fewer closed-in spaces. This is a small map, more suited to duels or small groups of players.

MIDGARD

Number of players: 6 to 8

Tight, bloody, and furious, this is an indoor map with a large arena in the middle surrounded by hallways and windows on all sides. There isn't much room to hide here, so keep moving and grab everything you can. The highest ridge overlooking the arena requires a little jumping to get to, but contains a Life Seed and Necroward powerups. This map slightly favors close-range weapons , but a skilled player can make use of any weapon on this map, as you switch between constricting hallways and the central arena quickly and constantly. This map is best suited to medium-sized groups, but can be a regular slaughter fest for larger groups.

CRYPT

Number of players: up to 15

This map is very similar to one of those you encounter in the single-player game. It's a twisting maze of crypts and crumbling tunnels. The fighting will all be right in your face for this one. A Willpower powerup awaits in the area where you fight the Behemoth in the single-player game. There's no sniping from high above or clearing those wide-open spaces with the Singularity Generator. Be careful using those area effect weapons on this map, unless you want to watch your score dip into the negative. It's best to rely on the Shotguns, Assault Rifles, Life Leeches, and other weapons more suitable for close quarters. This map is large enough for medium-sized groups of 6 to 8, and maybe even groups up to 15, but things get exponentially more hectic above that. But hey, that can be a good thing.

THE CHOSEN ARENA

Number of players: 4 to 6

There's nowhere to hide this time. This map is divided into two areas: indoor and outdoor. The outdoor area encircles the inside one, and basically consists of a circular alley with a ramp leading up to the entrance to the inside area. The inside area is a large arena with three ledges, atop of which are powerups. Take your pick of weapons for this level, although you'll probably want to have some sort of arca effect weapon for the indoor arena. This is a great map for one-on-one duels and small groups of 4 to 6, but gets too crowded with larger groups.

ROOFTOPS

Number of players: 4 to 6

This is a very intense map; the action takes place atop the Cabalco headquarters. It's all wide open on this map, so you'll probably spend most of your time with area effect weapons. However, don't overlook the Life Leech on this level, as its alt fire is great for knocking opponents over the building ledge to their deaths below. Like most smaller levels, this level is great for small to medium-sized groups of players who want simple, in your face bloodbathing without all the running and hiding.

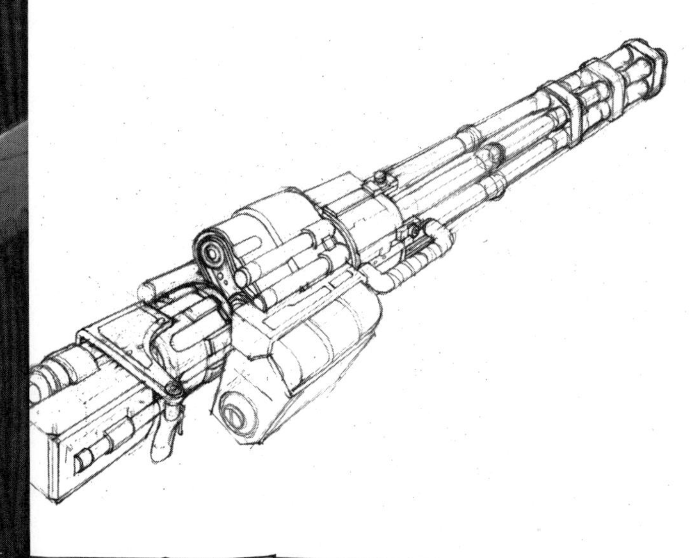

CONDEMNED BUILDING

Number of players: 12 and above

This is a large map set in an abandoned apartment building. It is divided into two areas: rooftop and apartments. The rooftop holds a lot of goodies, including a Necroward and lots of ammo, but it can be dangerous since it's easy to fall or get knocked off ledges to your death below. The stairwell leading to the apartments holds an Anger powerup at the bottom, as well as a few other items. This level is too big for small groups, who will find the action too sparse. Larger groups, however, may find it much more fun.

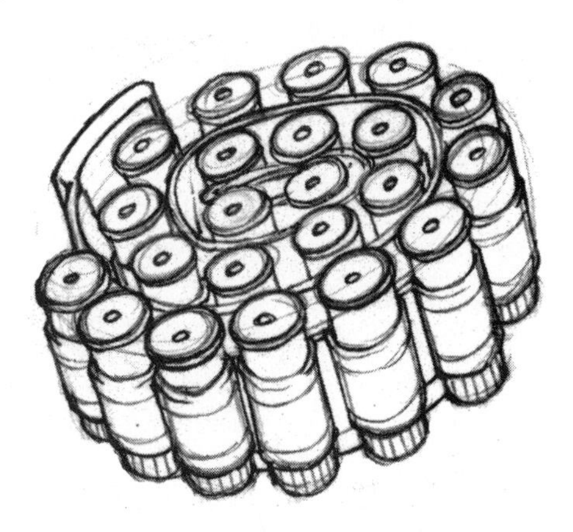

DUSTBOWL

Number of players: 6-8

This is a good medium-sized level with nowhere to run and nowhere to hide. It almost consists entirely of one large outdoor area, with a small structure dividing it in half. You can access the wall of the structure by running up the slopes of the bowl, then jumping up, or by climbing a ladder within the structure. Make heavy use of area effect weapons here, as there is lots of room to dodge and run. Also make use of the proximity and time bombs to control access to certain areas, especially the Life Seed in the bloody pool. Because this map is so open, it could be fun for small groups, but medium-sized groups are most likely to get the most fun out of it.

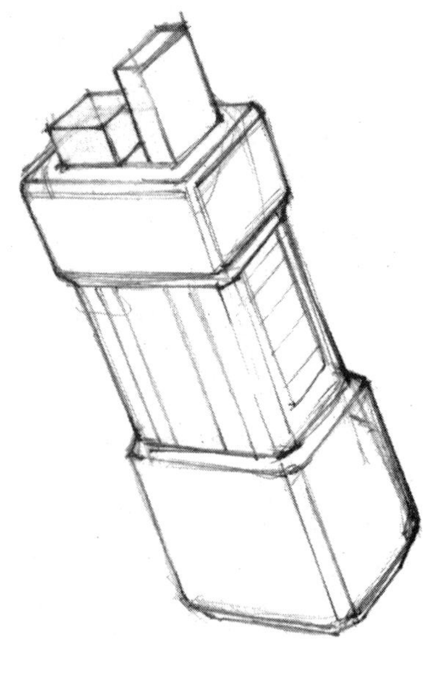

FIELDS

Number of players: 4 to 6

Who said good bloodbath maps can't be simple? There's really not much to say about this level, except that it takes place within a large, open field with ammo spread all around. Don't try wandering out of the confines of the battlefield, though, or you'll be dead in an instant. Use whatever weapon you like here, since it's so confined, yet you don't have to worry about hitting walls with your Napalm Launcher or Howitzer. This map is good for small to medium-sized groups of combatants.

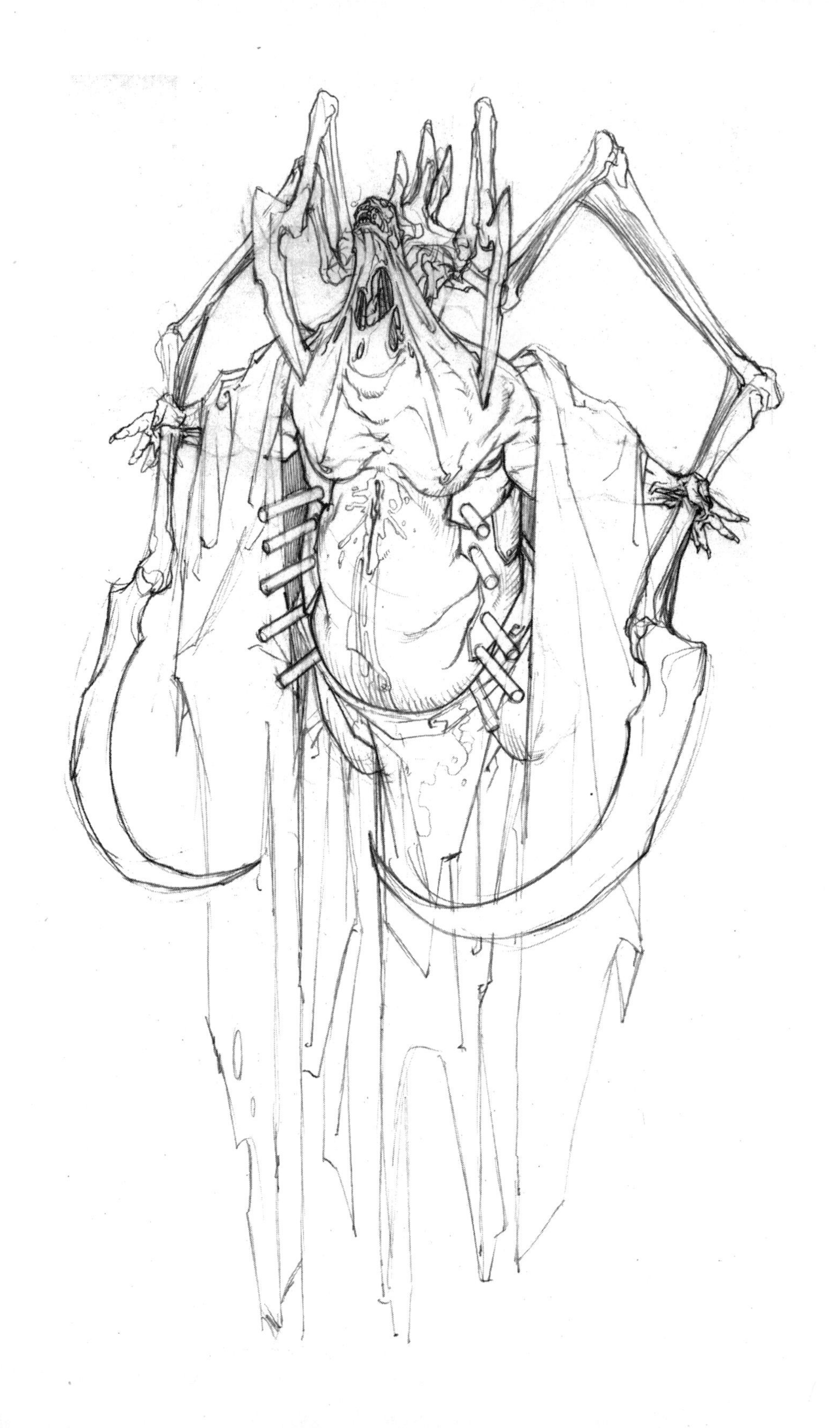

Part IV

BEHIND THE BLOODY SCENES

As you might suspect, Blood II: The Chosen was not dropped off by the Computer Game Fairy late one night at Monolith's studios. It was the product of months of grueling work by a team of dedicated designers, engineers, artists, programmers, managers, and pizza delivery guys. No one person can truthfully claim responsibility for all the fun you've been having playing this game. Now comes the time where we drag you kicking and bleeding behind the scenes to meet the people who made this ghoulish, heart-pounding, and gory phenomenon possible.

MEET THE BLOODY DEVELOPMENT TEAM

Here they are.Meet the minds behind *Blood II: The Chosen*. What? You expected some band of ghastly freaks dripping with the blood of their freshly slain opponents as they cackle and caw like madmen? Well, we caught them on a good day. Heck, they were even good spirited enough to share information on their favorite weapons, enemies, strategies, and PC games. Then they came after us with pitchforks. Well, just two of them, but we won't say which.

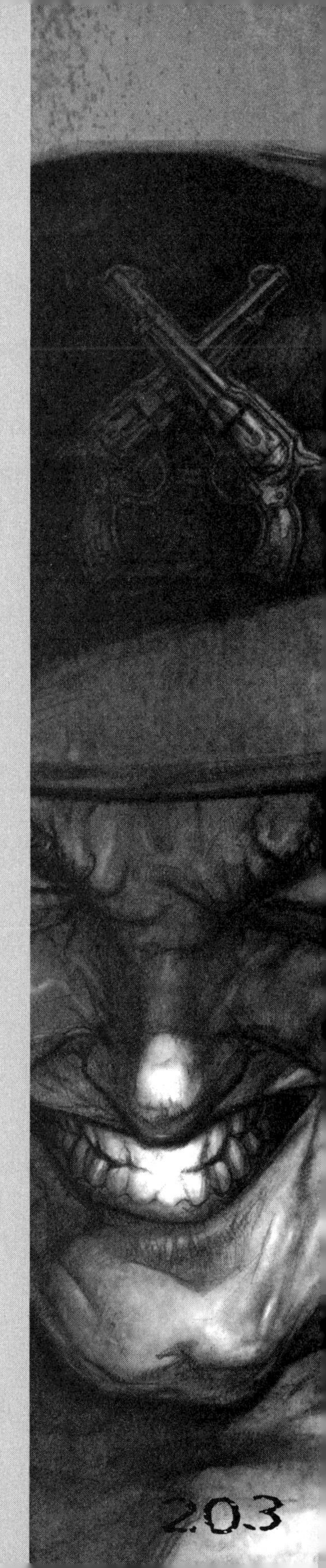

JAY WILSON

Job on the project: ..... Lead Designer

Handle: .... Shade

Favorite weapon: .... Probably the minigun. I'd been waiting forever for someone to make a "true" minigun, and one that fires at an insane rate and instantly chews up everything in its path, making it one of the most powerful weapons in the game. Well, let's just say I got tired of waiting.

Favorite enemy: .... The Drudge Lord, because he's badass and scary!

Favorite strategy: ...... When another player falls to their knees in humiliation, instead of blasting his (or her) head off I prefer to kick it off with a swift jump onto the opponent's head.

Favorite PC Game: .... That's really tough, but I'm going to have to say the original X-Com. No other PC game has enthralled me like X-Com's brilliant blend of resource management and squad-based strategy. I still fire it up from time to time.

Note: .... Jay was a level designer on the original Blood title.

KEVIN KILSTROM

Job on the project: ..... Lead Artist

Handle: .... Meddler

Favorite weapon: .... Proximity Bombs—because they annoy people.

Favorite enemy: .... Death Shroud

Favorite strategy: ...... "Set up camp and roast some weenies"

Favorite PC Game: .... Blood is my favorite, but I also love C&C Red Alert.

Note: .... Kevin was also one of the primary artists on the original Blood, creating detailed clay models of all the creatures for animations. On Blood II, Kevin's work can be seen in all the level texture art, creature textures, world models, and debris. Kevin has a distinct talent for blood and gore, and a bit of twisted humor.

GREG KETTELL

Job on the project: ..... Lead Engineer

Handle: .... The Godfather

Favorite weapon:....... It's a toss-up between the Howitzer, because it's precise, and the Singularity Generator, because it's unique.

Favorite enemy: .... Shikari, because he just looks cool.

Favorite strategy:...... Shoot the other guys first.

Favorite PC Game:....... Civ II, because it's never the same game twice.

SCOTT SCHLEGEL

Job on the project: ..... Engineer

Handle: .... Schlegz

Favorite weapon:....... Double-barrel shotgun. Most fights are in close and this delivers massive damage with no side-effects. Napalm cannon is a close second.

Favorite enemy: .... Zealot. Cool look. Cool attacks. Cool voice.

Favorite strategy:...... Lay proximity bombs all over the level. Most annoying tactic yet.

Favorite PC Game:....... Starcraft. I love RTS games and beating down punks on Battle.net was too much fun.

Note:................. Scott is the master of Blood II's AI system and the way cool hit detection.

Job on the project: ..... 3D Engineer

Handle: .... Kluggly

Favorite weapon:....... Napalm—cuz I like to burn things.

Favorite enemy: .... Female Cultist—cuz she has nice bunz.

Favorite strategy:...... Now I can't give out all my secretz ;-)

Favorite PC Game:....... Blood—cuz I like to burn people.

Note:................. Brian (Ernie) also worked on the original Blood. His responses above are direct quotes. He's really not that twisted, but I suppose working day and night can do that to a person. Ernie does the work of like three artists. He is the master of everything 3D.

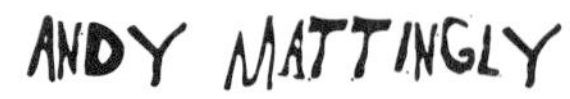

Job on the project: ..... Engineer

Handle: .... None

Favorite weapon:....... Lifeleech, because you can cover a large area with it, and it has defensive properties against projectiles and allows you to throw people into bad places!

Favorite enemy: .... Death Shroud, just because he flies around, looks very intimidating, and doesn't need a weapon to do major damage to you.

Favorite strategy:...... Use the decapitator to seek and destroy before entering a dangerous zone, then bounce some lasers or die-bug-die cans off the walls to weed out the area.

Favorite PC Game:....... The Complete Ultima 7 because it's got a gritty story, great game play, interesting characters, weapons, and spells, and most of all, a very detailed story and game world.

Note:................. Andy came onto the project when Paul Lord left the company in the Spring '98. You'd think he'd have a pretty brutal learning curve, but he seemed to take it all in stride, learning the engine becoming very proficient in the weapon technology. However, he still doesn't know the names of all the team members.

BILL VANDERVOORT

Job on the project: ..... Lead Level Designer

Favorite Weapon: .... Singularity Generator, because it has the coolest effect.

Favorite Enemy: .... Naga. It's the biggest enemy in a 3D game yet.

Favorite Stratety: ...... Hit 'em hard and fast.

Favorite PC Game:. ...... Doom 2—it provided countless hours of gaming and level design fun.

BEN COLEMAN

Job on the project: ..... Level Designer

Handle: .... Downinit

Favorite Weapon: .... Singularity Generator

Favorite Enemy: .... Zealot

Favorite PC Game:. ...... Doom 2

ERIC KOHLER

Job on the project: ..... Concept Art and 2D/3D Artist

Favorite Weapon: .... Proximity bombs; nothing beats racking up kills when you are not even on the same side of the map...they also annoy people more than any other weapon that I have found.

Favorite Enemy: .... I like the Zealot and the Soul Drudge the best. They look good and have cool attacks.

Favorite Strategy: ...... Put proximity bombs around every corner or behind powerups so they are invisible and then sit back and listen to the suckers cry.

Favorite PC Game: .... Blood (and I'm not just saying that). It has the fastest multiplayer and best weapon balance of any game I have played.

Note: .... Eric, and his totally awesome concepts, have really brought to life the very cool, gruesome creatures and weapons in Blood II. Many were cool months ago, but have been tweaked and refined to the "over the top" level they are now.

KAREN BURGER

Job on the project: ..... Product Manager

Favorite Weapon: ...... Life Leech, I just love the idle animation and the cool effect. Although I'm not very good at killing anything with it.

Favorite Enemy: .... Zealot; his animations and attack effect are very cool.

Favorite Strategy: ...... Cheating

Favorite PC Game: .... Solitaire

Note: .... Karen's unselfish dedication, product management skills, and late-night email exchanges and follow-ups not only made it possible for this game to come out in time, it also allowed us to put this book out in a timely fashion. No cheating here! Thanks, Karen!

JONATHAN STEIN

Job on the project: ..... QA Manager

Favorite Weapon: ...... The Singularity Generator has the best graphic of any weapon ever in a video game. Period.

Favorite Enemy: .... I'll go with the spiders. When they jump on Caleb's head and their legs wrap around Caleb's eyes, I jump out of my chair and hide under the desk. Spiders have always given me the willies. This isn't going to get printed, is it?

Favorite Strategy: ...... Pick up the Eye and a Bomb and go to town. Place the Eye next to a Bomb and then park yourself in a dark corner. Activate the Eye and sit tight; your opponents will soon run by and you go can send them to a higher plane from afar. This is brilliant design.

Favorite PC Game: .... Golden Eye 007. It's the only game based on a film that actually captures the essence of its source material. Additionally, the mission-based objectives provide structure and motivation without breaking the action. The animations are stellar, the AI smart, and, most of all, the player is rewarded for stealth and ingenuity.

Note: .... Jonathan has only been at Monolith since late summer. He joined our crew just as Shogo was starting its furious trip down the testing path. Guess there's nothing like jumping right in to the fire. He controls quite a group of energetic testers.

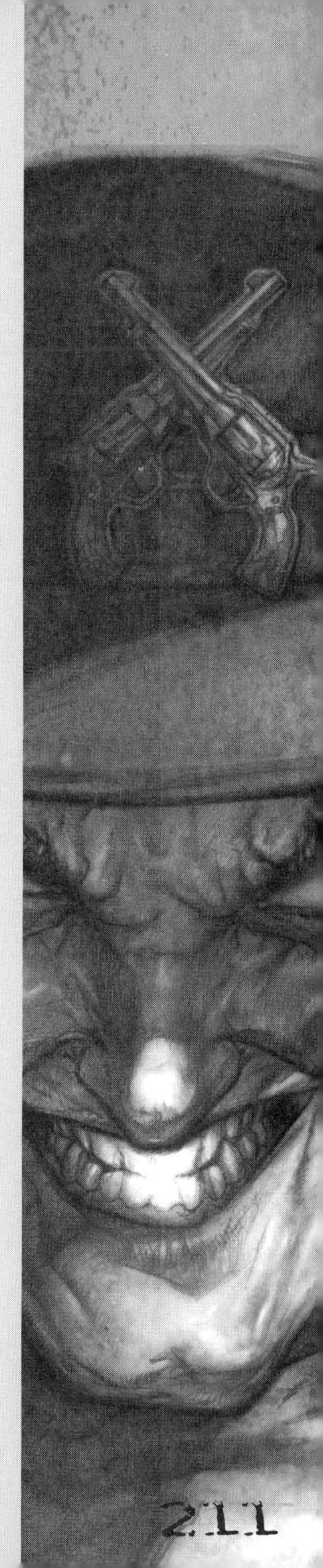

AN INTERVIEW WITH THE HEAD CHOSEN

Jay "Shade" Wilson, the Lead Designer for *Blood II: The Chosen*, was generous enough to sit down and answer some of our questions about his experiences working at Monolith and on the *Blood II* project. He has some very insightful comments about the gaming industry in general, as well as predictions about where it is going. He also shares some inside tidbits about *Blood II*, and describes the road it took from initial concept to final product.

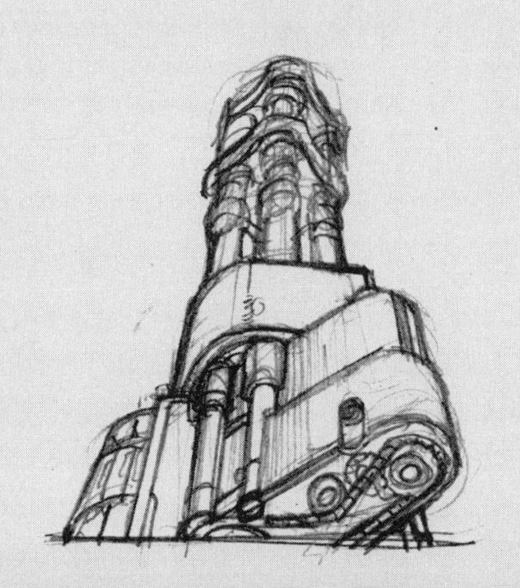

GW Press: *Why don't start off by telling us who the heck you are and how you became involved with* Blood II: The Chosen.

Jay Wilson: Hi, I'm Jay Wilson, *Blood II* lead designer. Before *Blood II*, I was a level designer on the original *Blood*. When *Blood* ended, doing a sequel was pretty much a given, and I had a whole bunch of ideas about *Blood II* and the direction it should go, so I basically decided to shut myself in my office and refused food and water until they gave me the project. This tactic failed miserably, so instead I actually wrote down some of those ideas, and, well, here we are.

GW: *The* Blood II *team has gone to a lot of trouble to maintain a strong presence in the online community. You guys set up a web page, and you personally have gone to a lot of effort to participate in online discussion forums. You've even taken your products to high profile LAN parties. Why do all this? Is this a deliberate strategy on your part, or something you just like to do? What do you think have been the rewards of doing it?*

JW: I think being a presence in the gaming community is more out of habit than anything else. Lots of companies say they are filled with gamers, but I think few companies could back up that statement like Monolith can. Most of us have always been active online, frequenting gaming forums and irc channels, going to LAN parties and competing in frag fests. I got my job in the industry from being an active member of the Doom mod community. This is something we've tried to hold onto even as Monolith has grown. I think many of us feel like we make games because we enjoy them and like being part of the gaming community.

Taking our games to LAN parties and staying closely in touch with the community can certainly be construed as a strategy, but it's a strategy that shows we're willing to put our money where our mouth is. The members of the gaming community are our customers, and nobody knows what they want better than they themselves. By staying in touch with them we are better able to understand what they want, and that makes our games more appealing. By taking our games to LAN parties we're going right to the gamers, where we'll get the most critical scrutiny we could possibly get, something we're not afraid to do because we believe in our games.

In the end, the rewards are tremendous. I believe it has had a strong effect on building our fan base and has been one of the main forces behind generating excitement for some of our upcoming titles. But in the end, it just feels satisfying to know that you're involved, and that people appreciate it.

GW: *In your opinion, what does* Blood II *have over the hoard of other first-person shooters (FPSs) on the market? What makes it stand out?*

JW: Lots of people will give you different answers to that question: the Lithtech engine, the horror theme, the gore, or many other numerous features; but for me it all comes down to one thing, and that's game play. I love games, and I particularly love 3D shooters, but almost none of them satisfy me completely. No shooter is as fast, violent, and satisfying as *Blood* or *Blood II.* With other shooters either the movement is too slow, the control isn't tight enough, the weapons are too weak, the physics aren't exaggerated enough, or a myriad of other little details that make the Blood games so special. I think more than anything what makes us stand out is that we play different than any other game out there. Some people can say that *Blood II* is just another FPS in terms of features or graphics, I don't agree with it, but the argument can be made. But no one can say that *Blood II* plays like any other shooter out there, and that's what makes me proud to put my name on it.

GW: *What were the top one or two things in* Blood II *that made you say "Woah, that's cool!" when they were finished?*

JW: I'd say the top thing is the motion-captured movement. Coupled with the superb hand animation our 3D team has done I really think it brings the creatures to life more than any other shooter I've seen. It helps that the creatures look so good as well.

The next would be the singularity generator. When Andy showed me that one I nearly fell out of my chair.

GW: *What's your favorite map or set of maps in the game?*

JW: That's tough, but I think I'm going to have to go with Bill's Cathedral. It really captured the feel of a mythical cathedral somehow skewed into something that's just, wrong.

Of the maps I created, my favorite has to be Horfolk Station. I just like how it turned out.

GW: *Computer games usually take a lot of twists and turns on the road from initial concept to final product. Can you describe some of the major changes (compromises?) that* Blood II *went through from its beginnings to final product? Were these changes for the better or worse?*

JW: *Blood II* definitely went through major changes, but I generally view it as cutting of the dead wood. Most of the things we cut were cut because they just weren't good ideas, or didn't work the way we'd planned. We struggled to keep everything that we knew was a really good element of the game. I'd

say the most major thing we cut was the spell and binding system, which allowed you to select defensive spells and special powers for your character. This may sound like it would have been a great enhancement to the game, but what we found upon implementation was that all those abilities just got in the way of the action, making everything over-complex and less satisfying. Gone were the fast kills of the original *Blood*, as every attack had a defense. That was our biggest change, and I definitely think *Blood II* is better off for having lost that detail; and I think we at Monolith are better game designers having burned that particular bridge.

GW: *Do you have any plans for patches or expansion packs now that Blood II is out?*

JW: We'll patch *Blood II* as needed, to either fix bugs or add minor feature requests we get from the public. As for an add-on, that's pretty much a definite thing. Expect more blood to come at the beginning of '99.

GW: *What lessons did you learn while working on* Blood II? *How will you apply these to future projects?*

JW: I think the most important lesson we learned is constraint. We already knew how to make great games, and make them fun, but we didn't really have a good gauge for what was possible, and how long some things take. For example, twenty really solid weapons are much better than thirty mediocre ones. Like with everything, experience leads to a better ability to manage your time and skills, and *Blood II* was a big, nasty plateful of experience. As a result I think our future products will look even more polished, and be even more refined. It only goes up from here.

GW: *When people are under a lot of stress, they do weird things. What's the weirdest thing you or anybody else at Monolith did during "crunch time"?*

JW: Well, Aaron St. John did something weird once, but it wasn't during "crunch time," so it doesn't count. I'd like to say that we hacked down someone's door, or set the building on fire, or made blood sacrifices to some dark god, but the truth is that other than the occasional mental breakdown, crunch time is pretty quiet around here. This is mostly because we can't afford to replace doors or buildings, and we're all sitting in our offices with our doors closed trying to get stuff done. Now after crunch time is over, that's another story.

GW: *Who are the unsung heroes of the* Blood II *team?*

JW: Hmm, this question is a potential landmine of hurt feelings. I think the main unsung heroes would be the families of all the team members for putting up with our long hours, our stress and frustration, and still being there when we get home.

And secondly, a big hats off to Nick Newhard, who created *Blood*, and came up with several concepts for *Blood II.*

GW: *What was some of your inspiration for the many macabre things that found their way into* Blood II? *Any particular books or movies that we should know about (so we can stay away from them)?*

JW: A variety of things contributed to the concepts in *Blood II.* Eric Kohler and Kevin Kilstrom came up with many of the visual concepts based on my half-baked design specs and descriptions, and most of my ideas came from playing other games. *Blood II* being a sequel, I think we pulled a lot of ideas from *Blood*, and I pulled a lot of my game design ideas from *Doom*, which in my opinion is still the best shooter ever made. I think HP Lovecraft's books are a big inspiration on the *Blood* universe, as are most horror films, but especially the *Evil Dead* series and *Return of the Living Dead*. I also take a pretty heavy amount of influence from the pen and paper RPG *Shadowrun*, which is where I got the idea for turning the Cabal into a corporation.

GW: *FPSs have come a long way since* Ultima Underworld *and* Wolfenstein 3d. *There have been huge advances in technology, and some moderate ones in game play. What do you think will be the next great development in the genre? What will a blockbuster FPS look like five years from now?*

JW: I don't think the technology race has run its course yet, but I'll be glad when it has. For me, I'd like to see the FPS of the future include more thought into game play overall. I think there will be major refinements to the interface, and new ways to interact with the world and control your persona in it. Personally, I'd love to see the FPS genre expand into other genres, like RPG's and adventure games. I'd love to make a FPS that was completely non-linear, where you worked your way through a story like you would in an adventure game, only instead of puzzles to solve, you'd have to kill things. I also think we'll start to see FPS's expand in scope to include different types of action. Jedi using a third-person camera for melee combat was a big step. Finally, I'm hoping that 3D shooters begin to move into new styles of play. Right now most shooters play like *Quake. Quake* is a great game, but variety is the spice of life, and it doesn't look like it is going to stop making *Quake* anytime soon, so I'm guessing they've pretty much got the market locked on that style of game play. More games that go for *Blood*'s breakneck speed, or the realism of games like *Golden Eye* or *Outlaws*, or completely break into a new style like our own *Shogo*. These are the things I'm hoping to see in the 3D shooters of the future.

When I tell people this, I often have people say things like, "but don't you want (*insert ground-breaking technology here*)?" Sure, that sounds good, but if there is one thing you can count on in the game industry, it's that technology

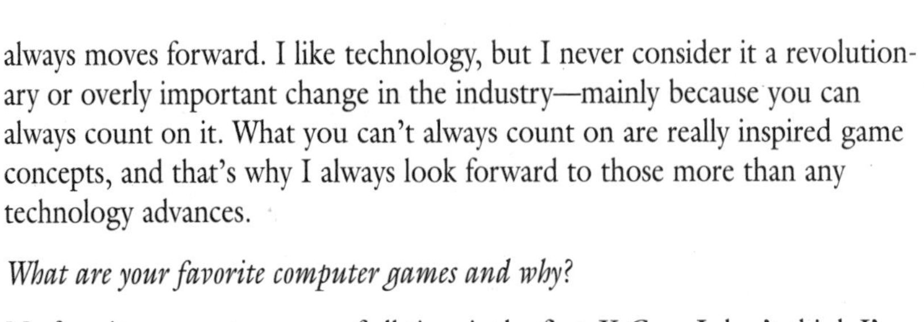

always moves forward. I like technology, but I never consider it a revolutionary or overly important change in the industry—mainly because you can always count on it. What you can't always count on are really inspired game concepts, and that's why I always look forward to those more than any technology advances.

GW: *What are your favorite computer games and why?*

JW: My favorite computer game of all time is the first *X-Com*. I don't think I've ever played a game that was so open-ended and so intriguing throughout. Everything about that game was superbly done, and it created a world that I got lost in night after night. I still play it, and I wish someone would make a new version that would do it justice. Then there's *Doom* 1 and 2, which again, I still play fairly often. The only shooter that I think even gets close to the speed and satisfaction of *Doom* is *Blood*, not to pat ourselves on the back or anything, I don't say that lightly. Many others come up, *Starflight*, *Tie Fighter*, *Magic Carpet*, *Syndicate...*

GW: *Where do you see the future of computer gaming? Is technology or creativity leading right now?*

JW: Technology is absolutely the leader, but there is still plenty of creativity in the works. I'm not pessimistic about the gaming industry, and I have a hard time understanding those who are. I constantly hear how everything's been done, and everyone is just making clones, and there's no originality out there. To hear all this, you'd think there wasn't a good game to be found on the shelves. But that isn't at all the case. Good games come out faster than I can play them, and I play through stuff pretty fast. What's the last game that really changed the industry? *Civilization*? *Wing Commander*? *Doom*? It just doesn't happen very often. But since *Doom* has come out I've had an awesome time playing a lot of really fun games, shooters and otherwise. Personally, I hope the future of computer gaming lightens up a bit, with less emphasis on re-inventing the wheel and more on taking solid ideas and creating awesome games out of them.

GW: *Give me the recipe for a successful computer game.*

JW: If I could do that, I'd put it in a bottle and sell it. There's no trick to it other than I can tell you that the best games will always come from gamers with the intent of making something that is first and foremost fun to them, without worrying about what anyone else says.

GW: *What advice do you have for people who want to get into the field of computer game development?*

JW: Nothing speaks more about you than examples of your work. If you want to be an artist, make art. If you want to be a programmer, write code. If you want to be a level designer, make levels. Always work with the latest technology available, and build a portfolio that includes lots of varying examples. For instance, if you want to be a level designer don't just make multiplayer levels. If you want to get a job with a computer gaming company they'll need more than that. Do a variety of things, and in a variety of formats. Examples of the excellent work you can do will get you a job in a heartbeat, and the jobs are out there.

Don't let Gideon catch you browsing through these pages!

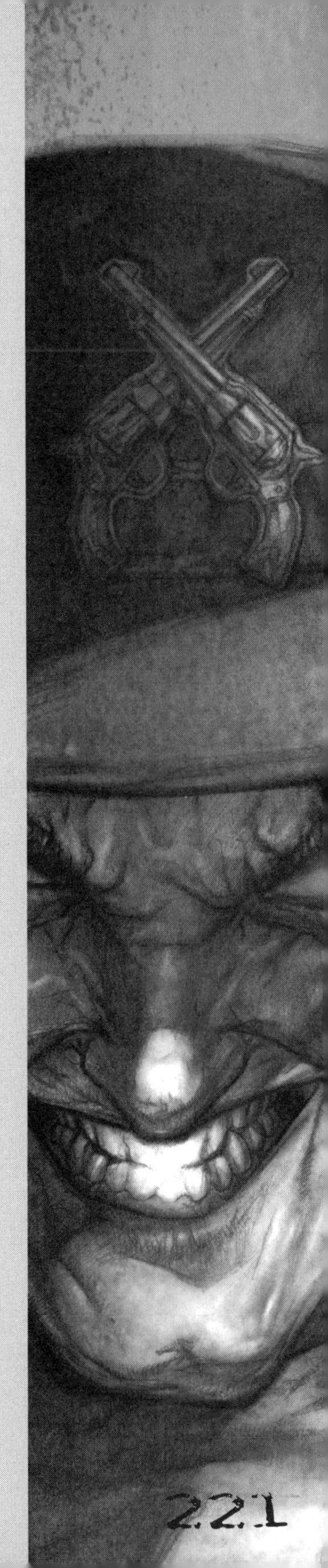

Appendix

CHEAT CODES AND CONSOLE COMMANDS

The LithTech Engine allows for a variety of commands to be entered directly from the game. Many of these are bizarre, and the results meaningful only to the programmers at Monolith. However, some of them, including the cheat codes, are interesting and fun to play with. These codes can be entered either via the console (which can be pulled down with the Tilde (~) key) or by pressing the "tell" button ("t" by default) and entering the command. In case you just can't make it on your own, the cheat codes are listed separately for your convenience.

NOTE

Please note that we don't know what all these commands do, or even if they will work in the version of the game you have. Just think of them as an unsupported bonus to play around with.

CHEAT CODES

Cheat codes can be activated two ways. The first is by bringing down the console with the Tilde (~) button (located above the TAB key on most keyboards), typing in the command, pressing ENTER, and then putting the console away by hitting "~" again. The second, easier method is to press the "tell" key ("t" by default), type in the code, and then press ENTER.

COMMAND	WHAT IT DOES
MPGOD	God mode toggle
BEANSOFCOOLNESS	Like MPKFA, but gives you a differnet set of weapons
MPKFA	Fills all weapon slots, and provides maximum ammo
MPAMMO	Full ammo
MPCLIP	Toggles clipping through walls
MPHEALTHY	Full health
MPWHEREAMI	Display current position
MPHIDEME	Invisibility
MPBEEFCAKE	Triple damage
MPSPEEDUP	Speed increase
MPSTRONGER	Strength increase
MPCALEB	Change your character to Caleb
MPOPHELIA	Change your character to Ophelia
MPISHMAEL	Change your character to Ishmael
MPGABBY	Change your character to Gabriella
MPKILLEMALL	Kills every creature in the level
MPGOshopping	Gives all items
NICENURSE	Health Powerup
HOTNURSE	Life Seed powerup
WARD	Gives you a Ward
NECROWARD	Gives you a Necroward
CARBONFIBER	Gives you the Willpower powerup
TAKEOFFSHOES	Gives you the Stealth powerup
HERKERMUR	Gives you the Anger powerup

COMMAND CODES

NETWORKING CONSOLE COMMANDS

Like cheats, these console commands can be entered in the console (hit "~" to bring the console down; hit "~" again to put it away), or use the "tell" key.

COMMAND	WHAT IT DOES...
FastInput <0,1> (default 1)	This causes the client to check input and send it to the server during rendering to minimize the response time.It costs about 0.2 fps in netgames but makes the input more responsive.
ForceRemote <0,1> (default 0)	Normally, the engine uses a different net protocol for a single-player game which is more efficient, but ForceRemote 1 will make it use a network connection.
LocalDebug <0,1>	By default, the transport debug doesn't tell about local connections. This will enable local connection debug.
TransportDebug <0-10>	Debug net transport layer shows lots of info about packet sending/receiving. LatencySim <amount> adds simulated latency in the networking layer. This takes up tons of memory and therefore should only be used for debugging. Set to zero to disable.
DropRate <0-100>	Percentage of simulated packet loss; useful for debugging.
DebugPackets <0, 1, 2>	0 = no debug output for packets 1 = basic debug output--new objects and removed objects 2 = verbose debug output
connect	Connect to the first available IPX game
connect <ip address>	Connect to the computer with the given IP address
ShowThruPut <0,1>	Shows how much data is being sent per second.
ShowConnStats <0,1>	Shows status information about all active network connections. Only shows info for local connections if LocalDebug is 1.

SERVER CONSOLE COMMANDS

Server-side console commands are done by entering "serv <command>" in the console, where command is like any normal command. Note: the server commands will most likely change and some will be removed.

COMMAND	WHAT IT DOES...
Portal <name> <val>	Open or close a portal (only used for debugging).
UpdateRate <rate>	Set the server's internal update rate. This defaults to 30 times per second.
TimeScale <scale>	You can scale the time on the server to make things go slower or faster. This is cool for some effects.
ShowUsedFiles	Spits out a list of all the files the server is using.
ObjectInfo	Shows a list of all the objects currently in the world.
ShowGameTime	Shows the game time progressing.
ShowClassTicks	Shows how many ticks were spent updating each class each frame (this slows things down a bit so don't have it on all the time).
DisableWMPhysics	Enables the FLAG_BOXPHYSICS flag on all objects so you can see how much the WorldModel physics is costing.

RENDERING CONSOLE COMMANDS

Like cheats, these console commands can be entered in the console (hit "~" to bring the console down; hit "~" again to put it away) or with the "tell" key.

COMMAND	WHAT IT DOES...
Bilinear <0,1> (default 1)	Enable/disable bilinear filtering.
FixTJunc <0,1> (default 0)	Some video cards show gaps between polygons at t-junctions. FixTJunc can make these look better by adding extra triangles which is a little bit slower.
ShowPVS	Draws geometry back to front so you can see what's in the PVS.

COMMAND	WHAT IT DOES...
LockPVS	When this is enabled, the engine will draw what's in the PVS for the area you're currently in no matter where you go so you can see how much extra stuff you can see.
LightSaturate <amount> (default 1)	Saturates all dynamic lights.
RCom <commands...>	This provides a way to talk to render drivers. Here are some Direct3d driver-specific render commands: "ListDevices" will spit out all the hardware accelerated devices that it can use. "ListTextureFormats" will spit out all the texture formats that the current card supports, as well as which texture format it's using.
Texture4444 <0,1>	Forces the texture format to be RGBA 4444. This is faster on some cards.
ShowFullbriteModels <0,1>	Draws models with a fullbrite texture flat-shaded.
ShowTextureUpload <0,1>	Shows stats on texture upload. Helpful for finding out if an area is using too much texture
.ShowFillInfo <0,1>	Shows how much screen area is being drawn. Helps determine how much overdraw you have. Overdraw is a large cause of slowness.
DrawAll <0,1>	Draws everything in the world, regardless of the visibility list.
ShowSplits <0,1>	If DrawFlat is 1, then this shows BSP splits on the flat polies.
DynamicLight <0,1>	Enable/disable dynamic lighting.
FastLight <0,1>	Uses a faster method to light things with dynamic lights, but doesn't look as smooth.
LightModels <0,1>	Should models be lit by dynamic lights?
ModelFullbrite <0,1>	Enable/disable model fullbrite colors (having fullbrite colors is slower).
LightmapsOnly <0,1>	Tells renderer to only draw lightmaps.
Wireframe <0,1>	Draw everything in wireframe.

COMMAND	WHAT IT DOES...
ModelBoxes <0,1>	Draws model physics bounding boxes.
LodBias <value>	Sets the mipmap range, so you can push those mipmapping lines back. Default value is 0.7. The lower you go, the further the lines are apart.
DrawSky <0,1>	Enable/disable sky rendering (default is 1).
FogEnable <0 or 1>	Enable fog (only in Glide).
FogR <0-255>	Fog red color (defaults to 100).
FogG <0-255>	Fog green color (defaults to 200).
FogB <0-255>	Fog blue color (defaults to 100).
FogNearZ <0-65000>	Where the fog starts (defaults to 0).
FogFarZ <0-65000>	Where the fog ends (defaults to 2000).
SkyFogNearZ <0-65000>	Where the fog starts in the sky (defaults to 0).
SkyFogFarZ <0-65000>	Where the fog ends in the sky (defaults to 200).
MaxModelShadows <number>	The engine uses a maximum of 3 shadows. You can disable shadows with "MaxModelShadows 0" or set it to 1, 2, or 3.
ModelLodOffset <offset>	This offsets all model levels of detail by the given amount. This should be used for a "low detail" setting for slower machines. (Note: You can set this to negative as well if you want to stop the models from using LODs).
ShadowLodOffset <offset>	The LOD that shadows use is the model's level of detail (which is affected by ModelLodOffset) + ShadowLodOffset. This defaults to 150, which saves 300 triangles for shadows.
ModelAdd <r> <g> <b> (0-255)	You can brighten up the global model lighting with this command. FarDetailDist <dist> sets the farthest distance for drawing polies. Anything between 0 and FarDetailDist has its detail level scaled in between there. MaxDetailLevel <level> causes the renderer to not draw anything above the given detail level.
RenderDebug <0 - 5>	Helpful rendering debug information is printed in the console when errors occur. Higher numbers print out more information.

COMMAND	WHAT IT DOES...
MipMapOffset <0,3>	Offset the mipmap level that it uses by a certain amount. This helps on crappy cards with very little texture memory.
GroupOffset0 through GroupOffset9 <0,3>	Offset the mipmaps used for textures in each group (this offset is in addition to the offset applied with the "global" mipmap offset in MipmapOffset).
Dither <0,1>	Enable/disable dithering (best if it's on).
DrawParticles <0,1>	Turn on or off particle drawing.
DrawSprites <0,1>	Turn on or off sprite drawing.
DrawModels <0,1>	Turn on or off model drawing.
DrawLineSystems <0,1>	Turn on or off line system drawing.
ShowFrameRate <0,1>	Show frame rate info in the console.
ShowPolyCounts <0,1>	Tell how many polies it's drawing.
LightMap <0,1>	Enable/disable lightmapping.
FarZ <100,65000>	Far clipping distance.
ScreenWidth <512,640>	Video width and height (only useful on the command line).
ScreenHeight <384, 480>	Video width and height (only useful on the command line).
RenderDLL <dllname>	Use a different render DLL (only useful on the command line).
LODScale <num>	Scale factor for LOD values. Defaults to 1.0f
Force2Pass <0,1>	Forces d3drender.dll to render lightmapped polies in two passes, even on a card that can do it in one pass (like a Voodoo2).
TripleBuffer <0,1>	Enable/disable triple buffering. Triple buffering makes some cards run much faster.
Gamma <0-500>	Set the gamma value; defaults to 1.
WarbleSpeed <speed> (default 25)	Sets how fast the warbling effect goes.
WarbleScale <0-1> (default 0.92)	Sets how pronounced the warbling effect is. The closer to zero, the more pronounced the effect is.
EnvScale <scale> (default 1)	Scales the environment map so it looks blurrier.
EnvMapAll <0,1>	Environment maps all models, regardless of whether they have the flag set or not.

Sound Console Commands

Like cheats, these console commands can be entered in the console (hit "~" to bring the console down; hit "~" again to put it away) or with the "tell" key.

COMMAND	WHAT IT DOES...
DebugSound <0,1>	Tells when sounds are created.
DebugNumSounds <0,1>	Spits out how many sounds are currently being mixed each frame.
MusicEnable <0,1>	Disable/Enable music.
SoundEnable <0,1>	Disable/Enable sound.

Other Console Commands

Like cheats, these console commands can be entered in the console (hit "~" to bring the console down; hit "~" again to put it away) or with the "tell" key.

COMMAND	WHAT IT DOES...
TraceConsole <0,1> (default 1)	Puts console output into the debugger's trace window.
ShowFileAccess <0-4> (default 0)	Puts messages into the console when files are accessed.
ShowGameVars	Spits out a list of the game console variables and their values.
ListInputDevices	Shows a list of all the input devices and key names in the console.
Record <world name> <record filename (without extension)>	Records a demo on the world.
PlayDemo <record filename (without extension)>	Plays back a recorded demo.
TimeDemo <record filename (without extension)>	Plays back a recorded demo as fast as it can. This is good for measuring frame rate over a period of time.
ShowTickCounts <0,1,2,3>	Shows some performance data. The higher the number, the more detailed the info.
ShowMemStats <0,1>	Shows memory allocated and number of allocations.
DebugStrings <0,1>	Spits out messages when it can't find requested strings.

COMMAND	WHAT IT DOES...
ErrorLog <0,1>	Checked on startup. Causes all errors and console output to be logged to a file, Error.log.
AlwaysFlushLog <0,1>	Writes the log file to disk every time something is printed to it. Slow, but it'll guarantee the contents of the log are intact if the engine crashes or something.
ErrorLogFile <filename>	Specify an alternate file for the error log (default is error.log).
<varname>	Prints the variable name and its value.
Set	Lists all the console variables and their values.
ListCommands	Lists all the console commands.
NumConsoleLines <0-20>	How many lines of the console are visible in the upper left corner.
Video <0,1>	Enable/disable video; only useful if you do it on the command line.
MaxWorldPoliesToDraw <number>	Maximum world polies to draw; useful for unvis'd levels
world <worldname>	Switch to the given world.
Bind <device name> <trigger name> <action name>	Bind a key or other input to an action.
RangeBind <device name> <trigger name> <low range> <high range> <action name>	Bind a key or other input to an action. This is usually used if you want to hook up a joystick to act as a button. When the joystick moves in between the low and high ranges you specify, the command is considered on. You can repeat the last 3 tokens to add more actions with range bindings. Here's an example: RangeBind "joystick 1" x 0 22767 left 42767 65535 right.
scale <device name> <trigger name> <scale amount>	Scale an input axis to make the mouse turn faster, for instance.
addaction <action name> <action number>	Add a new action.
enabledevice <device name>	Enable a device (like keyboard or mouse).
ssfile <filename>	Set the screenshot filename.

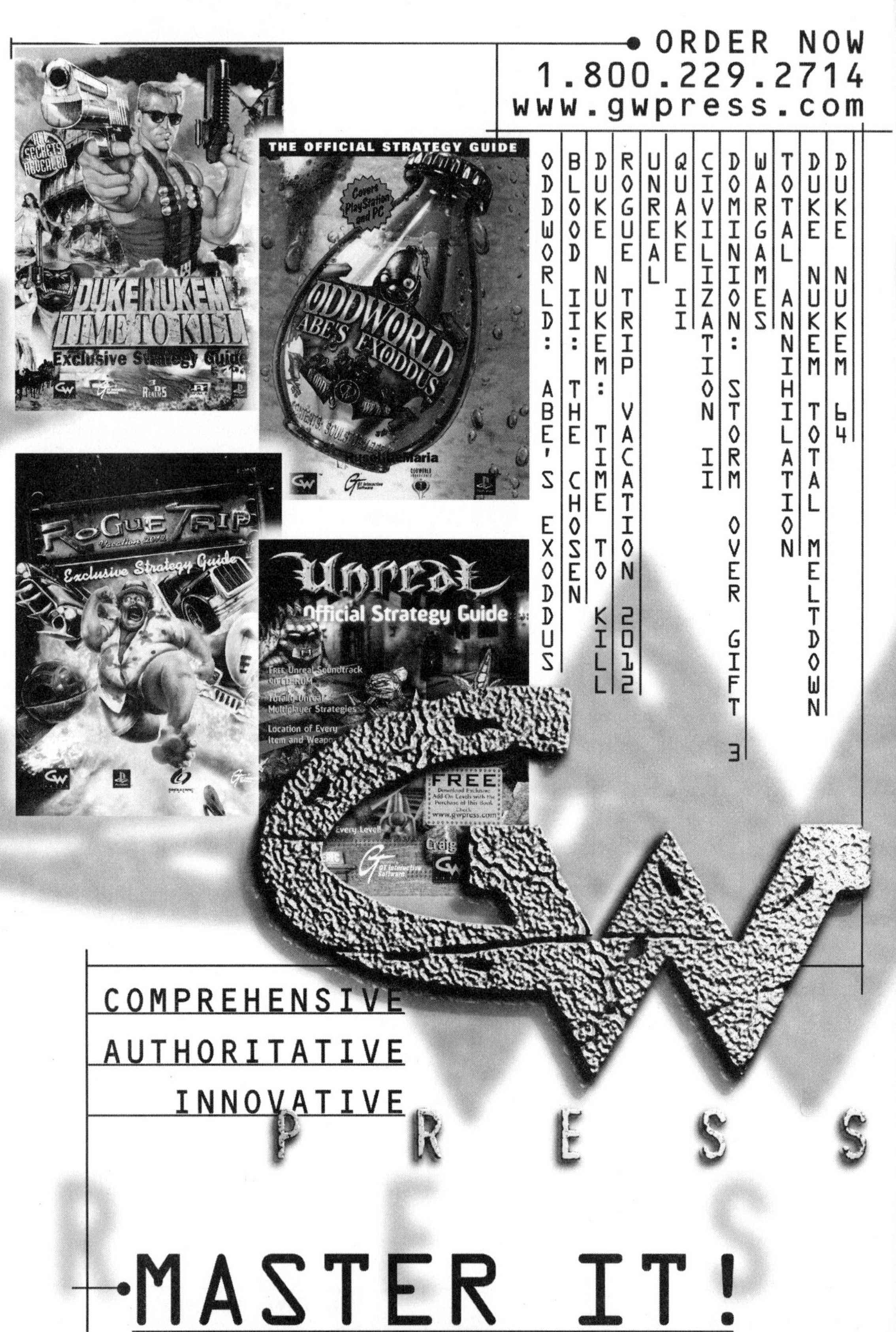

DON'T JUST PLAY THE GAME
ORDER NOW
1.800.229.2714
www.gwpress.com
ODDWORLD: ABE'S EXODDUS
BLOOD II: THE CHOSEN
DUKE NUKEM: TIME TO KILL
ROGUE TRIP VACATION 2012
UNREAL
QUAKE II
CIVILIZATION II
DOMINION: STORM OVER GIFT 3
WARGAMES
TOTAL ANNIHILATION
DUKE NUKEM TOTAL MELTDOWN
DUKE NUKEM 64
DUKE NUKEM TIME TO KILL
Exclusive Strategy Guide
THE OFFICIAL STRATEGY GUIDE
ODDWORLD ABE'S EXODDUS
Rogue Trip
Exclusive Strategy Guide
Unreal
Official Strategy Guide
COMPREHENSIVE
AUTHORITATIVE
INNOVATIVE
GW PRESS
MASTER IT!